PRAISE FOR
VIRTUAL LEADERSH

CW00326894

'I am so pleased that Penny has written this book and can share her skill and inspiration for really successful virtual working with even more people. When I met Penny I was working with three global companies and was spending half of my days (and lots of early mornings and late nights) on calls with colleagues. Penny taught me so much about how to make these into really successful meetings and reading this book reminded me of all that and more. Penny is also the master of communicating in a clear and simple way, even though the subject matter is complex. I recommend this book to everyone who needs to do business in a "same time, different place" context – I am confident that practising what Penny recommends will transform the quality of your work.'
Dr Ruth Murray-Webster, Director, Change Portfolio, Associated British Ports Ltd, UK

'Penny has done a magnificent job of covering every single element which you need to master. I've been managing virtual teams for over 20 years and thought I knew it all. I didn't. And you won't either until you have read this book.'
Pete Bennett, Founder, Buzz Conferencing, UK

'Penny's latest book is your own personal leadership coach. Pragmatic and practical, this book will help you avoid horrible conference calls and quickly boost productivity wherever your team are based. Targeted sections let you dive into solutions for issues you are facing with your virtual teams today. Highly recommended for team leaders, managers and those working virtually – whether in a formal leadership position or not.'

Elizabeth Harrin, business change manager and author of *Collaboration Tools for Project Managers*, UK

'When I first began to think about virtual working I didn't predict all the different factors that need to be taken into consideration and learned a lot by trial and error. I would have saved a lot of time and energy by reading this book! Even now, with several years' experience in virtual working, I found this book chock-full of useful tips and ideas that will help me to be far more effective going forward. I hope that this book will become a classic. It certainly deserves its space on my bookshelf as both a primer that I can lend to newbies and a very useful resource for me to use as I think through and address increasing the complexity of virtual working in multiple time zones in the world of work.'
Emma Langman, Head of Talent working in international retail, Kuwait

'In my role within a global organization, I see daily the need for better leadership for remote teams working towards a common goal. Dr Penny Pullan offers us all the help that we need in this with insight, practical guidance and a dash of inspiration, which is always welcome. Covering all the aspects of time, language, culture, and generations which make this a complicated leadership task, the book shows us all a clear path to success in this virtual world we all work in today.'
Peter Taylor, Head of Global PMO at Kronos and 'The Lazy Project Manager'

'Dr Pullan drills down on the world of virtual work teams to build a baseline for managers in the 21st century. Virtual teams are flexible in place and time, pull from the brightest talent and offer a 24/7 cycle, and yet have challenges that require knowledge for effective leadership. Pullan puts the benefits of virtual working in a context that managers can trust. *Virtual Leadership* should be required reading for every leader, project manager and executive, virtual or traditional. Get this book in the hands of your leadership team.'
Tom Wise, Quality Director and University Adjunct Instructor, author of *Trust in Virtual Teams*, USA

'As someone who has spent over twenty years living the virtual life, I loved this book! Penny's book has creatively captured the foibles and tricks and tips for success with virtual leadership.'
Professor Eddie Obeng, speaker, innovator and author, Learning Director of Pentacle The Virtual Business School and Professor of Entrepreneurship and Innovation at Henley Business School

'This book will guide you to becoming an effective and graceful leader of virtual teams. Penny Pullan hits all the key points around establishing, nurturing and working with diverse groups, wherever their individual members may be located. *Virtual Leadership* reveals the importance of a leader mindset, deals with technology and virtual meetings, lays out a path for managing virtual work in between meetings, and addresses the complications and pitfalls that every virtual worker faces. Throughout it all, the author shines a light on the often-overlooked truth about virtual work: that its most important aspect has nothing to do with technology, and everything to do with being human. Stop suffering through virtual work. Instead, transform it through applying the skills and practices in this essential handbook.'
Rachel Smith, Director of Digital Facilitation Services, The Grove Consultants International, USA

'*Virtual Leadership* is a real standout in an increasingly crowded field. Using scores of relevant real-life examples and hundreds of practical tips, Penny is an engaging writer who generously shares her deep wisdom and extensive experience on a complex and often confounding topic. Even those who regard themselves as virtual leadership experts will come away infinitely smarter for having read this terrific book. I highly recommend this for anyone who wants to master the art and science of leading a successful virtual team. You will thank me later!'
Nancy Settle-Murphy, author of *Leading Effective Virtual Teams*, USA

'This is a book for everyone who works in a modern organization, from a team member approaching their first encounter with virtual working, to an enterprise leader looking to transform to an effective, efficient, distributed organisation. Dr Pullan has provided everything from guidance for organizations looking to deploy communication and collaboration tools, to advice for users on how to maximize their effectiveness whilst avoiding destroying their lives by being "always on".'
John Greenwood CPhys MInstP PMP, Regional Risk Management Champion, CSC, UK

'In this book, Penny provides a very complete list of virtual teams' pitfalls that allows a better understanding of what is not working today. And before one gets overwhelmed by the sad reality of far-flung teams, she provides a 360° view of how we can make it work. By building on her own life and work experience, combined with an extensive survey of real-life practices and underpinned by several books and studies, she will inspire many to wake up their inner virtual leadership skills and engage people from afar to get things done together – and live happily ever after.'
Jean Binder, author of *Global Project Management*, Switzerland

'I have attended a number of Penny's Virtual Summits and spoken at one of them, and am thrilled that she has now put pen to paper on this important issue in modern workplaces. This book is a comprehensive handbook for anyone who spends time in the virtual world of work. A lot more than just insights into the technologies, it is a detailed, practical guide to all aspects of team building, managing meetings, engaging across cultures and styles, and so much more. It is indispensable and required reading for leaders in the modern workplace.'
Graeme Codrington, CEO of TomorrowToday, futurist and expert on the future of work, South Africa

'At a time of increasing globalization, virtual working is a very real challenge to organizations and to my own world of project, programme, portfolio and change management. Both the 24/7 global economy and mobile working without a permanent office means we have to find different but effective ways of working. We also need to find successful ways to collaborate and to build strong relationships, confidence and trust with clients and teams when we cannot meet face-to-face. *Virtual Leadership* helps to address and resolve these issues. Penny has a wonderfully engaging and straightforward way of writing, and her book looks across a range of sectors and situations for virtual working and virtual leadership. I certainly recommend *Virtual Leadership* to individuals and organizations grappling with the complexity of virtual working.'
Sarah Coleman, Project, Programme and Change Consultant and Educator; author of *Project Leadership*

Virtual Leadership

Practical strategies for getting the best out of virtual work and virtual teams

Penny Pullan

First published in Great Britain and the United States in 2016 by Kogan Page Limited

2nd Floor, 45 Gee Street	1518 Walnut Street, Suite 1100	4737/23 Ansari Road
London	Philadelphia PA 19102	Daryaganj
EC1V 3RS	USA	New Delhi 110002
United Kingdom		India

© Penny Pullan 2016

The right of Penny Pullan to be identified as the author of this work has been asserted by her in accordance with the Copyright, Designs and Patents Act 1988.

ISBN   978 0 7494 7596 3
E-ISBN   978 0 7494 7597 0

British Library Cataloguing-in-Publication Data

A CIP record for this book is available from the British Library.

Library of Congress Control Number

2016946118

Typeset by Graphicraft Limited, Hong Kong
Print production managed by Jellyfish
Printed and bound in Great Britain by CPI Group (UK) Ltd, Croydon CR0 4YY

CONTENTS

ABOUT THE AUTHOR

Dr Penny Pullan

Penny's first experience as a virtual leader was quite by accident. She had been planning to fly to New York on 13 September 2001 for the face-to-face kick-off of a global programme. Except it didn't happen. After 9/11, Penny and her global team were grounded for months. She had to find another way and that meant running the programme through virtual leadership. It went incredibly well and she was hooked. Since then she has been developing her own virtual leadership, especially on tricky projects, and helping others to do the same, initially within Mars Inc and then as a director of the consultancy she founded in 2007, Making Projects Work Ltd.

Virtual leadership is key to Penny's work supporting those who are grappling with tricky projects. Four aspects of these projects are:

- team members dispersed all over the world;
- a diverse mix of stakeholders, who need to be interested, engaged and involved;
- changing, complex, and often ambiguous, requirements;
- lots of risk!

Within this context, Penny brings clarity, confidence and powerful communication, making people more effective, projects more successful and work much more fun for everyone.

Penny hosts two virtual conferences each year, which are free to attend: the Virtual Working Summit (www.virtualworkingsummit.com) and the Business Analysis Summit (www.basummit.com), both attended by thousands of people from all over the world. She speaks regularly for professional associations and organizations. Her previous books include: *Business Analysis and Leadership: Influencing change* (Kogan Page, 2013) and *A Short Guide to Facilitating Risk Management*, co-authored with Ruth Murray Webster (Gower, 2011). She contributed a chapter on virtual projects to *The Gower Handbook of People in Project Management* (Gower, 2013).

Penny has a PhD from Cambridge University, is a Certified Professional Facilitator, has multiple qualifications in business analysis and project and programme management, and is a Chartered Engineer.

penny@makingprojectswork.co.uk
+44 (0)1509 821691
www.virtualleadershipbook.com

FOREWORD

Thank you Penny!

This is the book the world has been waiting for. Social media, global communications from anyone to anywhere, and virtual teams being the norm mean we are crying out for this book.

It is a how-to for the new way of life that we all live, at a thousand miles an hour. The techniques can be applied across all walks of life, as we gather together without actually being together to achieve a common goal. And Penny doesn't do theory, instead she takes you on a roller coaster ride of 'how-tos' that you can apply straight away; this book is far from 'virtual'! I also love the way Penny explains very complex ideas, thoughts and subjects in such a simple way that inspires us to do it.

I am very lucky to be asked to write many forewords, and I said yes to this one for three reasons:

- It will become the de facto Bible for leading people virtually.
- I knew I would get to read it in advance!
- Because I hold Penny in huge admiration. A few years ago I looked her in the eyes and said, 'Write a book,' and she has done just that. Actually, she has now written three!

Dear Reader: if I were you, I would stop reading my words and get reading Penny's. Very soon, I promise you, your virtual relationships, rapport and trust will be transformed forever.

David Taylor
Author of The Naked Leader Series

ACKNOWLEDGEMENTS

This book would never have been written without the support and collaboration of so many people including:

- My former colleagues at Mars, where I started to work virtually, especially Brian and the rest of the EBC team.
- Nancy Settle-Murphy, my very first virtual working mentor, supporter and now, I'm delighted to add, friend.
- All those who have supported my development as a facilitator over the past 20 years.
- The members of my virtual mentoring groups, my 'Outstanding Outsiders', who have shown me just how powerful life-changing virtual teams can be.
- All those who have spoken at my Virtual Working and Business Analysis virtual summits since 2010, sharing their knowledge and expanding mine.
- All the participants in my virtual summits over the years, numbering many thousands, for their interest, brilliant questions and interactions.
- To all my clients who work with me to develop leadership of change, whether using project techniques, business analysis, virtual working, graphics for communication and more. Those who work with me to run professional associations, usually virtually, especially Suzie and Merv.

I'm indebted to all those who completed my survey about virtual working challenges. Many of these and others contributed to the stories and case studies in this book including (using first names only): Amadea, Andrew, Brian, Carol, Carl, Charlotte, Chris, Cydne, Daniel, Eddie, Elizabeth, Emma, Evi, Ganesh, Gary, Graeme, Ian, James, Janet, Jim, Joanna, John, Judy, Julia, Karl, Laura, Lisa, Liz, Mark, Mauva, Michael, Pete, Rachel, Richard, Sarah, Simon, Tammy, Terrie, Thyra, Tomás, Tricia and Zoe.

Others have contributed anonymously. Thank you so much!

Many friends and colleagues shared their headshots to create the virtual picture map. Thank you to Clare, Cydne, Donnie, Gary, Emma, Liz, Mauva, Melissa, Nancy, Richard, Stephen and Steve.

Thanks are due to the Grove Consultants International, especially Bobby Pardini, for permission to use the Drexler/Sibbet Team Performance Model.

Others who helped with the book include Priya E Abraham, Eddie Obeng, Grace Marshall, Pete Bennett, Sarah Fitton, Nancy Settle-Murphy, Elizabeth Harrin and Rachel Smith.

Thanks are due to all those who have supported my development as an author, especially those who have written and/or edited alongside me especially Ruth Murray-Webster and James Archer. David Taylor gave me the initial idea for this book and has kindly written the Foreword; Jen Christie polished it; Jennifer Hall at Kogan Page honed it and agreed to publish it. Thanks to my editors Anna Moss and Amy Minshull for their support throughout the writing process, plus David Crosby, Emma Petfield and all those at Kogan Page who have transformed these words into beautiful books.

I'm very grateful to all those who read through drafts and proofs of this book. Their help and the time they invested in reading these words have improved it no end.

As ever, I'd like to thank my family for their support. Malcolm kept everything together at home and played Bach on the organ while I wrote. Kathleen and Charlotte have shown me how the rising generation are not just digital natives, but see virtual connections and communication as second nature.

Finally, I would like to dedicate this book to someone who has always been supportive even if, like much of his generation, he often has little idea about this virtual working malarkey. This book is dedicated to my father, Hugh Urry.

Introduction

Figure 0.1 A mind-map of this introduction

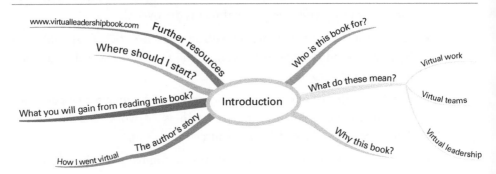

Who is this book for?

Do you work with others who can't always meet face to face? They might be based in different locations, far away, and have never met you. On the other hand, they might just be working from home for a day or two. You might be part of one or more long-term, virtual teams. You might just work with other people remotely, who wouldn't consider themselves as a team, just a group who work together occasionally.

Perhaps you lead virtual teams yourself or manage others who work virtually? Even if you don't consider yourself a leader, you will be able to make a lasting difference to the quality of virtual work through your own virtual leadership.

Do you strive to work well with people spread around the globe or even spread around your locality? Do you wonder how to overcome the challenges and frustrations of remote working? Do you want to see real and lasting benefits for your organization through your virtual work and that of your colleagues? If so, this book is written for you.

This book is for all those who want to develop their virtual leadership approach and skills, transforming their experience of virtual working and the results that they obtain from their virtual teams and other remote groups.

This book is written for all those who work virtually, whatever their job title, role or function. My own background is in helping organizations to change, often using skills such as project and programme management, and business analysis. Virtual working is becoming commonplace in these environments, and elsewhere. The insights for this book have come from a wide variety of people. Here are a few examples of virtual working across a range of different countries and industries:

- people working together across a range of companies and locations worldwide to deploy a stable, tested version of the latest anti-virus software shortly after every new threat is discovered;

- actuaries in Switzerland working with analysts in Zurich, IT specialists in Bratislava and India and marketing teams around the world to develop new insurance products;

- helpdesk staff in London answering calls to the computer helpdesk for a multinational company, who pass unfinished work to colleagues in San Francisco at the end of their shift;

- teams in a pharmaceutical multinational company working together across the world to launch a new medicine for cancer;

- workers based in a New York office, who 'hot desk' when they are in the office and often work from home, but who collaborate with colleagues from wherever they happen to be each day;

- entrepreneurs wishing to engage the best people for their new start-ups, regardless of location;

- doctors, consulting directly with their patients via video or telephone;

- clergy working with those who are unable to attend traditional Sunday services;

- job applicants, applying for jobs on other continents, whose only interview is via a video call;

- call-centre staff answering questions and solving problems for people they never meet, who might be calling from a different continent;

- small businesses working with virtual assistants around the world;

- groups of students around the world working with leading professors without ever meeting face to face;

- children doing homework during the holidays that their teacher has set for them online, and comparing notes with their classmates from their holiday location, wherever that might be.

The contents of this book apply wherever people work, whether in the private sector, public sector or for non-governmental organizations. It will be useful too for those who are collaborating across locations for leisure or educational activities, as well as for work.

This book will also be helpful for participants on internal and external leadership development programmes, as well as students on MBA and master's-level business courses such as leadership and international management. Human Resources (HR) and Learning & Development (L&D) specialists are likely to find it useful too as they grapple with the challenges of gaining business results from virtual teams and in flexible working environments.

With input from hundreds of people around the world, alongside my experience, I hope that you will find plenty in this book to help you reflect on your current skills and to support you to develop these further.

What do virtual work, virtual teams and virtual leadership mean?

There is an important point to make about the word 'virtual'. Be aware that the word 'virtual' has had a different meaning for centuries: 'almost or nearly as described, but not completely'. This meaning categorically does *not* apply to virtual work, teams and leadership! They are all very real.

In this book, when I talk about virtual work, I mean work done by people who are geographically distributed, working together despite the fact that at least one person is not in the same location as the others. Virtual work is supported by communications technology that helps people to connect when far apart.

A virtual team is simply any team that works in this way, with one or more team members apart from the others. Virtual teams are real teams working together over a network.

Virtual leadership is much more than merely using the appropriate communications technology. It is about being able to engage people from afar to produce results together. It builds on a shared vision of the future to help people to get things done together.

Why this book?

Why now? We are living in an increasingly virtual world, with a range of strong global trends all playing their part:

- There has been an explosion in the quantity and quality of collaboration technology. It is cheaper than ever before and access to the internet has grown worldwide.

- Our societies have changed rapidly, with people accessing technology for all sorts of personal use as well as work. (My own children 'chat' with their friends after school over an app, whereas I had to meet up with my school friends in person or else spend an inordinate amount of time on my parents' landline telephone to keep in touch!)

- The outsourcing of work early in the 21st century was a strong driver of virtual working. Many companies developed partnerships with providers in countries such as India, or even developed their own local branches in overseas countries, usually called offshoring. This outsourced work now ranges from answering customer queries on the telephone to designing and developing new IT solutions.

- Companies running global projects can bring together the best talent from around the world, which may include freelancers and partner companies, as well as their own employees.

- Homeworking or telecommuting is becoming increasingly common, where people – instead of spending hours each day travelling to and from their workplace – work from home or from a co-working centre nearby.

- Cost constraints in the global downturn of 2008 and beyond have also played their part. Companies have cut down on travel, saving on both the costs and the hassle involved (such as jetlag) in time spent getting from one place to another and the negative impact on work–life balance.

- Other factors have also affected travel, such as oil price volatility, the threat of epidemics, ash clouds and the need to reduce carbon emissions.

- In addition, virtual working allows the best people to work together, regardless of location. If you need round-the-clock cover for work, it is possible to achieve this through teams around the world in a 'follow-the-sun' approach. When one team finishes their working day, they pass unfinished work to their colleagues further west, who are just starting their day.

The trouble with this new world is that much of what works face to face does not translate directly to a virtual environment. Later chapters will explore this, but here's what is likely to happen:

- There will be lots of focus on technology, but even then, it will not always work and this will be annoying for everyone involved.

- Some people will love using video and others will hate it and try to avoid it as much as they can.

- The leader and the team become frustrated due to misunderstandings, some related to language, some due to different cultures and some as a result of team members coming from different generations.

- People will find that it takes a long time to communicate in written form compared with walking across and having a conversation with a colleague as they used to.

- Arranging live meetings may be difficult because of time differences. Once meetings are held, with so much to discuss, they can go on for a long time but with diminishing returns, as people switch to multitasking and are distracted by other things.

- It is likely that work will end up in e-mails, with different versions of documents residing in different people's inboxes and critical information hidden inside long e-mail threads.

- When the leader gives people work to do, they are likely to become disengaged gradually over time and focus more and more on other projects, typically activities with local colleagues.

- People may feel swamped with information, especially in a written form.

- Team members are likely to feel pressure to make themselves available outside of their own office hours to be able to interact with remote colleagues.

- People find it harder to feel part of the virtual team.

- If conflict is simmering, it will not be visible immediately but will likely only surface once a lot of damage has been done.

This book will help you to blend what already works from your face-to-face experience with the special aspects that help when you are working virtually.

The last decade has seen a number of excellent books on virtual teams. These are very helpful for those in a single, long-term, virtual team that has the time to set up slowly, perhaps even meeting face to face. Nowadays, though, one person might be a member of a number of virtual teams, some ad hoc and some long term. The same person could drop into other virtual groups as an adviser without considering themselves a member of a team. This book covers virtual work in all its forms and focuses on virtual leadership.

Too many people assume that they can overcome the challenges of virtual working and virtual teams just by getting to grips with the different technologies used for communication. That is just one part of the jigsaw and probably less than 10 per cent of what is needed. True virtual leadership takes into account the human side of virtual work, encouraging people to work really effectively together remotely while making the most of technology.

There are three aspects to excelling at virtual work:

- the skills of the specialism required to carry out the work itself;
- the ability to collaborate with and lead other people who are geographically remote (interestingly, this means that you need to start with yourself!);
- the ability to use the appropriate technologies to support each group and each situation.

The author's story: how I went virtual

Looking back, I had a good, early foundation for becoming an expert in virtual working. As a child I lived on three continents before the age of five; I was born in Malaysia, lived in the UK and then moved to South Africa. When I moved back to the UK, aged 11, I kept in touch with my best friend Susan through handwritten letters, even though we didn't see each other face to face for a decade. At Cambridge University, I got to know my now-husband Malcolm via the university mainframe computer, Phoenix. We were both graduate students and communicated through instant messages and e-mail before we met face to face. We're still together after 25 years, so it must have been a good foundation!

As a trained engineer, I have always wanted to break things down and understand the fundamentals and I applied this in my first job after completing my doctorate in the 1990s. The job was in the then-new field of 'Computer Supported Collaborative Work', which focused on helping existing, face-to-face teams to work better together, supported by technology.

It was in 2001 that I really got to grips with virtual working rather unexpectedly. I was due to fly out of London Heathrow to Newark, New Jersey on 13 September to run the kick-off for a new, major global programme for my then employer, Mars Inc. Does that date ring a bell for you? Well, to cut a long story short, the 9/11 tragedy put a stop to my travel plans. None of us were allowed to fly for months. I felt as if I had been thrown into the deep end as I had to learn how to make a programme kick-off meeting work, plus the subsequent programme, when I couldn't be face to face with all the other team members.

Suffice it to say, the programme went well, thanks to colleagues and others who helped me to translate what I already knew to this new, virtual world. As a trained and certified facilitator, I was able to tap into the human side of virtual work and apply and adapt my prior knowledge to this new situation.

Since that programme, much of my work has been virtual. I left Mars and founded Making Projects Work Ltd. My clients are spread around the world and I often work with them without travelling. I run international, virtual conferences such as the Virtual Working Summit (virtualworkingsummit.com) and the Business Analysis Summit (basummit.com) from my office in an English market town. My mentoring groups meet virtually, learning together and supporting one another, with discussions in a shared online space. I have taken part in academic research into building relationships online and I have served professional associations through mostly virtual special interest groups.

In my leisure time, I am learning to play the violin and even that involves a virtual group! I am part of a group of over 1,000 adult starters of string instruments around the world, who share tips and their progress online. I have played duets with new friends in places as far apart as Doha and Madrid as a result of getting to know them virtually.

What will you gain from reading this book

This book is designed to help you gain practical advice and ideas on how to develop your leadership of virtual work and virtual teams. It starts off with understanding yourself, working with others remotely in and out of meetings, introduces the range of technology for virtual work and continues into more complex aspects, such as working across cultures, generations, languages and time zones. This is shown in the virtual leadership model in Figure 0.2.

Figure 0.2 The virtual leadership model

Here is how the book is laid out chapter by chapter. In Chapter 1 I give an outline of the ups and downs of virtual work, drawing upon research on challenges faced by hundreds of virtual workers around the world. The rest of the book follows the leadership model from the centre outwards. Chapter 2 describes the core of the model: self. Before individuals can lead others effectively, they need to develop their own leadership mindset, skills and behaviours. This is especially true virtually. It is critical that people are aware of their own strengths and weaknesses, that they choose the most appropriate behaviours and attitudes, and that they come across as authentic.

Chapter 3 moves outwards to focus on working with others. It expands the ideas discussed in Chapter 2 to include knowing others, building trust and working with them effectively. We will explore how to set up a virtual team for success and how to take over leadership of an existing team, however dysfunctional. We look at mixed teams, part face-to-face and part remote, and cover how to create a level playing field. We touch on how the virtual leader can improve virtual teams from any chair.

Chapter 4 introduces technology. As I have already explained, many people assume that good technology is all you need to have effective virtual working, but this is not true. Technology is merely an enabler. Only with strong foundations of leadership of self and the ability to work with others can technology be used effectively. This chapter explains the different ways of working remotely and looks at which tools work best in different situations. It presents an overview of the practicalities of virtual meetings, as well as the use of social media, collaboration tools and other asynchronous technologies.

Chapter 5 focuses on leading virtual meetings: preparation for success; making virtual meetings work through engaging people and achieving action through virtual meetings. Chapter 6 considers virtual work outside of meetings, exploring how to lead your team between virtual get-togethers, keeping them engaged and in touch. We explore the challenge of productivity as a virtual worker. In Chapter 7, I dive into the complexities that affect virtual teams: working across cultures, time zones, languages and generations.

The book rounds off with Chapter 8, which focuses on several pitfalls of virtual work and how to overcome them. It is full of real, practical business situations and challenges faced by leaders, gathered from people from around the world. I draw content from across the chapters to weave together my response on how best to tackle each situation or challenge. This is designed to give quick, practical advice that you can apply straight away. The final chapter summarizes the key messages of the book and encourages you to take action by sharing stories of people who are using virtual leadership to transform their lives and the work that they do.

Each chapter contains a short introduction, summarizing its benefits. You will find strategies, practical tools such as checklists, case studies, stories, advice and visuals (tables and figures) to bring the material to life. At the end of each chapter, there are reflective questions to encourage you to think through the implications for your own situation and come up with actions you can take immediately to improve your virtual leadership and virtual working. You will find a list of references and further reading there too. Throughout the book, you will also find short stories, each giving you a window on one person's virtual world.

To support you even further, I have created a complementary website, www.virtualleadershipbook.com, where you can download many tools to use and colour mind-maps of each chapter in the book. You will find more information there and links to a wide variety of really helpful resources and discussions, with other readers and with me.

Where should I start?

The book flows from the beginning, as it builds from the centre of the virtual leadership model outwards. However, most virtual workers are very busy professionals, so each chapter can be read separately. For those with the tightest time constraints, I recommend starting by scanning Chapter 8 to find those scenarios that are closest to your own challenges, and then apply the suggestions that you feel are applicable to your context.

Further resources

This book, along with extra resources at www.virtualleadershipbook.com, aims to shine a light on all these areas, providing practical tips that can be applied straight away to make a difference. Please do report back on your progress via the book's website and also interact with me and other readers there.

I wish you all the best as you explore how virtual leadership could support your virtual work.

The ups and downs of virtual working

At the start of this book, we explore the world of virtual work. We will hear from people around the world about the joys and challenges of working virtually. We look at those areas where virtual work has similar challenges to traditional, face-to-face work and we explore the unique challenges that remote working requires. We will also hear more about and explore the results of my research for this book.

The benefits of reading this chapter will include:

- You will gain a greater understanding of the skills that you can apply from your face-to-face working experience and a wider knowledge of the challenges you will face in virtual settings.
- By hearing other people's experiences, you will become aware of what works well and will be forewarned of some of the potential problem areas.
- You will gain an insight into the experiences of people who work virtually.

Where virtual working works well

When virtual working works, it can be a fun, rewarding experience. It can give you access to the best people with the best skills, wherever they are in the world, as many global project managers and start-up entrepreneurs have found.

Virtual teams typically include more diverse people than local, face-to-face teams. This means a wider range of skills, knowledge, experience and culture, which can be invaluable when dealing with customers or staff from around the world and understanding their needs.

Figure 1.1 The ups and downs of virtual working – chapter mind-map

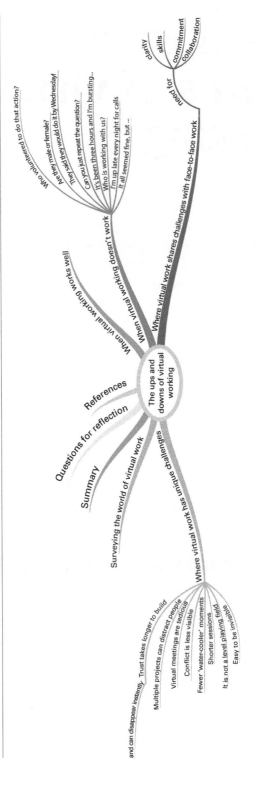

Virtual teams can be productive and provide support 24 hours a day, seven days a week by working with colleagues spread around the world. Using a 'follow-the-sun' principle, teams work to their own office hours and hand over the work to their colleagues at the end of their working day. With three teams on different continents, you can have continuous support without needing to employ people working shifts in one location.

For individuals, virtual working gives much more flexibility as to where they can work. A client of mine is based in the UK, with family members living in South Africa. She likes to spend time in South Africa with her family each year and is able to do so by working virtually. This flexibility of place and, to some extent, time, can be really helpful for those who are grappling with childcare or the need to be available for elderly parents, often women. A colleague from Greece works virtually for employers in the United States and Australia, thereby avoiding the turmoil of the Greek economy.

My cousin Carol is a doctor who loves travelling and working around the world. In 2014 she was serving a term as the resident medic on the remote Pitcairn Islands, which are located in the Pacific Ocean. The only scheduled way to reach these islands is by sea, travelling from French Polynesia. Apart from visiting cruise liners, the only ship visits 12 times per year.

As Carol's term on Pitcairn was coming to an end, she kept an eye out for her next appointment. She soon spotted an advertisement for doctors in Qatar. Although recruiters were visiting Australia and New Zealand to do face-to-face interviews for these roles, there was no way that Carol could leave Pitcairn for so long. In the end the whole recruitment process happened virtually with interviews conducted via videoconference. Carol impressed the recruiters with her wide experience and was offered a job in Qatar. It is lovely for me to have a relative to visit when I'm working in Doha and, without virtual recruiting, the hospital in Qatar would have missed out on an excellent doctor.

Virtual technologies allow people to do things together in ways that could only be dreamt of by previous generations. An example here was how General McChrystal of the US Army in Iraq used video links to share information with over 7,000 people each night. Rather than traditional command-and-control, which would have kept such information in the hands of the top leaders, he found that the complex environment in Iraq needed a new strategy where leaders on the ground knew as much as the top brass of the army (McChrystal *et al*, 2015). Another new way of working supported by virtual technologies is international recruitment: recruiters can interview people via video link from almost anywhere in the world. Technology can also allow academics to provide world-class education at a fraction of the cost and broaden access. Organizations are beginning to tap into these possibilities.

A year before writing this book, I tried out virtual education for myself and joined a massive open online course (MOOC) run by the University of Edinburgh and learnt all about music theory without having to pay a fee. This allows access to higher-level education to many who were previously excluded. My then 12-year-old daughter Charlotte was one of the 91,000 people who joined in and she gained 99 per cent in the final assessment, beating me in the process! Even a few years ago, high-school students just did not have access to university-level education like this, let alone have a chance of doing better than their parents.

With the widespread movement of family members and friends around the world, people are finding that virtual technologies are very helpful to keep in touch more easily. When I met my New Zealander husband in the 1990s, he had to limit phone calls home, as they were prohibitively expensive. Nowadays we can use free video calling to keep in touch with distant relatives without spending a penny. This means that people are becoming more used to the idea and the practical use of video and other virtual working technologies at home, as well as at work.

When virtual working doesn't work

Virtual working has so much promise, but it doesn't always deliver. Below are some very typical scenarios to show some of the ways that virtual working and virtual meetings can get tricky. In this section, names have been changed so as not to embarrass the individuals involved.

Who volunteered to do that action?

Kate organizes high-level, international conferences with senior people from governments and companies. She told me how, in conference calls, often a voice will pipe up and offer to take an action. Unfortunately, the person speaking usually does not identify themselves and so no one knows who they are. This means that Kate cannot record the action against anyone's name. Such actions cannot be followed up properly and are unlikely to get done. (See Chapter 5 for ways to prevent this and to challenge this behaviour diplomatically if it does happen.)

Are they male or female?

When I was consulting with a group in Spain, Tomás explained his dilemma: 'I had been working with someone from India via e-mail for a while, but had no idea if they were male or female. Their name didn't help me and I really didn't know. I thought that it would become clear as soon as we had a team conference call. Unfortunately, I still couldn't tell. The voice was completely neutral and could have been either male or female. In the write-up afterwards, I had to refer to this person as 'they' when everyone else was 'he' or 'she'. It was very embarrassing!' (See Chapter 5 for ways around this one.)

They said they would do it by Wednesday!

Over lunch in Switzerland, I heard from Daniel about his frustrations on his project. He was working with a team of software developers overseas: 'When I asked them if they could get some work done by Wednesday, they all said that they could. Now it's Friday and there is no evidence that the work has even started. It drives me mad!' This sounded familiar and I asked Daniel if his colleagues were based in the Middle East, India or elsewhere in Asia. He agreed that they were from India. I introduced him to the concept of saving face, a deep-rooted cultural characteristic that Daniel needed to know about and to phrase his questions accordingly. (See Chapter 7 for more on how to be productive across cultures, especially on working well with people of different cultures from your own.)

Can you just repeat the question?

I have spoken to large numbers of people about virtual working and most confess that they are not always completely focused on their virtual meetings. Zoe was particularly honest: 'I have a global management meeting at 10 pm on Friday nights. By then I am tired and ready for the weekend. My colleagues in the United States are all wide awake and at work, as it is still during office hours for them. I take a large glass of red wine up to my study and join in with the introductions. By the time they get into the meeting proper, I'm relaxing and sipping my wine. I only stop if I hear my name and then ask them to repeat the question.'

Most people wouldn't be quite as audacious as Zoe, but, even with the best intentions, virtual meetings are often tedious and other work, projects, social media and games can tempt people away from being completely focused. If you hear people ask you to repeat the question, it is a good indication that their attention had wandered away and only came back when they heard their name spoken. (See Chapter 5 for ideas about how to make your own virtual meetings really engaging and techniques to ensure that people are focused throughout.)

It's been three hours and I'm bursting...

I joined a project risk management review for a major international manufacturing company. This review ran all morning, using a conference call with a shared screen. The screen showed a few cells of a very large spreadsheet, which recorded all the risks. After three hours, I was desperate for a bathroom break, as the conversation hadn't stopped. As an observer, I wasn't an official participant, so didn't feel that I could ask them to stop just for me. It seems that many leaders of virtual meetings assume that people are able to operate like machines. However, we are all human and virtual meetings work much better when leaders take this into account! (Find out more about planning virtual meetings for humans in Chapter 5.)

Who is working with us?

In the same risk management review, I was an invited observer. However, due to technological challenges and mismatched software systems, it took me a while to join the meeting. This meant that I wasn't able to introduce myself at the start. No one invited me to introduce myself when I joined the call. As the meeting was already in full swing, I kept quiet. There were only three or four people talking, although I heard later that there had been at least 10 people on the call. Who was there? Had anyone else joined the call, perhaps uninvited? Were uninvited people hearing confidential company information? No one knew who was listening. This is quite common. (See Chapter 5 for more on how to make sure everyone is clear who else is in the meeting and how to deal with confidentiality.)

I'm up late every night for calls

Janet was exhausted. She works for a major pharmaceutical company on global projects. Many of her key contacts are based in the United States and she is based in the UK. This is true on many of the major virtual projects that she runs. 'Penny', she said, 'I'm permanently exhausted! There are always people in the team who want to ask me things. If they are based in Los Angeles, then they only arrive at work when I'm meant to be leaving.' As a conscientious project manager, Janet found that it was easiest to spend most of her evenings on one-to-one and group calls with her project team members from her home, but this was causing her to get more and more exhausted and was negatively impacting her work–life balance. (See tips for working across time zones in Chapter 7.)

It is interesting that, while virtual working gives more flexibility in the workplace, too often that flexibility has meant that working hours have extended well beyond their normal boundaries, as Janet has found. Where people are unable to work into the evenings, due to childcare or other responsibilities, they might find themselves at a disadvantage or even excluded entirely (Meyerson and Fletcher, 2000).

It all seemed fine, but...

While all the problems above are fairly easy to spot, this one is quite different. Everything seems to be going well. You are letting people know what work needs to be done. Everything seems to be progressing, as far as you can tell. The only indication that something might be wrong is that people are a bit quiet in meetings. When you ask in meetings if everything is going well, the universal answer is, 'It's fine', or, perhaps, silence. Finally you find out that major conflict has broken out and that some team members will not work with others. You wonder how you could have been so unaware of this for so long. Virtual conflict like this can be very hard to spot. Often it develops quite far before being spotted and is difficult to put right once it has been spotted. (See Chapters 5, 6, 7 and 8 for tips on how to listen out for and react to conflict when you do not have the advantage of seeing people on a day-to-day basis.)

Where virtual work shares challenges with face-to-face work

My experience and survey results show that there are many areas where the challenges of virtual work are the same as those of face-to-face work. These include:

- *The need for clarity.* People working effectively need to have a clear, shared purpose for what they are doing and a clear, shared high-level vision of the outcome of their work together. They should have clear individual goals and understand how their own goals fit with other people's goals to support the vision. At a detailed level, they need to be clear on the tasks they need to accomplish and to know who is doing what.

- *The need for skills.* People need to have the appropriate skills to carry out their roles effectively as part of a team or group.

- *The need for commitment.* However people are working, whether face-to-face or remote, they need to be committed to completing their part of the work, so that others can rely on them.

- *The need for collaboration.* In the 21st century, most professional work is now knowledge work. It is important that people can collaborate with each other and share information as required. I was disappointed to find out from my survey results that, in some traditional industries, command-and-control leadership is still thriving and that sharing information is not widespread.

Where virtual work has unique challenges

Virtual work brings a set of challenges, both management and technological, which differ from those faced in face-to-face environments. Below are some of these challenges that came up in the survey.

Easy to be invisible

With virtual groups distributed around different locations, it is very easy for individual members to become invisible and to 'drop off the radar'. In a face-to-face meeting, people will notice if someone is quiet and does not contribute. In virtual meetings, on the other hand, a core group can discuss a topic for a long time, get caught up in it and completely forget that there were other people present who did not contribute.

It is important as a virtual leader to monitor participation during meetings and in between, as this does not happen automatically. When you notice anyone in danger of becoming invisible, you can then draw him or her gently back into the group. (See more in Chapter 5 on virtual team meetings and Chapter 6 on working together between meetings.)

It is not a level playing field

There are likely to be people in a group working virtually who are closer to power and resources than others, who naturally have more influence. In virtual meetings where some people are remote and others are together in a room, it is all too easy for those at the other end of the line to be forgotten, as those who are face to face discuss things together.

As a virtual leader, it is your job to create a level playing field, where you adapt to those with the least connection, rather than let the face-to-face group dominate. Be aware of how people's locations will give rise to differences in influence and seek to mitigate these differences. (See more on creating a level playing field in team meetings in Chapter 5 and between meetings in Chapter 6.)

Shorter sessions

I try to limit the length of my virtual sessions to an hour if possible or 90 minutes at the most. After this time, I notice that people's attention starts to wander, even with all the tools I use to keep people as engaged as possible throughout virtual meetings! For this reason, it makes sense to keep virtual meetings short. If you need to cover a lot of ground, you will need to run several short sessions rather than convening an all-day meeting. (For more on virtual meetings, see Chapter 5.)

Fewer 'water-cooler' moments

Teams working at the same location have plenty of opportunities to chat around water coolers, coffee machines, in corridors or over lunch. This serendipitous meeting of colleagues tends to build up relationships between people outside of team meetings and formal work. This means that relation-ships between team members develop and that people get to know and trust each other. If there is any hint of a problem or conflict, people can go and find their colleague, explore what the matter might be and resolve any issues.

In virtual work, there are no shared 'water coolers'. While one person sips a warm cup of tea after a bracing lunchtime walk in an English winter, their virtual colleague might be licking an ice lolly to cool down at the start of a hot summer's day in Rio. There is no chance of bumping into each other and chatting in an unplanned way!

As a virtual leader, create planned ways to have informal conversations to build relationships. (See Chapter 3 for ways of working with others remotely and Chapter 6 for more about building the team in between meetings and how to create 'water-cooler moments' virtually.)

Conflict is less visible

In a virtual team, it is easy for people to remain silent and for this to be missed. Conflict can bubble away under the surface and lie undetected for much longer than in a face-to-face team. Once conflict does emerge into the open, sorting it out is much harder with people remote from one another.

In a face-to-face team, it is easy to deal with issues as soon as they arise. Conflict is visible on people's faces and/or in their body language. Between meetings you can gather people together to sort things out. In a virtual team, on the other hand, you are likely to miss out on many indications of conflict. It is important to always listen out for silence and for subtle indications of conflict, such as people appearing to go along with things but with reluctance in the tone of their voice. (See Chapters 3 for tips on working with others, Chapter 5 for meetings and Chapter 6 for working together between team meetings.)

Virtual meetings are tedious

Many virtual meetings are so boring that they cannot compete with other distractions, such as e-mail, social media or even games! Take conference calls, for example: in a call, a listener is only using their sense of hearing. The other senses are not involved. It is all too easy for something else to catch their eye and distract them away from the call. It seems that when human bodies are free to do other things, they will. There is a rumour that some people even go to the bathroom during calls – I have heard the occasional flush over the years.

Remote participants need to be actively engaged and kept involved in meetings so that they find it easy to keep focused and participate. Using richer forms of communication can help, such as visuals and sharing body language, as can the use of immersive virtual worlds. (You will learn strategies and techniques for this in Chapter 4 on virtual technologies and Chapter 5 on virtual meetings.)

Multiple projects can distract people

When people have multiple projects it becomes even harder for them to focus on any one piece of virtual work. In my work with project managers, I notice that around two-thirds of them are involved in multiple virtual projects, with around one-third having five or more projects on the go at any one time. With so many things to think about at once, it is easy for virtual projects to fade away and for local, face-to-face work to gain more attention in its place. It is natural that local work would gain more commitment as team members can just walk over to see how things are going or to ask questions.

As a virtual leader, awareness of this is important as you set the team culture and think of ways for people to stay focused and committed. (There will be more on this in Chapters 5 and 6.)

Trust takes longer to build and can disappear instantly

While trust can be an issue for face-to-face teams, it takes even longer to build trust between virtual colleagues. As a virtual leader, you cannot assume that, once you have trust, it is there forever. It can disappear without warning at any moment.

As a virtual leader, be very careful to generate a positive team culture and, wherever possible, build relationships between team members with a face-to-face meeting early on. (We will consider aspects of trust in Chapter 3 and how to apply these aspects to virtual meetings in Chapter 5.)

Surveying the world of virtual work

People use virtual working in a wide range of roles and organizations across the world. To gain an insight into this variety, I asked people to fill in an online survey summarizing the challenges they face with virtual work and then asked them about what really works for them virtually. The 169 participants came from 24 countries around the world, predominantly from the United Kingdom (66 per cent). Other countries represented included the United

States (10 per cent), followed by Belgium, Italy, Germany, Australia, Switzerland and Finland, all around 2 per cent. Participants filled in a short survey of nine questions. The survey included questions about their role and organization, their country of residence and their involvement in virtual work. Respondents wrote about their own challenges with virtual work and then, from a prepared list of typical issues – gathered from the author's consulting work, previous surveys and webinars – chose all those that applied to their work. The survey participants then gave their own tips for effective virtual working. You can find a link to the survey at the website to support this book: www.virtualleadershipbook.com. Over half of the respondents agreed to follow up with the author, sharing stories and case studies of their own experiences. In most cases, these were shared on the understanding of anonymity or only sharing first names. You can read many of these tips and stories throughout the book and in the story boxes at the end of most chapters.

The majority of participants in the survey worked for multinational companies (60 per cent), many for large organizations with more than 250 employees (46 per cent) although there were also people responding who were from micro-companies with 10 or fewer employees (18 per cent). Just over half were members of virtual teams and just under half lead virtual working.

Let's explore the results. The survey asked participants to choose from a list all the challenges of virtual working that they found applied to their situation. Participants then had a chance to comment on what they personally found difficult when working virtually. 'Engaging remote participants' stood out as the main challenge, ticked by 76 per cent of the survey takers.

Next on the list were a group of challenges, all rated very similarly:

- 'Missing out on dynamics and nuances of conversation' (58 per cent).
- 'Working across time zones' (56 per cent).
- 'Working across different cultures' (56 per cent).
- 'Building trust' (55 per cent).

These are key issues for virtual leaders, especially when dealing with the 'nitty-gritty' aspects of virtual working.

The next grouping included:

- 'Monitoring work done' (47 per cent).
- 'Different understanding of the same term or word' (44 per cent).
- 'Detecting and dealing with conflict' (42 per cent).

- 'I don't get to spend much time with remote people and so I don't know them as well as local team members' (42 per cent).
- 'Working across different languages' (41 per cent).
- 'Using technology' (41 per cent).

All of these will be addressed in the coming chapters.

The survey then asked what made virtual teams work together more productively. Answers were free form and the most popular answer by far was meeting up face to face, either once at the start of the project, once a year or more regularly. This was interesting and not entirely unexpected. Face-to-face interaction is what we humans are most used to and we have learnt to be effective communicators by using non-verbal cues. It is important to learn how to build trust virtually and how to handle difficult conversations when meeting face to face is not possible. Without this, virtual working will not be nearly as effective as it possibly could be.

Other common suggestions included:

- regular, clear communications, without lengthy gaps in between;
- clear roles and responsibilities;
- the use of meeting agendas;
- being clear about how the team will work together in meetings, and overall;
- shared vision, outcomes and sense of purpose;
- an open team culture, with each person listened to and able to ask for help from the others;
- time to get to know each other and build rapport and trust;
- understanding each team member's perspectives and how they prefer to work;
- technology should be easy to use and up to the challenge;
- the use of video over audio alone;
- widespread use of screen-sharing technology;
- the use of a common repository that everyone can access easily.

Interestingly, while some people preferred to use the telephone, others preferred to use instant messenger. Perhaps these people were from different generations? I did not ask for people's age, so I don't know for sure. Other than on this point, the feedback was very consistent. We explore these through the rest of the chapters in this book.

If you would like to add your own views to the survey, you can find a link to it at the resource site for the book: www.virtualleadershipbook.com.

Summary

Throughout this chapter, we have seen the great promise of virtual working: being able to work together regardless of location, and all the flexibility that can bring for organizations and for individuals. Of course, this brings opportunities, but challenges too, which we will deal with in the rest of the book.

Questions for reflection

Here are some questions to help you think through the ups and downs of virtual working for you personally and for your organization:

1 What success have you already had with virtual working? What has gone well for you? What have you learnt that you can apply in the future?

2 What have you found harder in your virtual work? What would you like to change in the future?

3 What does virtual working allow you to do that was not possible 20 or 30 years ago? What are you grateful for?

4 Where do you find virtual working tough? What scenarios in the chapter rang true for you? What scenarios of your own could you add? [Please write these down, as you will find these useful as you read through and apply the rest of the book.]

5 What insights did you gain from the survey results? How would your answers differ from those given by the respondents? What about your virtual team members?

References

McChrystal, S, Silverman, D, Collins, T and Fussell, C (2015) *Team of Teams: New rules of engagement for a complex world*, Penguin, New York

Meyerson, D and Fletcher, J K (2000) [accessed 29 February 2016] A Modest Manifesto for Shattering the Glass Ceiling, *Harvard Business Review* [Online] https://hbr.org/2000/01/a-modest-manifesto-for-shattering-the-glass-ceiling

Virtual leadership, mindset and approach

02

In this chapter I discuss virtual leadership, what it is and how it is critical to successful virtual working. We explore various approaches to leadership and see how virtual leadership needs a different mindset from traditional leadership. We consider what makes great leaders great and investigate what skills you need to become an outstanding virtual leader, whatever your role in remote teams. We explore the attitudes, behaviours and aspects of personality and identity that can make or break a virtual leader. At the end of the chapter, we touch on how you can use your environment to support your virtual leadership.

By reading this chapter, you will:

- anderstand what virtual leadership is and how it goes beyond more traditional forms of leadership;
- appreciate how any member of a virtual team can act as a virtual leader, not just the assigned leader;
- gain an insight into the mindset, attitudes and behaviours that you need to be a successful virtual leader;
- come up with new ways of using aspects of your personality and identity to support your work as a virtual leader.

Figure 2.1 A mind-map of this chapter

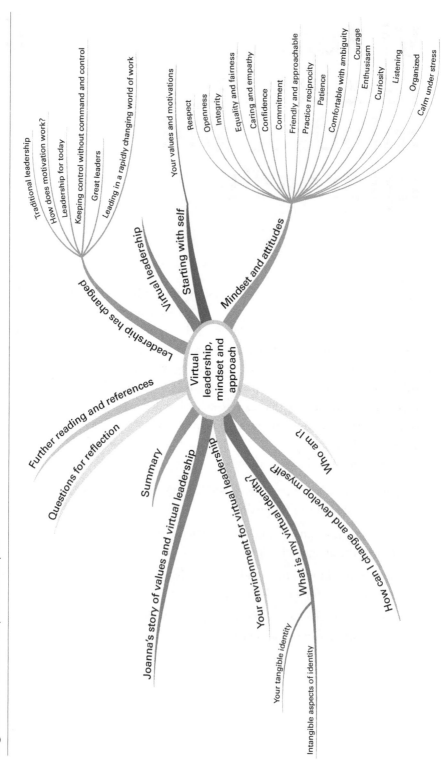

Leadership has changed

Leadership complements management and it is more than just getting things done. It is about sharing and agreeing a compelling view of the future, connecting with people and engaging them in the work, and together delivering results. There are many different ideas and models of leadership and probably almost as many books written on the subject! Searches on leadership come up with hundreds of millions of hits. Let's look back in time to understand a bit more about where leadership comes from and how it is evolving to cope with our rapidly changing world.

Traditional leadership

Traditional leadership around the world usually focused on particular individuals who led from the front. These were powerful people, usually men, who commanded and, when they spoke, others had to follow their lead, whatever that meant. An example of this was in the Charge of the Light Brigade in the Crimean War in 1854. The message 'Charge!' came through to the Light Brigade, a group of 600 lightly armoured British troops on horseback. They didn't question the order but followed though, leading to very high casualties and many deaths. Alfred, Lord Tennyson captured this well in 'The Charge of the Light Brigade':

> Their's not to make reply,
> Their's not to reason why,
> Their's but to do and die:
> Into the valley of Death
> Rode the six hundred.

In the 20th century, command-and-control was the primary way that managers worked, influenced by both the industrial economy of the time and the military leadership styles used in two world wars and subsequent conflicts. It especially suits areas with lots of repetitive action and unskilled labour, such as factories and mass-production environments. In this autocratic style of working, managers hold the influence, power and authority, along with the responsibility to deliver. Managers make the important decisions and relay these to workers to carry them out. While workers are unlikely to be asked to obey to death, as in the Light Brigade, they still are expected 'not to reason why' but to get on with the work instead. Managers supervise the workers closely and control the work done. Communication is predominantly one way, flowing from the manager to the workers, who expect to be told what to do. The manager is seen to have the wisdom, knowledge and experience. The workers comply.

The command-and-control style can be efficient, especially in crisis situations where there is not time for discussion and deliberation, and where problems are known and solutions are clear. The leader needs to deliver the results, using standard methods and experience. It can be useful today in hierarchical organizations for short projects, which do not require creativity and which generate lots of output by following standard procedures. Outside of these cases, command and control comes with major issues, the biggest of which is that it does not tap into the creativity and skills of the individuals doing the work. Henry Ford said, 'Why is it every time I ask for a pair of hands, they come with a brain attached?' This implies that Ford found each worker's brain to be a problem, rather than a rich resource to tap into.

Command-and-control leadership works best in situations where the workers are unskilled, the leaders have the knowledge required, and work is repetitive and routine in nature. In the late 20th century, as repetitive jobs were automated with the use of robots or computers, command-and-control leadership began to fall out of favour. With more and more workers handling knowledge rather than things, using thinking as a key tool, it no longer made sense not to harness their minds fully. Command and control tends to reduce workers' intrinsic motivation to do good work. It can create an 'us and them' culture, dividing managers and workers, as seen when workers take industrial action.

Command-and-control managers are likely to micro-manage the work done by workers, wanting to know precisely what is being done at any time and, preferably, being able to see the workers' progress with their own eyes. This is not going to work in a virtual world, is it? While micro-managing their team might give a manager the feeling of control, it can destroy individuals' motivation to work. How have you felt when people have micro-managed you? I suspect you didn't like it much. I certainly don't like it at all! In our virtual world, motivation is really important as it helps to keep remote workers engaged and focused on their virtual work.

So, command and control is not a sensible option for most virtual work. It cuts out the creativity and skills of most of the team, reduces their motivation to do a good job and creates division. It tries to keep control at the centre, with the manager, who needs to spend a lot of time monitoring what everyone is doing. Let's explore what might work better, starting by considering how to increase motivation.

How does motivation work?

With the complex working environment of the 21st century and with large numbers of repetitive jobs now carried out by robot or computer, many workers are now knowledge workers. They are well educated and have highly developed skills. This is especially true for those virtual workers who are recruited for the particular knowledge and skills they can bring, regardless of location. So how do we motivate virtual, knowledge workers?

Studies of motivation show that there are three key aspects that motivate workers engaged in non-routine tasks (Pink, 2011). These are:

- *Purpose*: the connection to a cause larger than ourselves that gives meaning to work. It is the yearning to do what we do in the service of something larger than ourselves and it gives our work meaning.
- *Autonomy*: the desire to direct our own lives.
- *Mastery*: the urge to get better and better at something that matters.

We now know that these three elements are far more powerful motivators for knowledge workers than the rewards and punishments often used, even today.

Traditional command-and-control leadership does not give workers autonomy, as the boss directs the work, but knowledge workers relish autonomy, virtual workers especially so. One study showed that virtual managers were very happy to have a remote manager themselves, as they were free to get on with their jobs rather than being watched all the time (Hall, 2007). (Incidentally, when the same people were asked how their own virtual teams felt, they were concerned that people reporting to them might feel isolated, forgotten and lonely. This is an interesting mismatch!)

So what sort of leadership styles will tap into these three powerful motivators and provide a good basis for effective virtual work? Let's look at some options.

Leadership for today

While command-and-control leadership is still practised in places, especially with routine work, most leaders find that a more inclusive approach works best. This empowers workers to take their part, not only in carrying out the work but also contributing to decision making. The wisdom, skill and experience of each individual team member are essential to the success of the team overall. Leaders value the input and contribution of each person. Leaders agree clear, measurable goals and timescales with their workers, instead of sending them orders and monitoring their output constantly. How precisely workers do their work is up to each individual. The leaders essentially get out of their workers' way, giving them the autonomy to achieve the work in the way of their choice. This helps to motivate workers and it works well virtually.

Some organizations take this even further and operate self-directed teams. These are empowered teams where managers support the team members rather than supervising the work. Each person shares responsibility for managing and doing the work and the team are jointly responsible for the quality of the output. Team members in a self-directed team tend to show high levels of commitment and motivation as the leadership is distributed across the team. Here, the leader becomes more of a facilitator and a coach, making it easy for the people in their team to achieve goals and to develop both individually and as a group. In a way, this turns the whole idea of leader from someone whose primary goal is to be the boss to someone whose primary goal is to serve others. Many writers have explored what this means for leaders, talking about servant leadership, authentic leadership, facilitative leadership and many other terms.

As a coach and facilitator, the leader asks questions to help people work out the solution for themselves, rather than telling them what to do. This works best with people who already have some knowledge and skills. Coaching moves them towards being more self-reliant in the future. Any solutions they come up with are their own solutions and so they are likely to be committed to making them happen. Their own solutions are more likely to work with their local context than something imposed from far away. This sort of coaching can be done just as easily over telephone calls as face to face.

This move away from traditional leadership helps to solve another problem. All the attributes required of a leader in our fast-changing world are highly unlikely to be found in just one person. It is far easier to cover these attributes with several people acting together, and a more distributed leadership achieves this. 'Intellectually, it is evident that the heroic leader cannot continue to exist in today's complex, dynamic organizations, no matter how talented and gifted... Leadership is a distributed phenomenon, not just emanating from the top' (Avery, 2004).

Keeping control without command and control

'But how do I keep control?' is a typical question for a manager who is used to command and control and is challenged to change their style. It is important to agree what the virtual team is trying to achieve, and the level of risk involved. The next step is to work out the level of reporting and the key measures that will help flag to the manager and the team as a whole when they need to get involved to support a colleague to deliver. Don't try to include a large number of controls – this would be counterproductive! One or two key controls or measures should be enough: the most important ones only. In addition, there might be regulatory or legislative controls imposed on the team, which you need to track. This move does not mean doing away with control altogether. It means letting each team member control the work that they are responsible for. Minimizing the manager's leader's controls like this needs a good level of trust between him/her and the team, which we will explore further in Chapter 3.

Many organizations try to control what happens by imposing rules on their staff. In a fast-changing world, fixed rules give people very little flexibility to adjust to changing circumstances and complex situations. Instead of a fixed rule, use principles to help everyone to do the right thing. When I worked at Mars Inc, there were five principles to follow. As long as we abided by these, we had great flexibility to do whatever we felt was right in any situation. Another example is Alphabet, the holding company of Google, which has the principle 'do the right thing – follow the law, act honourably, and treat each other with respect' (Alphabet, 2015). The use of principles over rules works just as well remotely as it does when everyone is in the same location.

Great leaders

What does great leadership look like? When researchers ask people about their leadership preferences and when election results come in, the results often come back showing that many people think of leaders as attractive, charismatic, white, older men, able to take risks and likely to be self-centred and somewhat confrontational.

In terms of effective leadership, none of these matter and some of these are the opposite of what is really needed (Chamorro-Premuzic, 2015). What does matter in leaders is that they are or have:

- competence;
- good judgement;
- integrity;
- vision;
- self-awareness;

- prudence;
- conscientiousness;
- intelligence;
- self-control;
- empathy;
- altruism;
- sociability.

A study in the UK explored the difference between outstanding leaders and good leaders (Tamkin *et al*, 2010). Their conclusions were threefold:

- Outstanding leaders think and act systemically, considering how different aspects of their organizations interconnect.
- Outstanding leaders perceive relationships as the route to performance and give huge amounts of their time and focus to people and the climate of the organization.
- Outstanding leaders are self-confidently humble, as they know that they cannot personally achieve any of the outcomes that they strive for, but only through their impact and influence on people.

In a study lasting three decades, Kouzes and Posner have asked about the characteristics of admired leaders. The answers have come out consistently over time and are: honest, forward-looking, inspiring and competent (Kouzes and Posner, 2011). These are rated far higher than any other characteristic. Interestingly, the same four come up all over the world, with people from five continents all choosing these as their top four, albeit sometimes in a different order.

As a virtual leader, consider these lists and think how you can be the best leader you can be. When team members are spread around geographically, it is especially important to engage people. Your own interpersonal skills will be crucial here to build good relationships with team members and to boost team morale, even at a distance. Honesty forms the basis for trust and means that your virtual team will accept what you have to say. Being forward-looking helps you to encourage your team towards a common, future goal together. Inspiration will help people to strive to do their best. Your competence means that you can do the job and that you will not let others down. Self-awareness of your own skills and abilities is the basis for your own development.

Kouzes and Posner present a set of practices that they have found when interviewing people about their best experiences of leading others (Kouzes and Posner, 2012). These are their 'Five Practices of Exemplary Leadership', to which I have added a little about how to apply each in a virtual context:

- *Model the way*: how you can set an example to your virtual colleagues, through what you do, what you say and what you write. Most of what they see will be via technology.

- *Inspire a shared vision*: help people to decide together on a common vision of what should be done, then build clear goals for the future that everyone has bought into.

- *Challenge the process*: getting to the essence of how things are done and articulating ways to improve. This can start with how you work together virtually but can go far beyond, to the processes and practices of your organizations.

- *Enable others to act*: build collaboration, even though you are far apart, engaging others and encouraging them to play their part. This means getting to know them and what makes them tick.

- *Encourage the heart*: recognize other people's contributions and celebrate successes.

How can you apply these to your own virtual work and your own virtual teams?

If you are wondering how you could possibly 'encourage the heart' in your virtual world, this story might give you some ideas:

Carl was invited to a baby shower in Canada. Family and friends of the mother-to-be were in two physical locations, so they connected by videoconference. The mother-to-be opened her gifts in full view of both groups, and people on both sites tucked into party food to celebrate the upcoming birth. This inspired Carl to lead a virtual celebration for his team's work.

Carl worked with 20 people on six sites across California. After the team successfully passed a major checkpoint for their project with a big deliverable complete, he hosted a virtual celebration. Booking two conveniently situated videoconference rooms, he encouraged people to

▶

travel to the nearest one to their site. With pizzas and soft drinks, the team celebrated their success together. Carl told me that he printed a big project timeline, 4 metres long, for each site – it was revealed at the meeting. The head of the department joined in to say how much he appreciated the team. Carl's final touch was to recognize individual contributions. But rather than do this himself, he invited each team member to share what they appreciated about two other team members, one they knew well and one they didn't know so well. He had planned an hour for this, but it went down so well that it took two hours, with people chiming in to acknowledge their colleagues.

If you cannot travel like this, you can still celebrate virtually. I used to send coloured sweets to each site on a large project and we enjoyed eating them and comparing which colours we preferred. We could have eaten pizza together, but with wide time zones, it would have been breakfast time for one person, who preferred porridge to pizza! Small chocolates seemed to work just fine.

Leading in a rapidly changing world of work

In the 21st century, we live in a rapidly changing world. Technology is transforming how we do business and allowing new ways of working. We have vast amounts of information available to us, which we can harness as never before. Cross-functional projects cut across hierarchies. New companies, with flatter structures than their traditional counterparts, are growing rapidly. Society is changing with a new generation joining the workforce who have grown up with the internet and cannot imagine a world without smartphones and mobile data. The context for leadership is more complicated than ever in our volatile, uncertain, complex and ambiguous world. Change is ever present and experience of the past does not always help.

There are two fundamental areas that any effective leader needs to explore, examine and understand in this rapidly changing world: themselves and their context. In the rest of this chapter, we consider the first, and the rest of the book considers the context of our work.

Virtual leadership

What leadership style suits virtual working? When team members are physically remote from one another, it is not possible for the leader to see what each person is doing. Another challenge is that people are very easily distracted away from virtual work to other projects, other work or even social media. So an autocratic and command-and-control leadership style will not work in this setting – with a few exceptions, even though some leaders are still trying their hardest to force-fit it.

When team members are remote, they need to be self-motivated to keep working. No one can glance over to see what they are doing and so it makes sense to give them autonomy on how they carry out their tasks. Engaging people's hearts and minds is key to keeping people feeling part of the team. A style that shares the wider purpose of the work and allows the people to do their best, and develop mastery, will motivate people further.

From my experience, the best leadership style for most virtual work is one where the leader servers the other people in the team, making it as easy as possible for each person to achieve their best for the team. The leader acts as a facilitator, literally 'making it easy'. They facilitate engagement of individuals in the team and the tasks, as much as doing the work. They create an environment where the team and the individuals can thrive and develop.

How would this facilitative leadership play out in reality in a virtual team? Of course, it would vary from person to person! Here are some of the things you might notice:

- A new team member joins the team. The leader asks in their one-to-one video call what the new member would like to get out of their time in the team. What skills would they like to develop and what experience would be useful to them as they progress? What help would they need to participate fully in the virtual team? What technology support would they need to get going? This discussion leads to a shared set of goals for the individual that support the overall goals of a team.

- When the leader calls a team member, they ask questions such as: 'How are things going?' 'How do you plan to get this done?' 'How can I help you to achieve your goals?' 'What can each of us do on our own sites that would be helpful for you?'

- If something goes wrong, instead of blame, the leader and the team will explore what is needed to put things right. If processes need changing, they will work together to come up with a better way to do things in the future.

- When things go well, the leader will give praise where it is due. Some might send handwritten thank-you cards to their team members, individually encouraging them by praising them for their hard work, highlighting the difference each has made. Perhaps the leader might arrange a virtual party, arranging for a small pack of celebratory food and drink to be delivered to each team member, to share together over videoconference. Of course they would need to take into account any dietary and cultural requirements!

Did you notice how the facilitative virtual leader used open questions, as the leader is exploring rather than telling people what to do?

This type of virtual leadership does not need to sit with any one person. It can be shared amongst team members, who can facilitate and coach each other. As a member of a virtual team it is possible to lead from any chair by contributing questions and making helpful suggestions.

Starting with self: your values and your motivations

To be the best virtual leader you can be, start working on yourself. Understand yourself. Reflect on what you do. Work to improve and learn.

What motivates you? What is important to you? What would you stand your ground for at work? These are intensely personal questions, which help you to understand your purpose. Once you know what makes you tick, you can align what you do with your values – you will find that it is much easier to make the right decisions as a leader, and in life. You will be more motivated as you are fulfilling your purpose. You will also be more aware of times when your values do not align with other people's values or your organization's values, giving you helpful insights as you plan what to do next. Leading with values makes you more authentic as a leader and helps to create a consistent climate for your team. Unfortunately, understanding your own values is not simple and can take a lifetime of thought and testing.

Values are what are important to each individual and are unique to that individual. One of my values is integrity, but how I express this value will be slightly different from someone else using the same word. In my virtual teams, *integrity* means that I need to be transparent with each team member and not adapt information so that different people hear different messages from me. Of course, this is more of a challenge virtually where people cannot observe my everyday behaviours, but they can see me on video at team meetings, listen to me speaking on conference calls and read what I have written on team collaboration tools, in e-mails and in instant messages. These need to be consistent to show integrity. It's harder than face-to-face, isn't it?

At the same time, my value of *empathy for each person* will also come into play, meaning that, where some people might find information hard to hear or to understand, I would make sure that I knew their situation, communicating the same message but in a way that lands well, leaving them clear on what to do next and aware that I understand their perspective. Once again, this is more of a challenge virtually, where I cannot see as clearly how a team member is doing. In a co-located office, I would know if anyone was struggling, just by changes in their behaviour, appearance or patterns of working. I don't have that luxury virtually, so I need to focus more on listening carefully for changes, noticing what is happening with people and asking them how they are.

All this listening, noticing and focus on team members presents a dilemma for me. I could ask to connect to them on social media outside of work, which would give me a wider perspective on their lives, but perhaps that might be going too far? I don't want to appear to stalk team members. I don't want them to feel pressurized to comply with a request from me to see their personal information, photos and friends. It seems that the limits between caring, empathy and stalking are becoming blurrier online and much more open to perception and interpretation! It's not easy, is it?

How does virtual working affect your values? For me, it allows me to keep in touch with a large network of people all over the world. Collaboration is an important value for me – working with others to produce outputs of value. Some of my collaborators have never met me face to face, even my first virtual working mentor, Nancy Settle-Murphy, despite being friends for over 15 years!

Virtual working helps me to do much of my work without needing to leave home. As I have teenage children now, it is helpful to them for me to be available when they need me and this fits with my values: my family is important. Sometimes values clash, though. I wrote this paragraph on a flight from Birmingham to Munich, on my way to work in Basle, Switzerland, for a client. While I enjoy the rich interaction over three days, it comes at a price. My value of making a difference to my clients clashes with my value of family and these two need to be kept in balance or I feel uncomfortable and my work suffers.

Finding your values

How can you find out what your values are? Let's begin to explore the answers now. Grab a pen and paper and go through these questions step by step:

1   Think back to peak experiences in your life, taking into account your home life as well as work. These are times when life couldn't get any better and you felt that what you were doing was just right. You felt happy, satisfied and maybe even proud too. Perhaps these were times when you were really effective and efficient? Bring each experience back to life by exploring what you could see at that precise moment, what you could hear around you and what people were saying, what you could feel on your skin and inside your body at that particular time. What was happening and why? What do you notice looking back over time? What values were in play? Write them down in a way that suits you: in a list or a mind-map.

    If you need inspiration, you might find that a list of values is helpful to trigger your own thoughts. You can find hundreds of values listed online (Pavlina, 2004).

2   An alternative way to approach this, is to think about times in your life when you felt that something was really wrong. You felt uncomfortable with what was happening, even if you didn't know exactly why. You probably had a gut reaction as well as thinking that there was something wrong. Looking back, which values were being compromised? Write these down too.

3   You might find it helpful to talk this through with others, as they are likely to notice values that you would miss, especially ones that you think of as normal. Ask them what they consider to be particularly important to you.

4   Once you have a full set of values, the next step is to sort them. Which ones are most important? Which ones would you want to prioritize? The best way to do this is to focus on a couple of values at any one time. Which one is more important? A useful question here is, 'If I could only satisfy one of these, which one would I choose?' If the more important one is not at the top, then swap them over. Then move on to the next pair down the list. Repeat this from the top of the list, until you have your values in order of priority from the most important at the top to the least important at the bottom.

5   Once you have your values listed and prioritized, test them. Are they right? Would you be happy to share the top three with your boss, your

partner (if you have one) and other family members? Do they make you feel proud and inspire you? If you find that one of your possible values could hurt you, or if your values contradict each other, then there is more work to be done!

6 What do your values mean for your virtual work? What will you keep doing that works well and fits your values? What things will you stop doing that conflict with your values? What do your values suggest that you could do differently as a virtual leader?

Once you have identified your values, review them regularly to remind yourself about what is most important to you. You might like to put them on a screensaver or a Post-it note that you will see every day as a natural reminder.

Your mindset and attitudes

What sort of leader are you? What behaviours do you use? How could you change to become a better leader?

Let's consider a range of attitudes and behaviours that are helpful to the virtual leader in turn, drawing from Brake (2008), Coats and Coddrington (2015), Settle-Murphy (2013) and others.

Respect

As a virtual leader, treat others with consideration. This means understanding their local context, their perspectives, their culture, their generation, their nationality and language and other aspects of their identity, and then choosing to act appropriately. An example of lack of respect came from Bob, completely unintentionally. He manages a global virtual team from Texas, United States. He once asked everyone to attend a conference call on Friday morning, his time. While the time fell at an appropriate time of day for each member of his global team, Bob had forgotten that Mariam, from Doha, Qatar, would not be at work. Friday is a holy day across most of the Middle East and the weekend runs from Friday to Saturday, rather than the Saturday to Sunday that Bob was used to in his home state of Texas.

As well as treating people considerately, value what they bring to the team. Respect their skills and the work they do. Show your appreciation, in a way that suits their culture, of course!

Openness

Be receptive to ideas from others, even if they are different from what you might come up with yourself. In a complex world, having diverse inputs and insights strengthens your team. Listen carefully to input from your team members, making sure that you are clear on their contribution and their reasoning before making judgements. It is very easy to dismiss an idea because it might not work where you are based, whereas it might work very well in the culture where your team member is based.

Integrity

Be straightforward with others, being transparent and open wherever you can, especially in a virtual team as you are less likely to meet people by chance at the water cooler or coffee machine for a chat. Instead they will encounter you mostly through video and audio conferences, phone calls and reading what you have written. Be authentic and avoid hidden agendas. Be honest in your dealings, even when no one else will know what you are doing.

Equality and fairness

Be fair to each member of the team and others who you encounter, without bias. It is important to treat people equally and fairly whether they are located far away from you or not, even though you may know the local people much better than those based elsewhere. Equal treatment of each person in your team is a key element of virtual trust, as we will find in the next chapter.

I was once part of a team that had one person based in Australia when the others were based in the UK and the East Coast of the United States. When we had our live team meetings, the best time to talk for most of us was late at night, for Keith, our Australian colleague. Instead of expecting Keith to join our meetings in the middle of the night every time, we made sure that some of the meetings were held during Keith's office hours even though the UK and US team members were inconvenienced. By sharing the pain, we showed how we were treating each member fairly. Keith really appreciated it, felt that we valued him as a member of the team and trusted us to care for him.

Caring and empathy

Show consideration for the wellbeing and happiness of others in your virtual team. Take time to understand other people and their unique perspectives and circumstances. Be kind and understanding of their challenges and celebrate their successes. Be sensitive to their needs. Empathy is stronger than just understanding and caring about people's feelings. It means the ability to *experience* their feelings. Of course, there is a line to draw between caring and empathy, which are both good, and virtual stalking, which is completely counterproductive!

Nuo once had something to tell me, but seemed a bit anxious about it. She was in my virtual team and lived in Singapore. 'I have some news', she said. 'I've been promoted and so I'll be leaving the team. I'm so sorry!' Nuo knew that a vacancy in the team would lead to extra work for me, so she was concerned that I might be unhappy. I was delighted to show empathy for Nuo and congratulate her for her long-awaited promotion. I knew how hard she had worked and was pleased that the achievements that I had encouraged had now been recognized by the wider organization.

Confidence

Show that you trust your own abilities, qualities and judgement – show this in your writing and in your virtual team meetings. This will help others in your team to feel that they can have faith in you and trust you too. Of course, make sure that you model integrity, authenticity and transparency as well – if you really don't trust yourself, don't pretend that you do!

Commitment

Show that once you agree to do something, you deliver. This means carrying out the actions that you have agreed to in virtual meetings and in one-to-ones with team members. This models the behaviour that you expect from your team. As well as committing to actions, commit to your team members. Show them that, once they are part of your team, you will stand by them and support them.

Friendly and approachable

Be sociable and friendly to work with. This is probably easier to do naturally in a face-to-face team than when team members are spread around the world! You can't just go out for drinks or dinner or even chat over coffee in the office when people are in different places, so it takes a little more creativity to create social interactions outside of work meetings in a virtual team.

Many years ago, while working for Mars Inc, the makers of M&Ms® candy, I belonged to a virtual team of eight people spread across four continents. We met up face to face at least once a year and we met up by videoconference on a regular basis. I can remember how we arranged for a bag of M&Ms® to be delivered to each of the videoconference suites. At the start of the meeting, we discussed which colour M&M each of us preferred and then we all ate a few.

Practise reciprocity

Be willing to share what you gain. Practise give and take. While this is fairly standard good team behaviour, Professor Cialdini's work on the psychology of influencing people shows that reciprocity is very powerful when it comes to persuading others (Cialdini, 1984). It is a natural way of influencing others, where they are instinctively more likely to respond to you. Around the world, people tend to return a favour given to them. Model this with your virtual team and you will find that strong connections develop between team members, even though they are far apart geographically.

Patience

When things are delayed or there are problems, take this in your stride without getting anxious or angry. This is really helpful – you cannot just wander over to find things out from a team member as you would in a co-located team. Patience helps too when technology plays up, as it so often does! With virtual work, it can be useful to allow some extra buffer time for these sorts of situations.

Should you find yourself dealing with problems beyond your control, don't panic. Here are some tips for escaping from the despair of technological issues (Smith, 2015), which apply just as well to many problems when working virtually. Instead of giving in to panic, breathe and stay calm. This allows you the best chance of thinking clearly and to come up with good solutions. Then acknowledge the problem and state it. Try one thing to solve the problem. If this works, great! If not, try your back-up plan. Once the problem is sorted, you can think about what went wrong and how you could avoid this particular problem in the future.

Comfortable with ambiguity

In our complex world, there are not always simple and easy solutions to problems that occur. Instead things are often ambiguous, with added uncertainty about what is going to happen next. For most of us, this feels stressful. As a virtual leader, you need to be able to cope with ambiguity even more than face-to-face leaders, as you will not be able to discuss things with your team members immediately.

You won't always know everything you would like to. Your team will not know everything either. That's fine – it is up to you as a group to work things through and come up with the best solutions.

Courage

Another attitude necessary in our complex world is courage: to ask, to challenge and to do the right thing, when it might be easier to stand back and leave things alone to slide. Old ways of doing things do not always work and it often takes bravery to try new things and to find new ways of working. As a virtual leader, you are likely to come across situations that you and your organization have not yet dealt with. Perhaps a situation arises affecting team members on different continents, with different terms and conditions because they are based in different countries. What should you do? There is no obvious way forward. By tapping into your courage, you will be able to choose to confront uncertainty, to challenge the status quo and to find a new way forward.

Courage is often associated with heroes and super-human bravery. But the courage required for virtual leadership does not need nerves of steel. It is more about a mindset and a choice to do what is needed and what is right. It is about caring about the outcomes enough to step out and do something different. Courage implies that there is a challenge to be pushed through and fear that needs to be overcome.

There is a particular area where many people need courage in virtual work. For some, speaking into a video camera is very challenging, particularly when they are being recorded. But we know that the use of video gives us access to a much richer communication medium than just using audio. Why is it so difficult? It seems that some people dislike talking to a mechanical device, rather than a person. Others realize just how well videos highlight nerves when they see a replay of themselves. Perhaps that has happened to you? Did you notice a tense body and voice, a flat face without expression or an obvious lack of energy?

So what can we do about this? The key here is to consider the people beyond the camera and to speak through the camera rather than at it. While you will not always have instant feedback as you would talking to people face to face, remembering that you are speaking to real people will help. Remember *why* you are doing this, and that it isn't just to give yourself a hard time. Imagine that you are preparing a short video to welcome people to the team and to explain how they can use different tools to communicate with each other. As you record the video, move the focus from you and your nervousness to the people who you will help through the camera. That changes things, doesn't it? One final tip: smile, especially at the start! People form first impressions within seconds and seeing a smile right at the start will set things off well.

Enthusiasm

To deal with the challenges of virtual leadership, enthusiasm goes a long way. If you show enthusiasm, you show you care about the team and the work done. You are interested in the tasks and people, and eager to do a good job with your colleagues. Enthusiasm implies energy and commitment to do what needs to be done, with wholeheartedness. Enthusiasm is catching and brings a positive feel to the team.

Curiosity

What makes people tick? What motivates each team member? What really inspires them? What might happen if we try new things? What might be possible? Curiosity is a desire to know or learn something. In a virtual leader, it would imply interest in remote team members and in exploring new possibilities for working together. I suspect that anyone reading this text is curious about virtual leadership and wonders what the practical strategies might be. Are you?

Listening

Actively listening to team members helps them to feel heard. It is much more than just hearing. The Chinese symbol for listening includes the ear, but also your eyes, undivided attention and heart. Do you always listen like that? Are you completely focused on listening? In a virtual leadership situation, even though team members probably cannot watch you listening, they will be able to tell when you are not listening as intently as you should.

Organized

As a virtual leader you will need to be organized, or, at the very least, committed to becoming organized. There is so much information that you will need to work with and so many different people to deal with, in many different ways, using different technologies. Organization is key.

Calm under stress

In calm situations, it is relatively easy to behave in positive and supportive ways with remote colleagues. However, when stress mounts higher and higher in humans, a physiological reaction occurs, generating a fight/flight/ freeze response due to a cascade of hormones. While this was really useful for our prehistoric ancestors, as virtual leaders we are unlikely to have to fight or run from an animal predator at work! Instead, the extra hormones are likely to pull us away from a helpful state, instead drawing us into a less useful state for working with others.

Shwarz applied this to facilitators working with face-to-face groups. He noticed that an interesting thing happened to almost all of them once under enough stress. They started behaving in a way he calls the 'unilateral control model' (Schwartz, 2002). You may have experienced this yourself. I know I have. My helpful desire to support the group to achieve its outcomes disappeared and in its place came a very strong desire to survive (almost) no matter what the cost. I kept my thoughts to myself and did not ask for anyone else's input. I had taken on a 'win/lose' mentality. That really isn't very helpful!

While running a virtual session is not quite the same as standing in front of a group face to face, it can still get very stressful. The unwanted, unilateral control model can cut in when under pressure. For me, when things get tough in remote meetings, I know that I am tempted to bluster my way through to the end, just to get through with it. However, as long as I can recognize that this is what is happening, I can intervene. I just have to notice that stress is about to push me into that unhelpful state, described by the 'unilateral control model'. I can choose to divert into a different state instead. Schwarz calls this alternative state the 'mutual learning model'. In this helpful state, rather than forging ahead, I test my assumptions with other people. I share my information with others and ask them for their different information from their perspectives. I explain why I am suggesting what I am suggesting and, together, we build a way forward. I ask questions of others as well as putting forward my own ideas. I focus on everyone's interests rather than their stated positions, especially if there is disagreement. If we need to make a decision, I will choose a way to do this that builds buy-in and commitment from everyone (ie not voting). All of these are really useful for building engagement in a virtual team, so I make a positive choice to stay in this state, especially when things get stressful.

In this situation, I tell people if things are not going as planned. I ask for suggestions for the rest of the meeting – all this takes courage, but at the same time it takes the weight of leadership from me and shares it with the rest of the team.

As a virtual leader, how willing are you to be open and transparent and to aim for the mutual learning model, serving your virtual teams?

Who am I?

The key to becoming an effective leader is self-awareness: knowing yourself and what makes you tick. It means building on your own strengths and overcoming your weaknesses. It means understanding your own personality and, with the help of others, your own biases and blind spots. And it means developing yourself so that you can be the best that you can be for the context where you find yourself.

How can you understand your true self? Many people hide behind a mask at work and rarely show their true self, so it can be revealing and take time and effort. The 'finding your values' box on page 38 is a good place to start. What are your own strengths and weaknesses? A useful tool for finding possible strengths is the book *Strengths Finder 2.0* (Rath, 2007), which includes an online assessment of potential strengths and talents. I use this with the people I mentor as they are often far clearer on their weaknesses than their strengths. The assessment comes up with strengths such as strategy, maximizer (taking people from good to great, rather than mediocre to good) and communication, which are three of mine. People often underplay their strengths, assuming that what is easy for them is easy for everyone else too. It is helpful to stop and assess whether these really are things that everyone can do easily or whether they are unique, individual strengths.

As well as your strengths, what are your weaknesses? Where will you need cover from others in your team in order to work effectively together? Assessing all this will need you to dig deeply and to reflect on the past. You will not be able to analyse yourself fully, though. Check with other people who know you well – what do they assess as your strengths and weaknesses? What biases and blind spots do they describe? How would you adjust your initial assessment to take into account what they feed back to you?

Another aspect of your self is your personality. Many businesses and organizations use personality-profiling tools to help people understand their own personality types and how they are similar to and how they differ from other team members. These tools can be very useful as you seek to understand yourself.

How can I change and develop myself?

'Too many people separate the act of leadership from the leader. They see leadership as something that they do — rather than as an expression of who they are. If we want to be more effective with others, we first need to be more effective with ourselves' (Labarre, 1999). Do you notice the theme of being authentic coming back again? People who understand who they are, strengths and weaknesses included, and use this knowledge, will be more effective as leaders, virtual and face-to-face.

Reflection is an important way to change and develop, by looking back and thinking about how you can apply what you have learnt. That is why this book has questions at the end of each chapter to help you to stop and reflect on what you have read. Reflection takes time and effort – to reflect, slow down, then stop and think before diving into action. In our fast-paced world, though, it often seems that there is no time to slow down. It is an active choice to stop and reflect. Listen to others as well as to yourself: what do they have to say that you can learn from? Reflect on how you can build on your strengths and cover your own weaknesses. Reflection can help people to confront their fears and to do something they would not otherwise have done. Good leaders reflect, change things and develop over time.

Practising reflection

Much of 21st-century life runs at a fast pace. So, in many parts of the world today, it is countercultural to stop and reflect. So here are some tips to help you:

- Take time to be still. Some people find meditation helpful. Others find prayer useful. Still others find walking slowly through nature helps them to slow down, stop and reflect. Whatever it is, whatever works for you, why not schedule it into your diary so that it will happen?

- Another way to reflect is to write a journal each day. Some people choose three pages and just write, first thing in the morning, without thinking too much. Others spend time mulling over what has happened throughout the day and write down their reflections. It is another way of stopping.

- I mentor people virtually and one of the most effective aspects is a regular exercise in reflection. I ask my mentees to answer five questions each week in an online module. I ask them:

  - What has been your biggest success?

  - What has been your biggest challenge?

  - Reflect on your week in three or four lines here.

  - What are you committed to achieve in the next seven days?

  - What help do you need from me now?

  This helps people to review their week and to make a change for the better in the next seven days. It seems that, knowing that their mentor will read reflections and support them, helps them to make changes.

Whatever you do, make reflection a new habit. If you repeat something often enough, eventually it will become second nature.

We need to learn from what works and, significantly, from what does not work. Reflecting helps us to learn at a much deeper level. Too often, people focus on improving the way they already do things, looking at their strategies and behaviours. This is single-loop learning. Reflection helps us to access much deeper learning: double-loop learning. This goes back further, challenging our assumptions, our beliefs, our mental models and the core of ourselves. See Figure 2.2 to see this drawn out.

Figure 2.2 Single-loop and double-loop learning

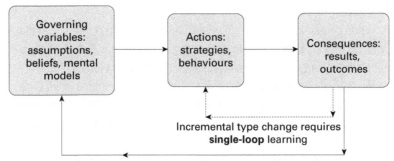

SOURCE: Pullan and Archer (2013)

What is my virtual identity?

In face-to-face meetings, people see each other in physical form. When you walk into a meeting room, people notice your appearance, your gender, your race/ethnicity and which generation you belong to. All of these are key parts of what they remember about you. They are tangible parts of your identity. However, when you work virtually, new colleagues cannot pick up these aspects of your identity quite as easily as they would face to face. Instead of glancing across the room, people in your virtual sessions need to work quite a bit harder to pick up clues as to who you are. Of course, they can still hear your voice. Your accent may give clues as to your origins and your voice might convey your gender and age. If you use a headshot photo or share video, they will see more, but still less than they would face to face.

Here we consider the different aspects of identity, how these feed into other people's virtual experience of you and how you can choose to present appropriate aspects of your virtual identity.

Who is Penny Pullan?

When people meet me face to face, they see a woman in her forties with blonde hair (perhaps a few grey ones!) who is medium height and solidly built. My eyes are blue and I have a tendency to develop freckles. I choose to wear comfortable clothes that suit the context I'm working in, but only ever flat shoes, as I'm often on my feet all day. Unlike many of my clients, I don't wear black.

When people meet me on a conference call, they don't see any of that. What do they pick up? Probably the strongest thing is my British accent. People from many parts of the world have told me that I am easy to understand. Perhaps this is because I have lived all over the world. I talk slowly and clearly. I don't have a strong regional accent. Most people can tell that I'm female, although my voice isn't very high. If I'm introduced as Dr Penny Pullan, that will hint at my educational background.

I wonder which aspects of my identity you have noticed from reading the book so far? I'm sure that some of the more intangible aspects have come through. Perhaps you picked up on my focus on learning and developing, along with my interest in change? What else? Only you can answer that!

In recent years, anthropologists who used to study indigenous tribes in far-flung parts of the world have begun to apply the same tools to the new world of virtual working. One such is Priya E Abraham and we will be applying some of her ideas on identity in the virtual world in this chapter and the next.

Your tangible identity

The tangible parts of your identity are those that are immediately visible and can be seen by the naked eye. These include (Abraham, 2015):

- appearance: what you look like;
- ethnicity: which may encompass nationality, culture, ancestry, beliefs, languages;
- generation: your age and more;
- gender: whether you are male or female.

Many of these characteristics are immediately visible in face-to-face meetings, but are not as clear virtually. If you joined a conference call with me tomorrow,

I wouldn't see you and would have to rely on your voice tone and possibly your name for clues as to your ethnicity, generation and sometimes even your gender. This is potentially very useful for virtual leaders. Instead of being labelled instantly, you can consider which combination of aspects of your identify would be useful for the group you are leading and bring these into play. Some will be more intangible aspects of identity, which we consider below.

Intangible aspects of identity

The intangible aspects of your identity are those that are not immediately visible to people. They develop over time and are harder to discern than the tangible elements. These include (Abraham, 2015):

- wellbeing: both physical and psychological;
- mobility: your own physical mobility, whether you have moved around the world, plus your use of mobile technology;
- sociability: your fun activities with others beyond work, your networks both physical and digital;
- communication: your communications styles and preferences;
- geopolitics: how your identity has been shaped by politics, region, climate, history and how you deal with differences with other people;
- lifelong learning: your approach towards learning and further development;
- employability: the value of your role and organization in the broader community;
- inclusion: at work, in networking and in flow of information, both traditional and digital.

How could you bring these aspects of your identity into your virtual communications? Let me give you an example. I work quite a bit in the Middle East, in countries where, in the past, the vast majority of women stayed at home rather than enter the professions. So my identity as a woman might be received differently from in my home country. On the other hand, people in the Middle East seem to value education highly, along with a commitment to lifelong learning. So, in a conference call to new people in the Middle East, I will always ask to be introduced as 'Dr Penny Pullan, the author of several books', amongst other information. It brings the lifelong learning intangible identity aspect to the fore.

For most new virtual groups, being welcoming, sociable and inclusive at the very start mean that people will notice these intangible aspects of your identity, as well as the tangible ones.

Your environment for virtual leadership

When working virtually, there is usually no need to be in a particular place, unless you need to use a high-end videoconference room. So you can choose the environment that will support you being the best leader you can be for your virtual meetings.

Perhaps you will not choose just one environment, but work in different places, depending on the tasks you need to accomplish. Perhaps you will cover the wall with inspirational posters. Perhaps not! Don't just do what you have always done – work out what supports you to be the best leader you can be and then take advantage of working virtually and create an environment that works for you.

Your environment is not just physical. What else is important for you to act at your best?

Joanna's story of values and virtual leadership

Joanna Pieters is an entrepreneur based in London. In 2014, she faced a dilemma that brought her values to the fore and tested them. She was very busy: about to launch a new product in partnership with another business. Joanna had not yet created all the content for her 'Brilliant Hiring' online programme, which was designed to help small businesses grappling with either not hiring people or hiring badly. Just as her workload was piling up, Joanna heard some bad news. Her father had been admitted to hospital. It didn't look good and Joanna wanted to support her parents. But at the same time, she had lots of work to do to meet her commitments, to her business partner and all the people who had invested in her new product. How could she drop either? How could she possibly do both?

A challenging situation? Absolutely! Ironically, Joanna's product was about using temporary, virtual workers to help grow a small business. So she decided to apply her own product to the situation and, within 48 hours, had recruited a team of people to whom she could outsource everything she didn't have to do herself. Joanna's virtual team members were spread all over the world, from Hampshire in England to the Philippines, Serbia, Canada and India. Joanna was able to spend time at her father's bedside in those last few months of his life. Her product was delivered on schedule. Joanna told me that the quality of the product was probably higher than if she had proceeded as planned beforehand. Her business partner was delighted with the results.

So what advice does Joanna have for other entrepreneurial leaders faced with a task to achieve with a virtual team of freelancers in very little time? She shared some of it with me:

- Be very clear about what you want, and what you don't want. Joanna created detailed briefing sheets for each task covering all aspects of the outcomes needed and processes to be used.

- When hiring people, find them quickly and try them out with short tests to prove they can do the work. Joanna asked prospective audio editors to edit a two-minute recording, and for other tasks created clear stages so she would be able to spot problems early. She included specific instructions in her advertisements and then only considered hiring people who followed them to the letter.

- When working with a new team for a project under pressure with a short time frame, directly managing people in a 'star' team helps. As the communications hub, you will find it easier to keep control. It reduces the scope for misunderstandings. (In Joanna's case the individual team members didn't need to contact one another as they worked directly for her. With everyone tackling different aspects of the work, this made sense, as virtual team meetings would have slowed down the work, with no added benefit.)

- Don't assume anything when working with people who don't know you or your business. People cannot deliver without support, and a freelancer may have other clients who want the same task done in a totally different way.

- If there are challenges, and there will be, raise them immediately as a shared challenge. Have the perspective that people want to do a good job for you and then work together to get it done. Allow people to come up with suggestions on how to improve things as well as offering your own ideas. However, if someone still fails to deliver, let them go quickly and find someone better suited to your needs.

You will notice that the best leadership style for virtual working depends partly on the situation. What suited Joanna's short, high-pressure project was more focused and directive than what would suit a much longer project where every team member needed to work with all the others. I explore this further in the next chapter, which focuses on leading others.

Summary

I have covered a lot in this chapter – starting off exploring how leadership has evolved, what great leadership looks like today and how to apply this to virtual work and virtual teams. Outstanding leadership starts with self: values, mindset, attitudes and behaviours. I explored how you can find out more about yourself and develop as a virtual leader, plus how you can use your personality and identity to express yourself virtually.

Questions for reflection

1 What type of leadership works best with the virtual teams that you lead? What type of leadership do you prefer? What will you do about any mismatch?

2 How can you tap into purpose, mastery and autonomy as powerful motivators of knowledge workers?

3 What is good leadership? Where have you seen it before? What can you bring into your own leadership style?

4 Of the long list of leadership behaviours and attitudes starting on page 39, which ones come naturally to you? Which ones are more of a struggle? What will you do about these?

5 What do you find stressful as a virtual leader? How do you deal with stress? How might you switch to the 'mutual learning model' from the 'unilateral control model'?

6 Who are you? What are your values? What have you learned from discovering these?

7 What elements of identity are you presenting to your virtual teams, both voluntarily and involuntarily? Which other identity elements would help to build common ground with your team members in the future?

8 What would be the best environment for your work as a virtual leader? How can you move your current environment a bit closer to your ideal one?

References and further reading

Abraham, P (2015) *Cyberconnecting: The three lenses of diversity*, Gower Publishing Ltd, Farnham

Alphabet code of conduct https://investor.google.com/corporate/code-of-conduct.html accessed on 7th October 2015

Avery, G (2004) *Understanding Leadership*. Sage Publications, London

Brake, T (2008) *Where in the world is my team?* John Wiley and Sons Ltd., Chichester

Caulat, G (2012) *Virtual Leadership: Learning to lead differently*, Libri Press, Faringdon

Chamorro-Premuzic, T (2015) [accessed 2 November 2015] What You Think Makes a Good Leader Probably Doesn't [Online] http://www.fastcompany.com/3051525/what-you-think-makes-a-good-leader-probably-doesn't

Cialdini, R (1984) *Influence: The psychology of persuasion*, Collins, New York

Coats, K and Coddrington, G (2015) *Leading in a Changing World: Lessons for future focused leaders*, TomorrowToday Global, Johannesburg

Hall, K (2007) *Speed Lead: Faster, simpler ways to manage people, projects and teams in complex companies*, Nicholas Brealey Publishing, London

Kouzes, J and Posner, B (2011) *Credibility: How leaders gain and lose it; why people demand it*, 2nd edn, Jossey-Bass, San Francisco

Kouzes, J and Posner, B (2012) *The Leadership Challenge*, Jossey-Bass, San Francisco

Labarre, P (1999) [accessed 2 November 2015] How to be a Real Leader, Interview with Kevin Cashman [Online] http://www.fastcompany.com/37235/how-be-real-leader

Loehr, A (2014) [accessed 17 September 2015] How to Live with Purpose, Identify Your Values and Improve Your Leadership [Online] http://www.huffingtonpost.com/anne-loehr/how-to-live-with-purpose-_b_5187572.html

Pavlina, S (2004) [accessed 2 November 2015] List of Values https://www.stevepavlina.com/articles/list-of-values.htm

Pink, D (2011) *Drive: The surprising truth about what motivates us*, Cannongate Books, Edinburgh

Pullan, P and Archer, J (2013) *Business Analysis and Leadership: Influencing change*, Kogan Page, London

Rath, T (2007) *Strengths Finder 2.0*, Gallup Press, Washington DC

Schwarz, R (2002) *The Skilled Facilitator: A comprehensive resource for consultants, facilitators, managers, trainers and coaches*, Jossey-Bass, San Francisco

Settle-Murphy, N (2013) *Leading Effective Virtual Teams*, CRC Press, Boca Raton, FL

Smith, R (2015) [accessed 1 October 2015] Escaping the Despondent Pit of Techno-Despair, *Grove* [Online] news.grove.com/?p=8203

Tamkin, P, Pearson, G, Hirsch, W and Constable, S (2010) *Exceeding Expectations: The principles of outstanding leadership*, The Work Foundation, London

Working virtually with others

03

This chapter focuses on working with others. It expands the ideas discussed in Chapter 2 to apply them to building relationships with others virtually, finding common ground and working with people effectively. In this chapter, I explore the crucial role of trust in virtual teams and how to develop it. I look at the structure and size of virtual teams and how this should match the needs of the work. I cover how to set up a virtual team for success and how to take over leadership of an existing team. You will find a range of practical tools and strategies to help your virtual team to work well together. Finally, I share two stories of getting to grips with virtual working. This chapter forms a foundation for later content on using technology (Chapter 4), running effective virtual meetings (Chapter 5) and keeping everything progressing outside of meetings (Chapter 6).

By reading this chapter, you will understand:

- Which aspects are important as you get to know and work with others in your virtual team.
- How trust works virtually, with three strands based on personality, cognition and institution.
- How virtual teams vary in size, structure and complexity.
- How to start out with a virtual team, whether forming a new team from scratch or taking over a pre-existing team.
- How virtual teams develop, including details of the team performance model.
- A variety of strategies and tools to help you lead your team.
- Key steps in closing your virtual team.

Figure 3.1 A mind-map of this chapter

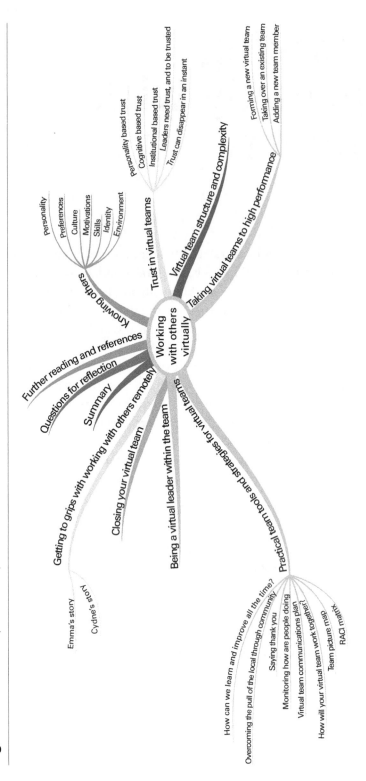

To be a great virtual leader, it is important to start with yourself first. Build on the leadership mindset, attitudes and behaviours that we covered in Chapter 2, as well as aspects of your own identity.

There are many different contexts for working with others virtually, from a one-off meeting, where there is little chance to get to know everyone involved, to a full-time virtual team, with time to develop deep relationships with each person. In between the two extremes, you might belong to one or many virtual teams, perhaps alongside face-to-face work. Which applies to you?

Knowing others

Your own virtual leadership should vary, depending on the individuals involved. Each person will have their own unique mixture of personality, preferences, motivations, skills and identity, along with the context in which they work. You will also find differences between you due to distance. Let's consider some of these now.

Personality

There is usually a mixture of personalities in teams and these can cause misunderstandings when people do not understand what makes the others tick. An example is introversion and extroversion. Introverts gain energy from being alone in a quiet place and often prefer one-to-one conversations to larger group sessions. They are likely to contribute only after thinking things through, which means that an introvert can often have great ideas and suggestions, but may hold them back in groups. On the other hand, extroverts have a preference for being with other people and gain energy from groups. Extroverts may well contribute ideas before thinking them through properly. They often exude enthusiasm and energy.

There is a wide range of personality preference tools available, such as the Myers Briggs Type Indicator (MBTI), which can be useful to find out about the different preferences of members of your virtual team. These rofiles give people the language to talk about differences and understand colleagues better.

Preferences

People will have different preferences in others areas too, including:

- *Communication with the team.* Make sure that you know people's communication preferences – ask them what they would like to receive and how. Some things to consider:
  - Do they prefer to receive all the details or are they more of an overview person, preferring a quick call to sort things out rather than exchange information in writing?
  - How do they process information best? Do they opt for visuals, metaphors, text, a one-to-one meeting, a phone call, a recording or a large meeting?
  - Would they like to be given options or just informed of decisions made?
  - What language do they prefer to work in? What is appropriate for their culture?
  - Would they rather receive the full facts before proceeding or get going quickly?
- *Hours of working.* Are they early birds or night owls? Do they prefer to work at a standard time for their location or would they rather flex to suit the team? Would they prefer only to be contacted during their own office hours?
- *Technology.* What do they prefer to use and feel most comfortable with? Some people, particularly in younger generations, feel very happy with instant messages and collaboration tools. Others prefer to talk one-to-one on the telephone.

Motivations

What is important to each member of your team? What is of interest to them? For some, if others care about them enough to ask about their children it makes a huge difference. Others would prefer to leave their family at home and not discuss them at work.

Remember the three elements of motivating knowledge workers from Chapter 2? What is their *purpose* in life? How does the work you do together help them to fulfil their purpose? What would they like to *master*, to develop really good skills in? How can you give them the *autonomy* that so many crave?

The way to find out team members' motivations is to ask them. Have a discussion about what they would like to achieve while part of your team.

Skills

What skills are needed for virtual workers? These are very similar to skills needed for virtual leaders. Virtual workers should be able to communicate effectively in writing and speak clearly, as both the written word and audio form a large part of virtual communication. Listening is key, as they will need to grasp what others are saying, and perhaps what others are not saying. Speaking clearly is important so that others can hear them over the telephone.

Virtual workers should be willing to share information rather than hoard it, so that others can build on their work. They need to be self-disciplined and self-motivated so that they do not need constant supervision. They must be able to use the technology that you will communicate with, or be willing to learn and practice it! Of course, on top of all of this, each virtual worker needs to have the appropriate skills for their role, whether they are a software developer working far away from their colleagues, or a copywriter working for a start-up business.

Identity

Remember the different aspects of identity that were introduced in Chapter 2? There were four tangible elements, which are easy to see: appearance, ethnicity, generation and gender. These were joined by eight intangible elements, which are harder to detect and may change over time: wellbeing, mobility, sociability, communication, geopolitics, lifelong learning, inclusion and employability (Abraham, 2015). We explored these, suggesting that every virtual leader would do well to understand these and consider emphasizing those aspects of their own identity that build connections with others in their team. In virtual working, the tangible identifying elements are less to the fore than in face-to-face work, allowing us to use the intangible elements of our identities to help build common ground with others.

As well as building bridges to our team members individually, we can use aspects of identity to help build common ground amongst and between team members. To do so, find out about your team members and look for areas of overlap, especially amongst the intangible, hidden, elements. For example, if you discover that the members of your group are keen lifelong learners, then you could share ideas for conferences, book recommendations and courses with one another. Perhaps one member has completed an online course and found it really useful? They could let others know about it. They might even help each other to gain professional certifications. This common ground can build bridges across difference through people identifying as lifelong learners, even if the members of the team are spread across the world.

Why is it so important to find common ground across virtual teams? You might think that diversity would be a good thing, bringing a broader perspective. This is true. The trouble is that human beings have a tendency to classify others as either in the same group as themselves, the 'in' group, or a different group, the 'out' group. Social psychology studies consistently pick up that people see the 'in' group as a very varied group of people and act more favourably to them. On the other hand, people judge the 'out' group to be much more homogeneous than the 'in' group and act less favourably to them. Misunderstanding and prejudices far too often prevent good relationships and can get in the way of working together.

Stereotypes can be useful as a starting point in our information-overloaded world, but they tend to oversimplify things. Applying stereotypes to individual team members is likely to be unhelpful and will lead to bias. How will you help other team members to overcome the stereotypes they may have of their colleagues, and even of you?

It can take a while to change your initial reactions to people. To do so, ask yourself the question, 'What is it about me that sees them in that way?' (Abraham, 2015). If you are aware of your own biases and build trust over time, your reactions can become more accurate. Your relationship with each person will build and develop as you observe them in action and as you collaborate with them. Observe, record what you see, listen and reflect to help build your own understanding of each person.

As a virtual leader, build a positive climate in your team where people and ideas can flourish. Listen carefully and encourage others to listen deeply to one another. Develop individuals' interpersonal skills. Use different bridging strategies to create a sense of belonging, while respecting the diversity of the group. Build connections through encouraging people to have informal conversations and to share stories, as well as doing the work.

Environment

The context where virtual work takes place has quite an impact on how people work together. Abraham uses her 'environmental lens' to explore this further, going beyond the shared location that people are familiar with in face-to-face work. She suggests the following aspects to consider:

- *Ethno*: taking a helicopter view of identity and ethnicity.
- *Idea*: looking at the politics, ideologies and power interests that act on the environment.
- *Media*: taking into account the media surrounding each person, whether traditional or technological.
- *Tech*: looking at the technology arena.
- *Finance*: taking into account the financial context of the interaction.

Abraham suggests that a combination of knowledge, skills and behaviours around these different areas will help to build interconnectivity in your group through finding common ground and shared experiences (Abraham, 2015).

Trust in virtual teams

It can take much longer to build trust between virtual colleagues than in face-to-face teams. As a virtual leader, you cannot assume either that, once you have trust, it will stay. Trust can disappear without warning at any moment.

When people spend time together at work in the same location, they get to know each other as individuals. They probably share the same mother tongue and culture. If they work together, they have lots of time to interact, to get to know each other and to build trust. They are likely to bump into each other for a chat at the coffee machine or water cooler.

Now let's switch the context to a virtual team. Suddenly there are no shared coffee machines or water coolers, so the chances of building social capital and a feeling of community are much reduced, as compared with the people who work in the same location. This is incredibly important as trust forms the basis of good working relationships in virtual teams and achieving outcomes together.

Let's explore trust a bit more. People's awareness of trust builds up from their very earliest experiences. We build a sense of trust through our experiences of others. If they meet our needs and expectations, then we learn that these expectations and needs are likely to be met in the future. At school and, later, at work, we experience how our peers treat us. Over the years, we store up data on which to base our decisions about other people's trustworthiness. Even small children expect life to be fair and, as we grow up and move into the world of work, we notice whether or not equality is built into the way we are treated at work. These build into layers of trust, which involve personality, cognition and institution. Thomas Wise, in his book *Trust in Virtual Teams* (Wise, 2013), explores how these layers work virtually and I will consider each one in turn:

- personality-based trust;
- cognitive-based trust;
- institutional-based trust.

See Figure 3.2 for a mind-map of these three layers of trust.

Personality-based trust

Our personalities are laid down well before we start our working lives, shaped by our experiences of people we meet and how they treat us and other people that they come across. If people are consistent in their behaviour, we are more likely to be able to predict how they will react to things, which builds our trust in them. We are also much more likely to trust those with whom we have good relationships. This personality-based trust is based on three things: perceived trustworthiness, how consistently people behave and the relationship with the person doing the trusting.

Each person will have their own expectations of what trustworthy is and their own propensity to trust people or not. As a virtual leader, you are unlikely to be able to change this very much! But what you *can* do is to help people build relationships, to understand each other's personalities and behaviours. While this would happen naturally over time with a face-to-face team, it takes thought to achieve this in a virtual team.

How can the individuals in your project team build relationships with one another, as real people, not just disembodied voices on an audio call? As a first step, you could provide a safe environment for open communications between team members, where, if they wish, they can relate to each other both on work topics and beyond. Instant messages can help, but can also interrupt work. Don't forget simple one-to-one phone conversations. To help relationships develop, ensure some face-to-face time in person or via videoconferencing technology. Building a shared experience of community like this develops trust day by day. Communication, reciprocation and open disclosure to others can build a strong feeling of belonging to the virtual group and creates a solid foundation for the other types of trust to grow.

One of my clients holds a team lunch via high-quality telepresence videoconferencing every couple of months. Team members bring their lunches and eat together, able to view and hear their colleagues. They talk about anything except work. This has helped to build the relationships and therefore the trust in her remote team.

Cognitive-based trust

Cognitive-based trust is a trust that we choose to place in a person or group based on the information that we have gathered from our past and other sources. It seems to be stronger if we are sure that we will be working with the person or group into the future. Cognitive-based trust is based on three things: expectation of a future relationship, knowledge and experience.

To build cognitive-based trust, remember that individuals need to know enough to be able to make a decision to trust each other. How can each person access the knowledge they need on the project? By building a collective memory, you can enhance the sense of belonging. So I suggest that you build a project team space, where your project documents and more can be shared with everyone. Make sure that everyone in the team has equal access, wherever in the world he or she comes from and whichever organization they are part of. Perhaps your team space could share stories and information about each team member and their previous experience, to help build up each person's credibility with others? Plan your team space together with your team so that everyone can gain the information they need.

As they work together, people will begin to establish feelings of belonging to a group. Help this by building a common vision and a shared sense of purpose. People will gather information about each other's strengths and weaknesses and build expectations about what each other is capable of and how they work best together. Cognitive trust comes from connectedness as a team.

Institutional-based trust

This layer of trust concerns the institutions that we deal with. From our earliest years, we have dealt with schools, sports teams, clubs and other groups. How can we judge if they can be trusted? Well, being treated fairly and applying rules equally to everyone are important. We should be treated consistently over time and in line with our expectations. The three elements of institutional-based trust are: consistency, equity and expectation.

In a virtual team, institutional-based trust is very easy to get wrong. How equitable is your virtual team? For a start, if your team members are spread across different countries, they are likely to have very different local policies in many areas of employment. One example is annual leave. Many employees in the United States start with two weeks' leave per year whereas in Europe this is much more likely to be four or five weeks. This inequality is built in, so people based in the United States may feel really unfairly treated when their European team members go off for long holidays that they cannot take. Working hours and working practices can vary hugely around the world and you are unlikely to be able to change them.

Use what flexibility you have to make things as equal and fair as you can. This means applying rules to everyone and creating, as far as possible, a level playing field for team members. If one has to get up in the middle of the night to attend team meetings, then vary the times so that this hassle is shared around the team. Show that you are predictable in the way that you deal with people.

Another all-too-frequent example where remote people are not treated equally is the hybrid meeting. Some people are present in a meeting room face to face and others join remotely by speaker phone. I have seen the results: far too often, the conversation in the room becomes animated and the people on the end of the phone are completely forgotten. They cannot hear very well because the speakerphone is too far away from the speakers. Even worse, people in the room write ideas on flipcharts or whiteboards that the remote people cannot see. Surely it would be far more equitable to have a conference call line with a shared screen? That would send a powerful message to remote participants that they were equal, valued members of the team and would increase their trust in the leader.

Another factor that comes into play in institutional-based trust is job satisfaction. People who are happy and satisfied at work are likely to feel more trusting of their employer. So, as a virtual leader, it might be possible to use job satisfaction to balance organizational policy issues that you have no control over.

Leaders need trust, and to be trusted

In a virtual team, it is not possible to glance over to see what your colleagues are doing. You cannot tell if they are working or not, even if you can see that they are active online. So trust is imperative, between all members of virtual teams and especially between leaders and those they lead. Without trust in their team members, a virtual leader is unable to delegate work to others and to give them the autonomy to deliver the work. So consciously aim to

Figure 3.2 A mind-map showing the three layers of trust

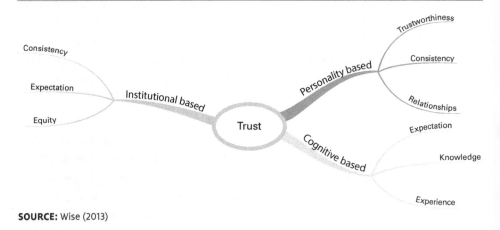

SOURCE: Wise (2013)

build all three layers of trust: personality, cognitive and institutional. As trust develops in a virtual team, members are increasingly likely to ask difficult questions and to challenge each other, finding better ways of doing the work. When stress builds, a virtual team who trust each other will have more resilience and more ability to handle and deal with conflicts that inevitably arise.

As a virtual leader, beyond trusting your team members, how can you encourage others to put their trust in you? You can draw on all the layers of trust described above, acting consistently, with equity and building relationships with individuals. In addition, consider David Maister's formula for trust, shown below (Maister, 2001). It shows you can boost trust by being credible. Show how you can be relied upon to do what you say you will do. Be friendly. And remember that if you come across as being primarily interested in yourself, this will damage trust. Maister's formula for trust is:

$$\text{trust} = \frac{\text{credibility} + \text{reliability} + \text{intimacy}}{\text{self-orientation}}$$

Trust can disappear in an instant

Once trust is built in a team, it can break down rapidly, derailing the team in the process. In a virtual team, it can be quite tricky to notice, as the body language that communicates trust breakdown cannot be seen at all, or, at best, not very clearly. After all, how do you know if silence in a conference call is happy silence or deep disagreement? You cannot assume anything!

How will you sort out problems? It is no longer a simple matter of wandering over to have a quick chat with individuals. If people are behaving in an unhelpful way, I suggest that you assume good intent. I find it useful to ask myself, 'What could their circumstances be that would mean that they were acting with integrity and still doing this?' If you need to, challenge them, asking them to conform to your team's agreed ways of working.

> Years ago, I was annoyed by a virtual colleague repeatedly arriving at work late, who was getting further and further behind with his actions. When I queried his behaviour, I discovered that his wife was suffering from breast cancer, and the whole family was really struggling to keep going as the arduous chemotherapy took its toll. Instantly my annoyance was replaced by empathy and the desire to support my colleague. As the North American proverb goes, it's best not to judge a man until you have walked a mile in his moccasins!

Virtual team complexity

There are many different types of virtual teams. Some people work for just one team, whether virtual or face-to-face. Most virtual workers are in multiple teams, some face-to-face and some remote, sometimes as leader and other times as a team member. Some people interact on the fringes of loose virtual groups to which they offer specialist expertise.

Let's explore the make-up of a single virtual team. If the work to be done is short and focused, with steps and outputs clearly defined upfront and

Figure 3.3 A simple virtual star group

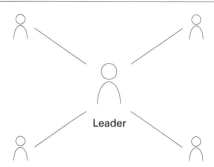

each person carrying out a specialist role, there is little need for group members to interact with one another. In this case, it makes sense to have the leader as the hub of a *star group* (Hall, 2007), as shown in Figure 3.3. It is shaped like a star with the leader at the hub. Each group member only interacts with the leader. An example is Joanna Pieter's team, described on page 52 in Chapter 2, a team of specialists brought together to create a predefined product very quickly. These teams are simple in structure and tend to be short-lived. If you are the leader of a team like this, then directive leadership styles might work for you – in contrast to more complex teams where facilitative leadership is best.

Figure 3.4 A more complex, networked, spaghetti virtual team

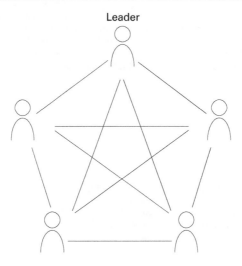

In this more complex situation, a team work closely together with a shared vision, but without a predefined path to reach it. Each team member needs to interact with everyone else. The team leader is no longer a central coordinator. This team is closely networked, with the leader playing the role of a facilitator and leadership is likely to be distributed. The work together will probably last longer than the simple star team and so the leader needs to invest time in building effective working relationships and common ground between everyone. The leader can take time to encourage people to develop their skills. Communication within such a networked team takes a lot of time, which is why they are sometimes called *spaghetti teams*, as shown in Figure 3.4, indicating the many connections each member has (Hall, 2007).

The virtual mentoring groups that I run are examples of this. Individuals come together for a year to develop themselves and their businesses without meeting face to face. Group members develop strong bonds with one another as they support each other's growth. My role is that of a facilitator and mentor, and often team members come up with ideas to everyone's benefit.

Many business projects use these virtual, spaghetti teams, especially where the work is complex, each project is unique, the tasks are not predefined and the timescales are significant, as shown in Figure 3.5.

Figure 3.5 Different types of virtual teams – the scale of complexity from star to spaghetti

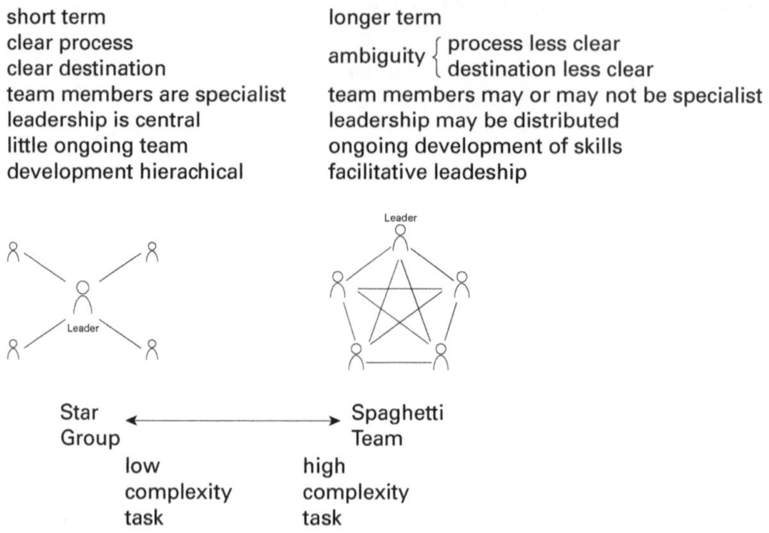

short term
clear process
clear destination
team members are specialist
leadership is central
little ongoing team
development hierachical

longer term
ambiguity { process less clear
destination less clear
team members may or may not be specialist
leadership may be distributed
ongoing development of skills
facilitative leadeship

Star
Group
low
complexity
task

Spaghetti
Team
high
complexity
task

Within a spaghetti team, the complexity of the interactions increases rapidly as the number of members goes up. A team of three have 3 connections, a team of four have 6 and a team of five have 10, as shown in Figure 3.6. The formula for the number of connections is:

$$\frac{n \times (n - 1)}{2}$$

– where n is the number of team members. Once a team has 10 people, there are 45 connections! Just imagine all the time and effort that the team of 10 would need to put in to keep each other up to date, especially if they do this with one-to-one phone calls or e-mails! This is why team collaboration tools make a lot of sense. If you lead a spaghetti team, though, think carefully about the size of your team, remembering that each increase in the size will add a large number of connections, making the team less efficient (see Figure 3.6).

Figure 3.6 How the number of connections goes up with the number of people in the team

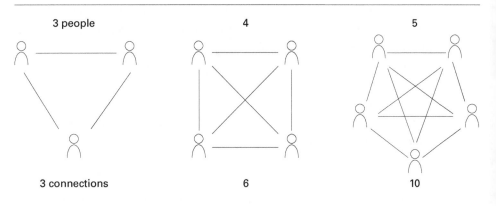

As a virtual leader, ask yourself where on the star-spaghetti scale your teams should lie. It is easy to fall into the trap of using a spaghetti team where a star group would be faster, cheaper and less complex. It depends entirely on how you need to work together, for how long and on what. A spaghetti team is the right choice if you are working on complex, shared tasks together over time, using a range of skills, where each person is essential and interdependent on everyone else.

Figure 3.7 A mixture of spaghetti teams across four hubs, connected with each other and the central leader via a star group structure

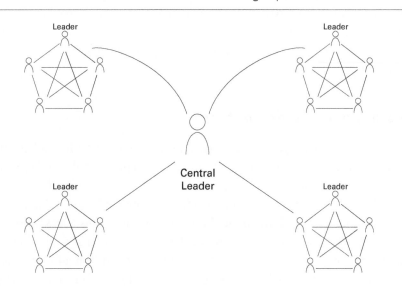

If you do not need everyone to connect with every other person, then choose a star group of people working independently via a central hub. Another option would be to combine the two, with a small spaghetti team for the central core and with other members less involved. A third option uses local spaghetti teams in different locations, with the leaders of each hub then connecting to the central manager (Binder, 2008). Figure 3.7 shows this with a group of 20 people split across four hubs, with the four hub leaders reporting to the central leader. This arrangement has only 44 connections. In a pure spaghetti team, there would be 210 connections, absorbing much more time and effort to maintain.

> While I was writing this book, I spent some time working with people involved in delivering change globally for a large bank. When I asked them about their work, they agreed that they have so many meetings, mostly online video or conference calls, that there is very little time left over for actually doing the work and completing actions before the next meeting. I wondered whether some of these teams were overcommunicating and if a star or mixed star–spaghetti structure with a central information hub would save time, cost and effort.

Taking virtual teams to high performance

In this section, I am talking about interconnected, virtual, spaghetti teams, which need to work together closely, rather than star groups where only the team leader needs to build good relationships with each individual group member.

Forming a new virtual team

What happens when you form a virtual team from scratch? If you have this luxury, make sure you follow the quickest steps to high performance. This does NOT mean knuckling down to work straight away, though. The Drexler/Sibbet Team Performance Model® is shown in Figure 3.8 and helps people to understand how to build high-performing teams (Drexler/Sibbet, 1990–2016). I find that it works particularly well for virtual teams. Let's go through it now, thinking about how you can build a high-performing, virtual team from scratch. The model works step by step through the stages of development of a team, using the metaphor of a bouncing ball.

Figure 3.8 The Drexler/Sibbet Team Performance Model®

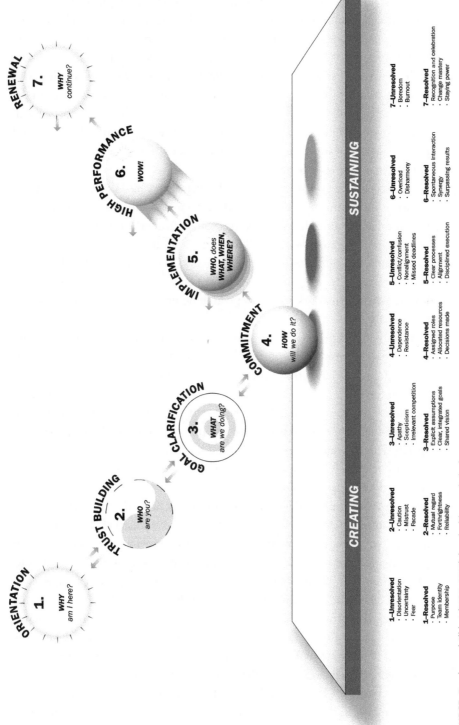

SOURCE: Drexler and Sibbet (1990–2016) (used with permission)

The model emphasizes how important it is to orient people at the start, by answering the question, '**Why am I here?**' The next step is to build trust by answering the question, '**Who are you?**' of the other team members. Note that this needs to happen *before* clarifying goals. All too often virtual leaders rush their teams straight to goal clarification or, even worse, assigning who is doing what. It seems to be human nature to bypass the initial steps in the model when under time pressure, but this is a big mistake, especially in virtual teams. There is little chance to develop relationships informally and answer these questions in a chat over coffee or the water cooler, as might happen in a face-to-face team.

So, make sure you start properly. Ensure everyone knows why they are a part of the team, what they bring to the (virtual) table and what part will they play. Make sure they get to know who the other team members are and what they bring to the team. If you are able to gather people together face to face, this can accelerate team formation. (Of course it will only happen if you use the time together productively by getting to know one another, not just sitting in a darkened room watching projected slides – as too many teams do!)

Once people are properly oriented and have built trust together, only then does it make sense for the virtual leader to introduce goals, asking, '**What are we doing?**' What is the purpose of the team? What are our goals? Do not just impose this on the team but discuss it and agree it. Listen to your team members' points of views. Make sure that everyone interprets your team purpose the same way. When you come up with goals, make sure these are specific and measurable, not woolly and unclear.

Once team goals are sorted, then the team needs commitment. Ask '**How will we do it?**' Here the leader and the team assign and agree roles, allocate resources and make decisions. Now the team is ready to work together, implementing their plans and carrying out actions together. They know the answer to, '**Who does What, When and Where?**' The next step is '**High performance**'. Of course this does not last forever and questions arise as to '**Why continue?**' At any stage, the team can go back to previous stages.

Most team models consist of a sequence of stages such as 'forming, storming, norming, performing' (Tuckman, 1965) or 'pseudo-community, chaos, emptiness, community' (Scott Peck, 1990). The Team Performance Model is different; it uses a visual metaphor of a bouncing ball to represent the team. The harder you push a ball to the floor, the higher the ball flies into the air on the rebound. When you add this understanding to the model, it reinforces how important the early stages are in bouncing your team up to 'high performance'. Can you see that the ball (the team) hardly exists at the start, gradually becoming more substantial until it becomes three-dimensional at the commitment stage, to bounce hard against the floor?

The model is helpful for diagnosing problems in team development too. You will notice words at the base of Figure 3.8 that describe what each of the seven stages looks like when resolved and when unresolved. This is very helpful for virtual leaders assessing existing teams, providing guidance as to where to focus. If a stage is unresolved, it needs more focus. Make sure that each stage's key question is answered before you move on.

Ian works virtually on major projects around the world. A few years ago, he was working on a troubled project and found his portfolio manager very difficult to get on with. She was based in a different country and the two had never met face to face. They both came across as hostile to one other. Her telephone manner 'got on his nerves' and conversations were fraught. I suspect that this feeling was mutual!

Together they agreed that this working relationship was not working and made the decision to meet in person for a couple of days. It made all the difference. They were able to build rapport and find out what each could bring to the project. Finally, they had answered the question 'Who are you?' which, once resolved, brought mutual regard, forthrightness and reliability. Ian tells me that they are still the best of friends, long after that project had finished.

I suspect that Ian and his portfolio manager could have answered this question virtually had they taken the time to do so right at the start. However, on a troubled project, they started on the work straight away, as most people would. Once the relationship had deteriorated so much virtually, it was a good idea to repair it face to face.

Taking over an existing team

What advice is there for leaders taking over existing virtual teams? It is helpful to review what was working well before the change of leader. As a new leader, have phone or video conversations with each team member to get to know them and their individual preferences and motivations. What did they appreciate about the team before you joined and what do they wish that you would do differently? Recall the different elements of trust shown in Figure 3.2 and use the ideas introduced earlier to build trusting relationships with team members as quickly as you can.

I find the team performance model of Figure 3.8 really helpful for this situation. It is useful for diagnosing where existing teams were, what was working well and what needed resolving.

Remember, though, that changing the team composition means that the old team is no longer there – with you leading, there is now a new team. However tempting it may be, you cannot just add yourself as a leader and think that you can continue where the old leader left off. Any new member changes the team, even a new leader. To take the whole team to high performing means starting again from the very beginning, answering the questions as a new team and moving to high performance. If you plan this process carefully, it need not take long to get back to high performance.

Adding a new team member

If you are bringing a new person into an established team, remember that the team has changed with the addition of the new person. While it is very tempting to let the rest of the team carry on as they did before, especially if they are performing well, don't do it! The new team member would be isolated and feel left out. This is especially true if they are new to virtual working, so be very clear about what you expect from them and check in regularly at the beginning.

Take the whole team, including the new member, through the foundational stages of the team performance model. This will bring them into the team and make sure that the existing team members get to know the new member too. It can help to allocate the new person a buddy, local to them if possible, to ease their way into the team. Encourage one-to-one conversations between existing team members and the new addition in order to build connections and help to build relationships on the way to high performance again.

Conflict

Conflict arises in virtual teams and it is harder to detect and deal with than in face-to-face teams, as the leader is unable to see what is happening and cannot have a quick chat face to face to try to sort it out. In this chapter, I give an overview of what you can do to handle conflict, while I cover conflict in meetings in Chapter 5 and conflict outside of meetings in Chapter 6.

So what is conflict and how can you handle it remotely? Conflict can be as simple as a disagreement and as complex as a feud. There are three different forms of conflict: task, relationship and process. Task conflict involves differences in understanding about the task at hand, with different viewpoints and opinions expressed. This can be a very useful form of conflict as it ensures that the team hears multiple views about tasks and generally leads to better decisions, once all of the viewpoints are heard and understood. Process conflict is about how work should be done and, like task conflict, can be helpful at low levels by making sure that a range of ideas are heard.

Relationship conflict, on the other hand, is usually very unhelpful and can be destructive. It involves interpersonal relationship difficulties and even hostilities between people in the team. Unfortunately, with virtual teams tending to be far more diverse than face-to-face teams, relationship conflict can be even more likely to surface as people are different from one another. Listen out for sarcastic comments or angry words and intervene quickly and decisively as, once relationship conflict takes hold, it can be nigh on impossible to solve in a virtual team.

The good news is that there are things you can do:

- *Make conflict less likely by planning for it upfront.* This includes having a shared vision, clear objectives for your meetings, agreed rules by which you will work together and clear roles that each of you play. Ensure that your decision making is transparent and clear. It can help to discuss what you will do if conflict arises and how it will be handled. The diverse mix of your team will mean that there might even be conflict about the best way to handle conflict: some might prefer to avoid it and put up with tough issues for the sake of team harmony. I would encourage you to work things out rather than pretend that all is well when it obviously isn't. My experience is that virtual conflict accelerates out of control very quickly.

- *Monitor the situation before conflict arises.* As a virtual leader, keep an eye on how the team is running. How are people dealing with each other in and outside of meetings? How are people asking questions of one another in meetings and discussions? Encourage people to spot issues and mistakes and step in to sort them out early, before they cause problems. It is important to listen incredibly carefully as it is all too easy to miss out early signs of remote conflict.

- *Intervene, at the time that conflict arises.* My favourite face-to-face option of giving everyone a five-minute break so that I can talk eye-to-eye with the protagonists is not available remotely, but it is possible to stop and have a phone call with those in conflict. It can be helpful to break the tension in some way, perhaps telling stories that are relevant to the situation or reflecting what you have noticed happening. While it can be tempting to keep your own emotions hidden during conflicts, the opposite may be helpful: expressing your own feelings while staying respectful to others can be quite effective. If there are two sides to an argument, clarify both sides so that people understand the different perspectives.

- *Afterwards, learn from the conflict and make it less likely to happen again.* Remember that many models of team development predict conflict, such as Tuckman's 'storming' phase (Tuckman, 1965) and Scott-Peck's 'chaos' phase (Scott-Peck, 1990). Conflict can be a step towards high performance, even if it feels the complete opposite at the time! Conflict can be used to transform teams and to build relationships at a much deeper level once people are through it.

Practical team tools and strategies for virtual teams

These tools and strategies are simple, practical and easy to use, yet work powerfully for both new and existing teams, and help resolve issues.

RACI matrix

How will you ensure that there is no duplicated effort and that everyone will be clear on who is doing what? A very practical tool for this is the RACI matrix, which lays out roles and responsibility for every action. A RACI matrix clarifies who is responsible (R), accountable (A), consulted (C) and/or informed (I) for every action, as shown in Table 3.1. The different virtual team members and other key players are listed along the top, with one column per person or role, and the actions are listed, with one row each.

There is only ever a single person accountable for any action, so there should only ever be one 'A' per row. This identifies the person where 'the buck stops', who is personally accountable for the completion of the action. They would take the blame if it didn't happen. 'R' marks the person or people who will actually do the action. Unlike 'A', there can be one or more 'R's marked in each action row identifying who is responsible for carrying it out. 'C' marks anyone who should be consulted about the action and 'I' marks anyone who should be informed about it. There can be zero to many 'C's and 'I's – it just depends on what you decide that the action needs.

Table 3.1 A RACI matrix for this chapter, showing who in our virtual team was responsible ®, accountable (A), consulted (C) and informed (I) for each step

	Penny: Author	Mary: Designer	Amy: Editor	David: Publisher	Malcolm: Proof-reader
Write chapter	AR		I		
Provide initial sketches	AR		C		
Digitize pictures	C	R	A		
Proofread	C		AR		R
Accept the chapter	I	I	AR	I	

Team picture map

A picture map makes sure that everyone has an overview of the whole team and where each individual is based geographically. It consists of headshots showing team members' faces superimposed on a map (see Figure 3.9). Each person's photo is labelled with their name and location and is placed at an appropriate place on the map to show their geographical location. It can be very helpful to remind people of their colleagues in the team, their location and time zones. A useful addition is people's contact details. I find that having the headshots visible makes conference calls and shared screen meetings more effective as voices are no longer disembodied for me as I can see the people's faces.

How will your virtual team work together?

It is important to flesh out your virtual team's ways of working, your 'modus operandi', group norms and operating procedures. It doesn't matter what you call these – choose something that works for your particular team. What does matter is that you have thought through and discussed how you want to work together and agreed the answers to a whole set of questions. Here are a few for starters:

Figure 3.9 A picture map showing team members' faces

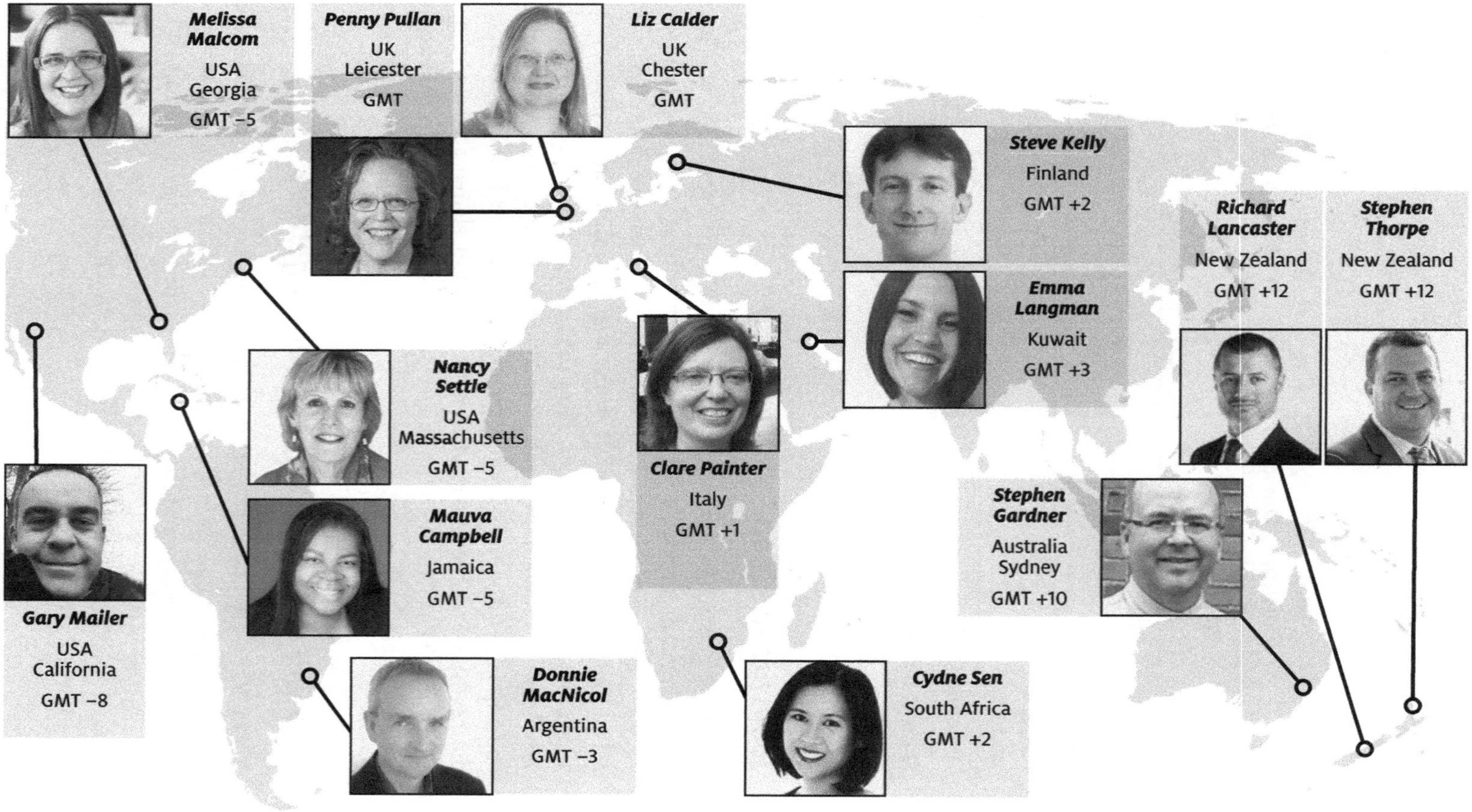

- What processes will you use as a team?

- When will you meet and what for?

- What will you use as a shared team space from the start so that everyone has equal access to information?

- What outputs will you deliver? How will you measure results? How will you know when you're done?

- How will you monitor progress?

- How will you make decisions? Will you use majority votes (not recommended where you need to create buy-in to decisions) or consensus? What decisions will the leader make alone and what will be team decisions?

- What group norms and operating principles will apply – how will you get things done together? How will you challenge one another? How will you deal with conflict? (An important insight here is that it makes sense to assume good intent from people.)

Virtual team communications plan

Communication is the lifeblood of virtual teams and a communications plan really helps this to flow in a planned, rather than haphazard, way.

Consider what particular information different team members need. Use the communications plan to note **Who** in the team needs to know **What, When/ How often** and in **What format**? Will the information be **Kept**? What is the latest **Status**? This can be captured in a simple table as shown in Table 3.2. When you design this plan with your team, remember that communication should be two-way: team members need to be listened to as well as updated with information. Add in ways to replicate the informal water-cooler or coffee-machine chats in face-to-face teams. Now put the plan to work! You will find that you need to adapt it as things change.

Table 3.2 A communications plan template

Who	What	When/ How Often	What Format?	Kept?	Status

Building relationships through informal conversations

As a virtual leader, create planned ways to have informal conversations with teams to build relationships. These do not happen by chance as they would in a face-to-face team, where you would bump into each other in the corridor or over the coffee machine or water cooler. When you do meet up, try not to cram every moment with operational issues, however tempting that might be – remember to make time for informal conversation. Encourage your team members to do the same.

Monitoring how people are doing

You will not see your team members in passing, as you would in a co-located, face-to-face team. You cannot sidle up to them to check how they are. What will your virtual equivalent be? How will they keep you updated with their results?

Your communications plan should provide the answers: regular meetings with your team and a shared area for information and collaboration. Remember to make a conscious effort to check: 'Is each team member engaged, or not?' 'Do they have everything they need from others, or not?' 'What help or support do they need from me?' 'What ideas do they have to improve our work?'

Saying thank you

When team members deliver results or show an extra commitment to the team, such as taking part in a meeting outside of their normal office hours, make sure that you thank them for their efforts and praise them for work done.

A very simple and deceptively powerful tool is a handwritten thank-you card. It costs almost nothing to write and send to a team member, but acts as a rare physical connection to the team. (It uses the sense of touch!) It shows that he or she is appreciated. Ironically, with more and more communication via technology, slow, old-fashioned mail through the post really stands out as special in a way that it would not have done to our grandparents!

Overcoming the pull of the local through community

Each virtual team member is likely to be involved with other teams and projects as well as yours. Some of these alternative teams might be local rather than virtual, involving people they know well and see every day. In busy working lives, there is not always time to do everything properly. If push comes to shove, which team will command their respect? Some aspects favour local commitments over virtual ones, and these include:

- Loyalty is naturally local for many people.
- Strong relationships built over time.
- Shared language and culture with local colleagues.
- Shared experiences going back over time.
- Line managers may be local.
- Urgency – an angry customer standing by your desk is more likely to gain attention immediately than a remote manager trying to reach you by phone.

With such strong local pulls on many members of virtual teams, how can such teams survive and, indeed, thrive?

The answer comes through creating a community in the virtual team, with trust between members and loyalty to one another. This builds a sense of engagement and of belonging. However, this does not happen by chance but through the leader and the team carefully developing trust over time. There are many tools and methods to support this. Choose those that will work for your situation. Some virtual teams meet face to face occasionally in order to get to know one another. Others try to have a chat session just before conference calls, to catch up on what is happening in each other's locations. Other teams meet up for lunch over videoconference, with a total ban on work conversations. If you were really pushing out the boat, perhaps you could arrange for a special lunch delivery to each location rather than people having to bring their own lunch.

How can we learn and improve all the time?

As a virtual leader, always aim to learn and improve. This does not need to be spectacular improvements to make a difference. It is more like checking your course and making little adjustments often. That is what airline pilots do. Thyra, a friend of mine flies planes for Air New Zealand. She tells me that her planes are slightly off course almost all the time, but that the navigation systems are constantly adjusting to make sure that the plane lands safely at the destination. As virtual leaders, we can use this idea too. Get into the habit of checking regularly to see how things are going and what changes we need to make to get back on track.

A tool I use to do this is a very simple 'lessons learnt' exercise, sometimes called a retrospective, which takes five to ten minutes. Here's how it works. Ask the following questions one by one, gathering answers from each of your virtual team members before moving on to the next:

- What's going well?
- I wish that...

Please note that I used 'I wish that...' instead of 'What's going wrong?' The positive framing of 'I wish that...' is key. It opens people's minds to the possibility of a better alternative. It welcomes feedback on how to improve. If I use 'What's going wrong?' – as many people do – it shuts people down and, at worst, leads to a whine session or complete silence.

When you ask for contributions from the team, it is sometimes useful to take these in anonymously. This means that people feel very free to say whatever they are feeling. It is especially useful in times of conflict or when the team is feeling under pressure. It is helpful if you have cultural issues that prevent people from voicing their concerns openly in a live meeting. It can be tricky, though, to take contributions anonymously via technology. There are options. If you have a team over multiple locations, then one person at each location could collect anonymous suggestions on pieces of paper. If not, then choose someone in the team who is trusted and liked by everyone. Ask people to send their 'anonymous' contributions to this person, who will then strip ideas of their originator's name and share the ideas with everyone else.

This 'lessons learnt' tool is easy and quick. It only takes 5 to 10 minutes but it is powerful. Try it at the end of a team meeting. Plan for five minutes or so to review the session, to help you learn what to keep doing and what to do differently next time. Remember to look at these lessons again at the start of the next meeting and put them into action. You will notice an immediate improvement!

Being a virtual leader within the team

One of the premises of this book is that virtual leadership helps virtual teams to work effectively and to improve over time. You don't need to be the designated boss to show leadership and to encourage the team to work well together. Any team member can model the way for others, ask great questions, and challenge unhelpful or unprofessional behaviours. Each one of us can builder deeper and more effective relationships within the team and help trust to grow and develop. If your role in your virtual team is as a team member, please do apply what you have read in this book. For starters, you will be ready to be an excellent team leader once you have been putting the skills into practice for a while!

As a virtual leader, my own dream virtual team would consist of very different people with a very diverse range of skills and strengths, all showing leadership in this way. Each team member, myself included, would be supported and also challenged to become the best they could be, by everyone else in the team. People would facilitate one another to develop, encouraging each person to take their full part in the life of the team. While I would have particular responsibilities as team leader, I would not need to be directive or to bear the weight of leadership all alone. Wouldn't that be wonderful? I have experienced this from time to time and it has always been a very positive experience, from which I have learnt a huge amount.

Closing your virtual team

Like any other type of team, there will come a time when each virtual team has served its purpose and needs to disband. The answer to the question, 'Why continue?' will be that there is no reason to keep going.

At the end, it makes sense to ensure that all the team information is tidy and accessible, in case anyone should need it in the future. Complete any formal closure procedures. Make sure that you have gathered the lessons from the team and passed them to others in your organization for which they would be useful.

Finally, remember to celebrate success and to take time to mark the change as the team disbands. These rituals can be very helpful for people going through change. They are too often skipped over in our fast-paced world. If you were co-located, it would be time for a party or a dinner out together. In the virtual world, you can celebrate too. What would work for your particular team and the individuals within it? (There are suggestions earlier in this chapter.)

As a virtual leader, how can you help those who are leaving your team? Can you provide them with a reference, a public review online and/or feedback for their appraisal? Can you let them know what you consider their strengths to be and what you value? What have you really appreciated about them and their work?

Getting to grips with working with others remotely

Cydne is a freelance lead business analyst working in the UK and South Africa. Emma is a senior HR manager based in the Middle East. Both work in and lead virtual teams:

Cydne's story

When I initially started working virtually, there was a lot of trial and error! There are many challenges, but now that I'm aware of them, I have adjusted my approach.

I aim to have productive and positive virtual working experiences by being prepared, having strong positive communication with team members and being committed to working productively.

Conflict happens in virtual teams! Try to address conflict immediately, perhaps by the group agreeing on an action plan to resolve it. Active listening is especially important when conflict arises. Listen for the 'non-verbal' cues of hesitation, long pauses or team members being more silent than usual. There will be signs that you will begin to pick up on and knowing these signs will help you to be aware of what is happening.

Agree your office hours so that your team members know when you are working. Use shared calendars so that people can see when you are available or booked, which is especially useful for collaborative work. Seeing others 'online' creates that sense that you are working together and can contact them if required.

Emma's story

For many years, I thought that virtual working was 'less than' face-to-face; a poor compromise when money or time were too tight for anything else. I resisted trying to use technology at my fingertips, thinking that jumping on a train or in the car was somehow more logical than sitting in the comfort of my own home or office to interact with others.

Nowadays I am a major fan! For coaching or mentoring, I even prefer to work over a simple audio connection. For me, this means I can concentrate on subtle communication signs, such as breathing patterns and tonality. I can also walk around during the conversation. For me, this combination of physical movement and limited sensory stimulus from the other person enhances my listening skills and I find it easier to give my full attention to the other person. I guess this is a skill I have honed over the years but it has been a surprising upside of working at a distance.

Another way that virtual working helps is in forcing me to think through multiple ways of sharing key messages with others. Delivery by video, webcast or recording forces me to really think about what I am saying, and reduce it to the key points. It makes me cut out waffle and noise, and prepare more thoroughly for my audience.

Ultimately, I have found that if you have a shared purpose that you really care about, ie you are aligned emotionally and mentally, then distance is no barrier to building relationships and working effectively with others - no matter where you are physically.

Summary

This chapter has explored working with others remotely. To do so takes far more than just technology. We will focus on that in the next chapter. It is about building connections, understanding, trust and community, so that, together with your colleagues as a high-performing team, you can do great work, even when you are far away from one another.

Questions for reflection

1 How well do you know the other people you work with virtually? What aspects would it help you and your team to know better?

2 How much trust is there in your virtual teams? What can you do to increase your own trust in your team, trust between members, and their trust in you?

3 For each of your remote teams, how are they structured? Should they be spaghetti teams or star groups or a combination of the two? Given your answer, how many connections do you need to make?

4 How did you find the Drexler/Sibbet Team Performance Model®? What is your assessment of your virtual teams against each of the steps of the bouncing ball? Where are the steps resolved? Where are they unresolved and need more work?

5 What has worked well for you taking on new or existing virtual teams? What about adding team members? What would you do differently after reading this chapter?

6 Which of the practical team tools and strategies do you use already? Which other ones would be helpful? When will you try them out?

7 How are you encouraging others in your team to develop their own virtual leadership?

8 What has worked well when closing virtual teams? What would you do differently next time?

9 How did you feel about Cydne and Emma's stories of getting to grips with virtual working? What did you take from each one?

References and further reading

Abraham, P (2015) *Cyberconnecting: The three lenses of diversity*, Gower, Farnham

Binder, J (2008) *Global Project Management: Communication, collaboration and management across borders*, Gower, Farnham

Drexler, A and Sibbet, D (1990–2016) *The Drexler/Sibbet Team Perfomance Model®*, The Grove Consultants International, San Francisco

Hall, K (2007) *Speed Lead: Faster, simpler ways to manage people, projects and teams in complex companies*, Nicholas Brealey Publishing, London

Lipnack, J and Stamps, J (2010) *Leading Virtual Teams: Empower members, understand the technology, build team identity*, Harvard Business Press, Boston

Maister, D (2001) *The Trusted Advisor*, Touchstone, New York

Scott-Peck, M (1990) *The Different Drum: Community-making and peace*, Arrow, London

Settle-Murphy, N (2013) *Leading Effective Virtual Teams: Overcoming time and distance to achieve exceptional results*, CRC Press, Boca Raton

Tuckman, B W (1965) Developmental sequence in small groups, *Psychological Bulletin*, **63**, 384–99

Wise, T (2013) *Trust in Virtual Teams*, Gower, Farnham

Technology for virtual work   04

This chapter looks at how technology underpins virtual working. It considers the range of different types of technology that people use for virtual work, looking at what works best in different situations. Please note that I will not refer to specific technologies, except in case studies or stories, in order to keep this book fresh. Instead, this chapter looks at the key concepts, applicable to whichever particular proprietary tool or application you choose to use. I explore how to use technology in ways that harness the powers of our own human technology, our brains.

By the time you have finished this chapter:

- You will have an understanding of the wide range of technologies available to you as a virtual leader.

- You will be able to choose the most appropriate type of technology for the different constraints that you face in virtual work.

- You will be prepared for the inevitable mishaps with technology that often delay virtual meetings.

- You will know how to use technology in ways that works best with the human brain.

- I hope too that you will be inspired to make the best use of whatever technology you have available to you and perhaps even try out something new.

Technology is only an enabler

Recent advances in technology and widespread broadband have allowed a huge number of people around the world to connect with one another and work together in new ways. Technology underpins virtual working.

It is important to remember that the technology itself is only an enabler. Alone, it does not make virtual working effective. It is more important to

Figure 4.1 A mind-map of this chapter

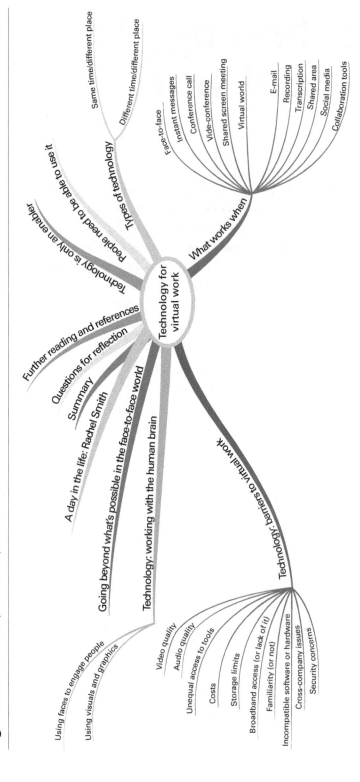

choose and use the appropriate technology to support the work that people are trying to do together and their communication preferences. Think of the choice between travelling to the office to use your company's top-of-the-range video suite for a 6 am meeting or taking the meeting from home as a conference call? Which would you prefer? I know what my preference would be – the conference call every time!

Don't fall into the trap, as many organizations do, of providing training for new virtual technologies, but not providing any support on how to work together effectively virtually. The culture of your organization and the behaviours of your people will have much more impact on virtual success than the particular tools you choose. There is even a 90/10 rule, which stresses how a virtual team's success is based 90 per cent on the people involved and 10 per cent on the technology (Lipnack and Stamps, 2000). Others agree, saying: 'It's never been easier to communicate or collaborate with people anywhere, any time. The missing upgrade is for the human mind' (Fried and Hansson, 2013). This book is designed to provide you with that upgrade so that you can show virtual leadership and gain improved results.

People need to be able to use the technology

However clever the technology, it is not going to work well unless people can use it effectively. Ensure that your teams are either: 1) already accomplished in the tools you wish to use; or 2) willing to learn, plus supported with everything they need to become proficient. Appropriate support might include training, a user guide and/or virtual learning. It depends on each individual and their situation. If you make assumptions that people will be able to use technology, they may never get to grips with it, which could hold you back. I find two extremes in my work: some people do not come forward to say that they need help with technology, while others assume they need lots of help, when they would be able to get started on their own.

Here is an example: I generally consider myself to be quite quick at learning new technologies. I've worked with technology for decades and used my first computer in the 1970s. However, I am part of a virtual group that makes extensive use of an online system for working together. The group is part of a professional association – a special interest group. I am not trained in the particular tool that we use and, as a result, I have muddled along over the years. I have not been as involved in online discussions as I should have. Is it about time I asked someone to run through the details of how to use the tool, or set aside time to work through the user guide? Definitely.

Types of technology

To separate out the different types of technology for different types of meetings, consider a two-by-two grid as shown in Figure 4.2. The top of the grid is labelled 'same place', which would align with traditional working in the same location, and the bottom is labelled 'different place', which means virtual working. The left column is labelled 'same time', which indicates live meetings and other types of synchronous work, and the right column shows 'different time', or asynchronous work.

Figure 4.2 The time and place grid

Same time, same place	Different time, same place
Traditional meetings	Display boards
Same time, different place	Different time, different place
Synchronous virtual working tools	Asynchronous virtual working tools

SOURCE: Adapted from an idea by Johansen (1988)

You can see that virtual technologies fall into either of the lower two quadrants. They are either different place/same time – synchronous – or different place/different time – asynchronous.

Same time/difference place

Synchronous virtual working tools include:

- **Chat,** such as text messages on a phone or instant messages.
- **Audio,** such as phone calls (one-to-one) or conference calls (for a group).
- **Shared screens plus audio,** which allow people to share their screens so that everyone can see what they are working on at the same time as discussing it verbally.
- **Smart whiteboards,** connected to each other between different virtual sites and sharing all of the markings made on each board to all the different sites.
- **Co-creation tools,** allowing people to work together virtually on documents, seeing changes made by others in real time (these tools can also be used asynchronously).
- **Live video,** where people are able to see each other in real time during discussions.
- **Live video** plus shared screen, where people can see the work and also small headshots of the speakers.
- **Telepresence,** which is made to appear as close to meeting face to face as possible but needs very sophisticated and expensive video and audio equipment and dedicated rooms. You can whisper to a remote person and only they will hear your message.
- **Virtual worlds,** where people use a virtual, three-dimensional world to meet up with others. Widely used in games, these can be really effective for business meetings and group events as well. In a virtual world, each individual is represented by an avatar, a computer-generated symbol that can be quite realistic, or alternatively just a coloured block. People can move around inside this world, moving backwards and forwards and turning around. By moving their avatars, individuals can move towards other avatars and then communicate with each other. These can be used for large, virtual conferences as well as smaller meetings. The difference with a virtual world is that they can be quite immersive, with individuals feeling as if they really are in the virtual world, interacting with others despite being miles apart.

These tools operate in the same box; however, they are very different. Consider instant messages and video conferencing as an example. The former only uses text to communicate whereas the latter adds in the speakers' tone of voice and their body language, which aid communication. Neither of these approaches have the richness of face-to-face communication in the same location, where people are able to shake hands and look each other directly in the eye.

It is important to choose the most appropriate tools for the job. While instant messages give short, written notes, which take little effort to write or read, they are not suitable for delivering complex information, building trusting relationships or dealing with conflict. If a simple technology is not working for your situation, try something richer. So, if instant messages are not working, try a phone call. If that isn't working, try a video call. If that doesn't work, maybe it is worth meeting face to face? We will explore which virtual tools work best in different circumstances later in this chapter.

Brian told me about his experience of telepresence. At the time he was working with colleagues in Singapore, Colorado, France and the rest of the UK from his base in Scotland: 'The room was set up with a semi-circular table facing a set of big monitors. When remote people joined, we could see everyone clearly, as if we were sitting around the same circular table. I found it a very good meeting experience; I could see body language clearly and even share eye contact with others. It was great when we could get the room, but of course, it wasn't always available.'

A conversation inside QUBE, a virtual world

Professor Eddie Obeng runs a virtual business school called Pentacle, where he uses QUBE. This is a virtual world where people can come together virtually to talk, laugh, brainstorm and share presentations together wherever they are in the physical world. I was intrigued and asked Professor Obeng to show me how QUBE works. He invited me to visit his virtual office on QUBE.

At the start of my visit, I installed the software and went through some induction training. This taught me how to move my avatar, my black and boxy virtual body. During the induction, I could see a huge, empty hall with large posters around the walls and, as I moved around by pressing the arrow keys on my keyboard, my view of the room changed just as it would in real life. I could look up or down, turn to the right or left, move forwards or backwards, nod or shake my rectangular head and even jump up and down. I found it quite easy to navigate, once I got used to it, and, on the whole, things worked just as I would have expected from the real world. I could sit down on chairs or stand up. I could see other avatars representing other people. I knew who they were because each had their name floating above their head. Some of them had company logos on their box chests. I could hear them speaking too. When I sat down at a table with other people, the conversation narrowed to the people sitting with me and I could no longer hear the others in the room.

Once I was able to find my way around, I headed for Eddie's office by clicking on a link, which took me straight there. My view changed instantly. I could see a window and posters on the walls. On turning my avatar around, I saw that Eddie was already there! He'd seen me appear from nowhere. The feeling of existing spatially relative to others mirrors the real world – this made QUBE immersive in a way that I hadn't experienced before from other technology. Eddie started talking to me. I could hear him through my headphones, just as he could hear me. We had a conversation about how this virtual world makes a difference to his clients. He showed me how his performance enhancement tools are embedded in the environment, helping people to be clear as they work together in groups. We used one of them during our conversation, where we added our hopes and our fears for the session to a large poster and then worked together to resolve the fears.

A couple of weeks later, Eddie invited me to be part of a large group session on QUBE led by Dr Tammy Watchorn, head of Service Improvement and Innovation in the NHS UK. She has used QUBE to work with people dispersed around Scotland to deliver improved and innovative services. Eddie facilitated the session for Tammy to speak on 'Turning Public Sector Reticence into Accelerated Innovation'. Being able to work with the entire group at times and break out into smaller groups was a very useful feature of QUBE. Sometimes Tammy presented to us as a large group, exploring the challenges that face the health service in Scotland. At other times, we moved into small groups, organized by the first letter of our surnames. When we were finished, the leaders pulled everyone back into a big circle to give our feedback. At one stage, to give us an overview, the facilitator pulled us up into the air so that we were all floating near the ceiling of the room. I was surprised to feel a bit nauseous looking down at the virtual floor below, which showed just how much it felt like the real world – I hate heights!

▶

Figure 4.3 A view inside QUBE

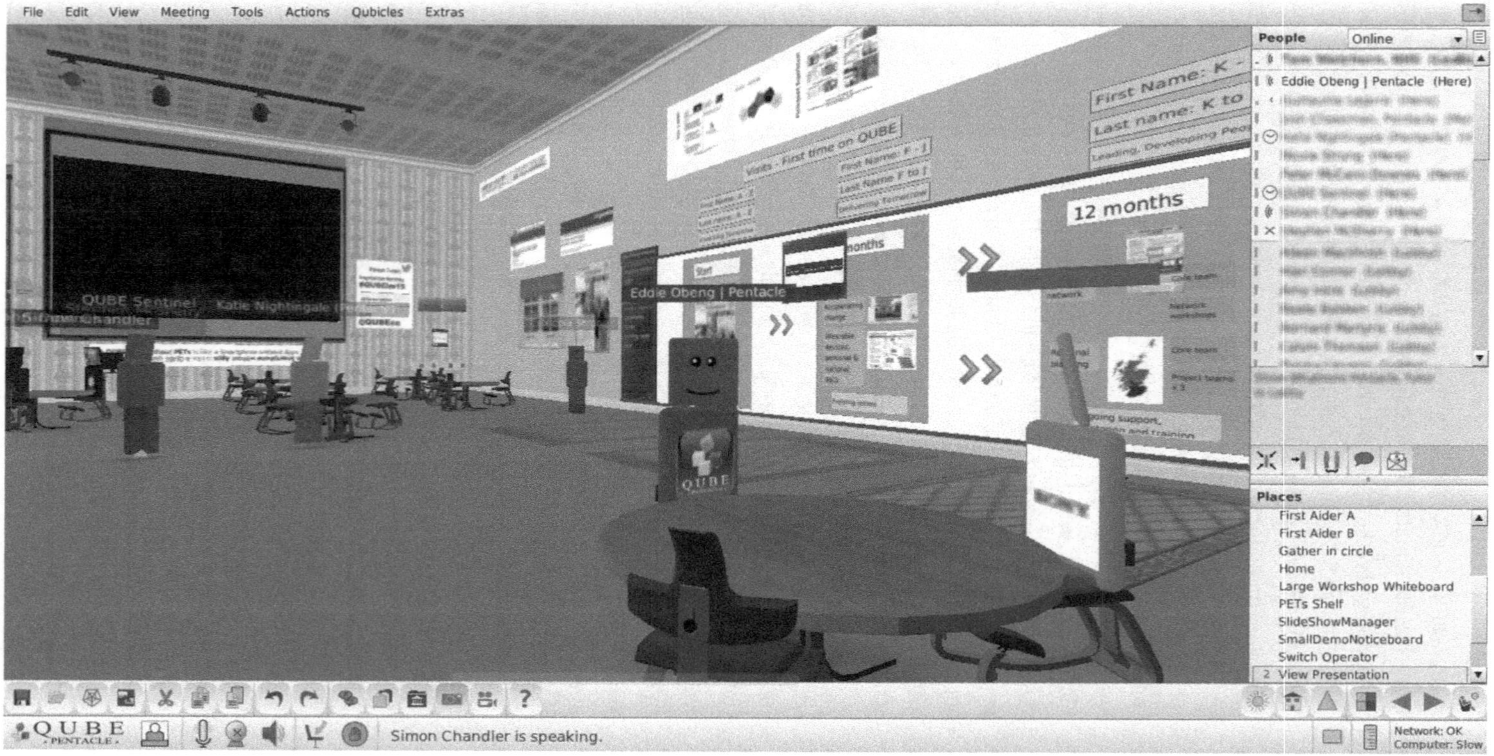

I found my QUBE experience quite different from the ways that most companies worked together virtually at the time of the interview in 2015. The biggest difference for me was that everything happening inside QUBE held my attention the whole time. This is rare indeed! Engaging remote participants consistently comes up as the number one challenge for people working remotely, and I think that Professor Obeng has solved that problem with QUBE. Although I didn't experience it myself, I could see that it would be possible to use QUBE in an asynchronous way too, for example by leaving posters on the wall of your qubicle or virtual office space and inviting others to contribute over time.

As with most technology, though, human misunderstanding can cause problems. I unwittingly managed to delete a poster by pressing an unexpected combination of keys. I hope that Professor Obeng has managed to put it back where it was without too much hassle!

Different time/different place

While synchronous ways of virtual working seem natural to people, not all interactions in virtual teams need to be live, especially when the team is spread across a wide range of time zones. There are technologies that support asynchronous interaction and these complement same-time interactions very well. Some examples of asynchronous technologies include:

- **Correspondence,** normally electronic, such as e-mail and texts and messages can be picked up later. While physical correspondence could *theoretically* be used for virtual work, there are huge time delays involved in using postal services. The only example I have seen of physical mail is handwritten thank-you cards sent around the world by a virtual leader. This had quite an impact on the team as people felt appreciated. Almost all of the team's interactions with their leader were over conference calls, so it made quite a difference to have something physical and personal to say, 'Thank you'.

- **Audio or video recordings,** such as the recording of a conference-call meeting made available for those not able to attend live. Video recordings combine audio with shared screens, so anyone who missed a meeting can see exactly what the team saw while listening to the discussion.

- **Transcriptions of audio and video recordings,** where a transcriber has listened to the words spoken and written them down. These are much quicker to read through than to listen to the whole meeting, but take time and skill to prepare accurately.

- **Collaboration tools** provide a hub for information, so that everyone can access the latest versions of files and documents.

- **Project management tools** allow teams to manage and schedule projects and provide shared to-do lists. Team members can monitor work and know what to do when.

  Often collaboration and project management tools are combined to provide a **virtual team space,** including a work plan, calendars, discussion forums, information and more. They take quite a bit of organizing to monitor and keep up to date and need good version control, but are much more powerful than information spread across individual e-mail accounts. It makes sense to assign an individual as the team space curator.

- **Social media,** such as micro-blogging sites, photo-sharing sites, blogs and wikis and much, much more.

- **Survey tools** allow people to give individual answers to questions.

- **Tools to support idea generation and other activities** – there are a number of tools designed to support specific activities, for example, generating ideas. For example, face-to-face teams will often use sticky notes when they are coming up with ideas, with one idea per sticky note. All the ideas can be clustered into groups and used to find the best ideas to take forward. Virtual tools exist that replicate this in the virtual world, allowing people to use virtual sticky notes to contribute their ideas. These can be clustered just like real ones. A key advantage is that the results can be output instantly, either graphically or in words, which takes much longer in the real world where each sticky note would need to be transcribed.

A conversation with Elizabeth Harrin, project manager and blogger

'I would recommend that virtual teams look at what problems they are trying to solve before diving into buying tools,' said Elizabeth Harrin. She works virtually with her teams in her roles both as a project manager for a UK health-care firm and on her blog, A Girl's Guide to Project Management. 'There are hundreds of online social and collaboration tools that are marketed at virtual teams. You really need to know your requirements before you invest, because the latest app might not be right for you. There are a number of issues that may be facing your team where technology can help, such as making sure everyone has the same view of their work allocations or to capture and codify as much organizational knowledge as you can before your baby boomers retire, taking everything they know with them.'

Author of *Collaboration Tools for Project Managers* (Harrin, 2016), Elizabeth has an interest in the use of social and collaboration technology in workplace teams. Her 2015 research amongst a group of nearly 200 project leaders showed that:

- 94 percent of people reported using collaboration tools to work with teams on projects.
- The main reason for using online tools was to share documents (27 per cent said they used their tools for this). Communication was the second most common reason, with over one in five respondents saying they used it for that. The third most common response was working with internal stakeholders (20 per cent).
- The other results looked like this:
    - Schedule or assign work: 17 per cent.
    - Work with external stakeholders: 11 per cent.
    - The final 3 per cent responded 'Other' and these included as a knowledge base, for transparency and audit trails, and document control.

'These findings tie in with the benefits from using collaboration and social communication tools at work, with the most common benefit being the ease of finding information. One-third of my respondents said this was the top benefit they see from their systems,' said Elizabeth.

'One-quarter of respondents reported that collaboration tools had been useful in creating a sense of team. I've done that myself through creating a virtual "trail" where employees had to seek out images on various intranet pages in a company-wide contest. In the survey I did in 2011 only 18 per cent of people said that they thought improved team morale was one of the benefits they were seeing as part of using social and collaboration systems at work. I hope this shows that businesses are getting better at finding ways to improve how virtual teams work effectively.

'Nearly 70 per cent of people reported that they would continue to use collaboration tools at work and they thought their use would increase,' said Elizabeth. She added that 32 per cent said they would continue to use them and their usage would be about the same as now.

'Interestingly, nobody said they would stop using them and their use at work would decrease, although one person wasn't sure,' she added. 'The

▶

more traction a tool has within a project team, department or company, the more useful it becomes. The trick is to choose a tool that really supports what your team is trying to achieve and how they work virtually. The most successful system implementations have a clear goal and clear requirements, and they integrate with your team's other communication channels such as face-to-face. There is no point in tech for tech's sake but if you are not using online collaboration tools now you will be soon. There is no sign that this trend is going away so the challenge for virtual leaders is to find the best way to deploy them to support productivity and effective working.'

The company Basecamp has produced their 'Basecamp' web-based project management collaboration software tool since 2004. Employees are free to choose wherever they want to live. Some work from an office in Chicago while others work remotely from all around the world. In 2013, Jason Fried and David Heinemeier Hansson wrote a book called *Remote: Office not required* to share their experiences of this way of working (Fried and Hansson, 2013).

Technology has allowed Basecamp to give individuals the freedom to choose how to live. If people want to, they can work in an office in a city and, if they don't, they live wherever in the world they wish to. Technology has freed people from soul-sucking commutes and the cost of running cars. Basecamp allows working hours to vary, as much of their virtual work is done asynchronously. They find many of their people are more productive outside of traditional offices, getting more done in hours that suit them and in an environment that they control. In fact, the authors consider typical offices as interruption factories, hampering creativity, which needs uninterrupted time. Unlike companies based in one location, Basecamp feels prepared for disasters – snowstorms or ash clouds in one location will not stop them operating.

Some people feel that they are missing out on interacting face to face with their co-workers, but the whole company meets two or three times a year for really high-quality human interaction. They do not have PowerPoint presentations at these special get-togethers! In between, employees have a shared online space and a virtual water cooler (a chat program) where they can hang out with their colleagues.

Overall, Basecamp find that remote working gives their people lifestyle choices while retaining high productivity. For them, remote working is a viable path to follow and they are keen to share what they have learned with others.

Considerations for choosing virtual technologies: what works when

There are quite a few things to consider when you choose technologies to support your virtual work. First of all, different technologies work well in different situations, so you will need to choose a combination. However, having too many different technologies in use at any one time will be overpowering for many people, more expensive to run, harder to support and counterproductive. So choose your mix of technologies carefully and remember that the right tool for you will vary from situation to situation.

The sections below show you what works best in what circumstances (Figure 4.4, Figure 4.5) and compares them all to face-to-face meetings. Thanks go to Nancy Settle-Murphy, who inspired this section with her practical 'What Works When' ideas.

Figure 4.4 Synchronous technologies

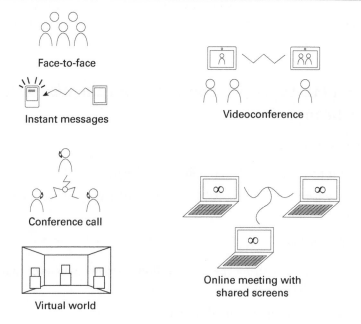

Face-to-face

Instant messages

Videoconference

Conference call

Online meeting with shared screens

Virtual world

Face-to-face meetings (for comparison purposes) (synchronous)

When it works best:

- Very useful for building relationships, dealing with sensitive issues or conflict.
- Also useful to show respect to team members by being present for them.
- It also works well for negotiation, getting buy-in, building trust and interactive discussions.

Things to consider:

- Likely to involve at least one person travelling, if not many, leading to cost, time and work–life balance issues.
- You can see people eye-to-eye in a way that videoconferences try to achieve, but it is not quite the same.
- If you have face-to-face time, do not waste it on looking at presentations in a darkened room or ploughing through lots of data. Far too many people do just this! Instead make time for spontaneous interaction – where people can catch up with one another and enjoy information conversation.

Instant messages (synchronous, but can also be used asynchronously)

When it works best:

- Great for asking a quick question of a colleague.
- Useful when not everyone is fluent in the language you use, as messages are written down.

Things to consider:

- A message can interrupt the receiver, slowing down whatever they were focused on beforehand.
- Constant messages are very distracting.
- While it is possible to mark yourself as 'active' or 'busy', not everyone uses these useful distinctions.

Conference call or phone call (audio only) (synchronous)

When it works best:

- People already know each other.
- Everyone is fluent at speaking the language.
- You do not need to share non-verbal input from people, such as slides, and you don't need to be able to see each other's faces and body language. It is not about sensitive issues, building relationships from scratch or dealing with conflict.
- It is convenient to use when your meeting falls outside normal working hours for some people, as they can take a call wherever they are, rather than having to travel into the office.
- Don't forget one-to-one calls! They are a normal part of working life and help to build relationships between virtual team members.

Things to consider:

- Send out in advance the overall purpose of the call, the objectives you would like to achieve, the agenda timings and any content.
- Audio quality makes or breaks a call. For this reason, use the best quality you can, so avoid mobile telephones, especially in areas with poor signal, and speaker phones.
- Use mute when not speaking, especially in larger groups or if you are in a noisy environment. I've heard airport and train departure announcements, lawnmowers running, children crying, dogs barking and, worst of all, toilets flushing when people have forgotten to mute their calls!
- State your name at the start of each point you make and agree upfront with others that they will do the same.
- Set up 'ways of working' for your call at the start. Some people call these ground rules or group norms. An example would be to state your name whenever you contribute.
- Can you add in text-based support? One way of doing this is to summarize key points and share them with everyone over instant messenger. This is particularly useful for those who are not speaking in their mother tongue. It adds a visual dimension for all those who can see the messages, meaning that they might be less likely to be distracted.

Videoconference (audio plus video of participants) (synchronous)

When it works best:

- It is important to see people's faces to gauge their reactions, as well as hearing their voices.
- All participants have access to the same high standard of videoconferencing technology and the bandwidth to support it reliably throughout the session.
- The meeting is to introduce new team members or to build better relationships between team members.
- You want to show people physical objects or models. For example, I had a notebook full of mind-maps, sketches and notes when I was planning how this book would fit together. I was able to show pages of my book to my friend Nancy Settle-Murphy in Boston, over a videoconference. This helped me to show her my ideas.

Things to consider:

- The more sites you have taking part in videoconferences, the more body language and visual feedback you will miss because fewer people will be clearly visible at any one time. Videoconferencing technology often focuses on people speaking, in preference to those who are silent.
- Don't expect people to travel to their office in the middle of the night to use a special, high-end videoconferencing system. In these cases, use a conference call or webcams so they can join from home.
- If the video quality is poor, you will not gain much as people's body language won't be very clear.

Online meeting, with shared screen and audio, and possibly some video (synchronous)

When it works best:

- Participants are working together on a document, presentation or shared drawing area.
- Everyone has equal access to the technology.
- All participants are comfortable with the technology.

Things to consider:

- If you have a wide range of time zones involved so that people will need to work outside of their normal office hours, will they be able to access the technology from home?

- There may well be technical glitches at the start, so make sure that you test the technology upfront.

- Focus on creating content that adds value, rather than tidying up or 'word-smithing' documents. Individuals can do tidying afterwards.

- Have a backup plan in case participants have problems accessing documents live. For example, you might place documents in your shared space and send links to everyone.

Virtual world, allowing people a three-dimensional view of the group, where they can see everyone else (synchronous; can also be used asynchronously)

When it works best:

- Everyone has the same level of access to the technology.

- All the participants have had training or put the time into becoming comfortable with the virtual world.

- You wish to break into syndicate groups. With its spatial view, the virtual world allows people to move into groups, see the different groups that have formed and to move between them if they want to.

- You know that people are likely to be distracted and so you would like a more engaging, immersive experience.

Things to consider:

- Will the tool work well for everyone?

- How will you ensure that everyone is ready and confident to use the virtual world? For example, the virtual world QUBE offers an induction session for new users before they enter the environment. However, if people have not allowed time for their induction, they can bypass it.

- Test upfront – have a practice run with the team before the real work starts.

A conversation with Pete Bennett, founder of Buzz Conferencing

'I advise people to go for the lowest common denominator across devices and protocols,' says Pete Bennett. He is the London-based founder of Buzz Conferencing, a global provider of free conference calls. We chatted over the phone while I asked him for his top tips as a provider of technology for virtual working. 'Keep the technology you use as simple as possible, as the more technically complex things become, the more likely the service is to be flaky and not to scale when you increase from a few people to tens of thousands on the line at once. With simple technology, you'll remove excuses that people were unable to join because of tech problems.' Despite being a technologist, Pete agreed with me that the human side comes first.

I asked Pete for his advice for people switching to virtual. 'Too many technology companies are guilty of telling people that they can replace all their face-to-face interactions with virtual technology. The trouble is that, to get to high-performing teams, there is a process: forming, storming, norming and performing. This happens naturally face to face but doesn't tend to happen online. I'd suggest replacing one in five meetings at first. My own experience with substantial global projects is that it is best to meet first face to face and get to know people properly. Then use virtual meetings for regular touch points, perhaps for weekly check-ins. In my company I host a weekly conference call at 9.30 am every Monday. Often it lasts five minutes or less, but it always happens on a Monday as a regular thing. It keeps people focused, as there is a deadline. In between these calls, people work asynchronously.'

Pete has access to mountains of data and trends about conference calls, so I asked him to share some of these with us:

- Most meetings start two or three minutes past the hour. Buzz Conferencing sees massive surges at this time and meetings tend to finish on the hour. Why do people start their meetings just past the hour, or at half-past, and why do meetings last an hour? Why are people a few minutes late? Perhaps people underestimate the time to find the bridge number and pin code and to get connected? Perhaps they were finishing their previous call? Pete starts his own meetings at 10 past and finishes them within 20 minutes, which works well for him.

- More and more meetings are happening outside the traditional UK office hours of 9 am to 5 pm. Pete notices that some calls are starting at 4 am UK time and others carry on until 11 pm UK time.

- Mobile traffic is growing strongly, despite the extra expense compared to a landline. Pete thinks that this might be for the convenience of being able to join a conference call when driving or commuting. Also many people have no landline nowadays.

- Why is Buzz Conferencing only providing simple conference calls, rather than online-video calling services? Pete feels that the key factors in their favour are reliability, audio quality and the fact that it does not need an internet connection or much user competence to work.

- When the London Tube train drivers went on strike in 2015, the tube network closed down almost entirely. Many companies allowed their employees to 'work from home' on these days. Pete had expected to see a spike in the use of his services, but instead saw the opposite: a reduction in the number of minutes used on these days. He suspects that the face-to-face culture of these workers means that 'work from home' might translate more accurately into 'stay at home without necessarily doing much work'. This is yet another indicator that the culture of the people is just as important as the technology!

- Pete is seeing a growth in the numbers of very large conference calls, with tens of thousands of people connected to each call. These give a wide reach in a secure way (via a phone pin number) to large numbers with good attendance rates. He is finding that people combine these broadcast-style calls with question-and-answer sessions, taking questions from tweets, e-mails or even texts. One example of this would be a legal firm who run large conference calls to update people on changes in pensions and allow those listening in to ask questions that are answered at the end of the call.

As with all those who have given their input to this book, I would like to thank Pete for his input and I'm also delighted about his observation that the human side comes first.

Figure 4.5 Asynchronous technologies

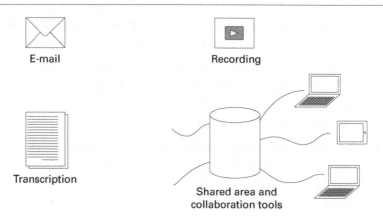

E-mail

Recording

Transcription

Shared area and
collaboration tools

E-mail (asynchronous)

When it works best:

- You are communicating uncontroversial information.
- You need a response, but not necessarily immediately.
- It would be useful to have a written copy of your communication.
- Working asynchronously will not slow things down.

Things to consider:

- It is quick and inexpensive.
- Avoid e-mail for emotive or contentious subjects.
- Summarize the content in the subject line, so that it is really clear what action should follow.
- Only send to people who really need your e-mail, so don't copy the entire team or work groups!
- E-mail can develop misunderstandings over time that, if not corrected, could grow into full-blown conflict. I know because I have experienced this at first hand!
- The generation currently entering the workplace tends not to use e-mail much.

Recording of the meeting (asynchronous)

When it works best:

- People need to come up to speed after a missed synchronous meeting, such as a conference call, videoconference or online meeting.
- The meeting contained complex information that cannot be picked up from reading notes or a transcription of the words spoken.

Things to consider:

- People do not always take the time to listen in to recordings of meetings they have missed.
- Listening to or watching recordings takes just as long as attending the original meeting, so you could use a transcription instead to cut down the time to absorb the information. This also makes it easier for anyone who does not speak the language fluently.

Transcription of a recording (asynchronous)

When it works best:

- People need to come up to speed quickly after a missed synchronous meeting.
- The words alone are enough. Hearing the tone of voice or seeing people's body language would not add anything.

Things to consider:

- Transcriptions are much quicker to read than watching/listening to recordings.
- Transcriptions are helpful for those who are not fluent in the meeting language as they can see the words used and can read at their own speed.

Shared area (asynchronous)

When it works best:

- Everyone has easy access to the tools.
- This is especially useful for teams with a wide mix of time zones, as everyone works when suits it them and they can access whatever they need.

Things to consider:

- Some people from different sites or different organizations may find it difficult to get access because of security barriers.
- It is important to keep the shared area organized so that people can access whatever they need quickly and easily.

Social media and collaboration tools (asynchronous)

When it works best:

- Everyone has easy access to the tools.
- The social side of these tools can help to build connections across virtual teams in an informal way.

Things to consider:

- Will everyone take part?
- Some people from different sites or different organizations may find it difficult to access.

These sections are available as a table to download from www.virtualleadershipbook.com.

Technology: barriers to virtual work

Let's consider issues that arise with technology in virtual work. There are almost always issues with technology in virtual meetings. A little preparation and thought upfront can help to overcome these. For technology barriers related to individual preferences, see Chapter 3 and for barriers related to generational differences, see Chapter 7.

Security concerns

With people working from a variety of locations, perhaps from home or their cars, from other organizations which might be abroad, the need for security becomes obvious. Who is joining your meetings? Who is accessing your virtual team space? Who is listening in to your conference calls? Are hackers able to access business-critical information that you have made available to your virtual colleagues?

There are two ways of tackling security issues. The first involves building security into the infrastructure and technology used. These include passwords, encryption and firewalls. The second is to remain vigilant. Ensure that people cannot join your conference calls to listen in without identifying themselves. Use a conference call system that shows all the telephone lines connected to the call, so that you can identify each participant and, if they are not wanted, exclude them from the call. Use logs to find out who has accessed your shared area and when. Ensure that people who leave your virtual team no longer have access to your team space.

It is important to consider the security of your data as well. Many individual entrepreneurs and smaller organizations do not think about this until something goes wrong and it is too late. Consider a cash-strapped start-up company, using a free tool to collaborate and sharing information quickly, including client names and other confidential information. While this might work really well for a while at no cost, there are considerable risks. Imagine if a team member left their phone unlocked on a train. All the confidential data would be accessible, with possible serious consequences for the start-up company and their clients. Often, the lower the cost of a technological platform, the less control the user has over the way their data is used and shared.

A few years ago I was invited to join a risk management review for an international manufacturing company. The review was held virtually, with participants from partner companies joining the session. They used a shared screen alongside an audio conference. Unfortunately I only managed to join the session half an hour late after slowly downloading several plugins to allow me to view the shared screen. When I joined the call, no one asked who I was or asked me to introduce myself. I'm not sure that anyone even noticed that I had joined in! There seemed to be three or four people talking to each other, but it wasn't clear who else was on the call. Perhaps there were 20 people? Or more? Who knows! If you have a session like this, especially if you are sharing sensitive information, make sure that you know who is on your call and who can see your screen.

Cross-company issues

Organizations often overcome some of their security concerns by installing firewalls between their operations and the outside world. However, when different organizations are working together virtually, this can become a problem, stopping virtual tools from working properly. The best way to get over this is to work with technical infrastructure people from all the companies involved to ensure that your tools will be able to work effectively.

You might find that these issues lead you to choose different tools. For example, conference calls are not affected by firewalls, so can be used instead of video calls or as a backup in case of problems. Prepare your Plan B in advance so that you have call-in details to distribute in case your video call doesn't work.

Incompatible software or hardware

Sometimes the tools are able to work across company firewalls but get stuck because of incompatible software or hardware. I find that most large companies in the UK prefer to use tried and trusted software and that this can be quite old. Once I was unable to use my shared screen system with a financial services company. It turned out that several people used a Windows operating system (Windows 2000) that was 15 years old and no longer compatible. I didn't expect that! We had to use a conference call as backup and, for future meetings, I e-mailed slides for people to look at.

Familiarity (or not)

If people are already using a technology and feel confident and comfortable using it, then it makes sense to stick with it if you can. My experience shows that, when presented with a new tool that is not straightforward or consistent with what they have used already, people are likely to ignore it or minimize their use of it.

Broadband access (or lack of it)

While broadband access is taken for granted in many parts of the world, it is not ubiquitous. I wrote this chapter on holiday in a remote area in the south of France and there was only sporadic, very slow broadband available at the villa where I was staying. Slow mobile data was only available if I walked over to a nearby field of sunflowers!

In a large, international virtual programme a few years ago, I worked alongside directors of chocolate companies and with governments in several West African countries. We wanted to use shared screens and video calls, but this just wasn't possible. One participant told us he had to drive for an hour to reach reliable broadband. Instead, we used conference calls, as mobile phones were reliable and worked well for everybody.

If you plan to use shared video and shared screens for your virtual meetings to allow for the best possible experience, make sure that everyone has the broadband speed for this to work properly. Have a backup plan, just in case.

Storage limits

For your virtual team space, it is important to make sure that you have enough storage for everything you will need to share. It would be very frustrating to reach the limit in the middle of uploading documents.

Costs

There are costs involved in virtual technologies, even 'free' ones. Take Buzz Conferencing, for example. While their conference bridge itself is free, Pete's company make money from a share in the call costs paid by people dialling into the bridge. For start-up companies, where people are likely to be using their own devices, the call costs would probably end up on individuals' bills. In larger companies, the costs would come out of their budget for telephony. Free online videoconferencing needs computer or mobile devices to work and will offer up-sells to premium offerings.

A UK-based charity wanted their employees to be able to work remotely. They saw the investment needed to do so as the cost of a laptop with webcam for each employee, which was quite significant. However, additional costs included access to the internet and conference calls, as well as training.

Some high-end tools require considerable investment just in terms of the technology alone. An example of this would be telepresence rooms used by some large companies. This provides very high-end videoconferencing facilities, which give a very clear view of each remote person and aims to make the experience as close to face-to-face interaction as possible. In a telepresence room, for example, you can whisper to another participant and it is likely that only they will hear your voice. As well as costs of the telepresence technology itself, this needs dedicated rooms at each site along with appropriate technical support to keep this complex technology working well. These rooms are less flexible than many other technologies as each participant needs to travel to use the dedicated room.

Accessing information

How will you ensure that everyone can find the information they need?

However good your own tools, if some members of your virtual team do not have the same access to information then it will erode trust as well as making it harder to work together effectively. If necessary, revert to simpler tools. A clear structure will help people to find documents and know where to put new ones. Searching, with filters, helps to find documents that are not immediately visible.

What about version control? How will people know that they are using the right version of a document? It is easy to end up with multiple versions of documents in different e-mail inboxes and no one knowing whether their own version is up to date!

Connectivity

Will people be able to access information and tools anytime, from anywhere (office, home, on the road, travelling abroad)? Can people access tools from any device, whether a computer or mobile device, such as smartphones and tablets?

Individual needs

Can your technology be tailored to suit individuals' needs and preferences? For example, a team member who is hard of hearing will need to be able to adjust audio volume. Consider preferences too. Most reporting tools rely heavily on text, whereas people often prefer visual summaries.

Audio quality

Without the possibility of seeing a speaker's body language, say on conference calls, the combination of the words spoken and voice tone will help you to understand the message and mood of the speaker. Put simply, the poorer the quality of the audio, the less that people can pick up. In my experience, the best audio quality comes from traditional corded telephone landlines; using mobile devices and/or VOIP phones can lead to poorer quality.

Another common use of technology that leads to poor audio is groups sitting around a board table with only one central speakerphone to talk into with remote participants via a conference call. When speakers are sitting close to the speakerphone, then remote participants might be able to hear clearly. Usually, though, as a meeting progresses, the people in the room tend to forget about remote callers and take less care. If the speakerphone cannot be passed around the room to whoever is speaking, then the audio quality will suffer greatly!

Video quality

While telepresence offers very high-quality video, many people use webcams and cameras in their mobile devices to provide video. This can be of highly variable quality, depending on a range of factors. One such is lighting, which can make or break video quality – make it if the subject is well lit with a dark background, or break it if the subject is backlit and visible as a dark silhouette.

Technology: working with the human brain

We have explored a wide range of technologies for virtual work. We have not yet considered how we can use these in ways that complement our own technology, our human brains. This is not discussed widely, although I find that it is key to overcoming many of the inherent difficulties of virtual working.

Consider the top challenge for virtual work from my research for this book: 'engaging remote participants'. It is easy to see how remote participants lose focus. For a start, many people work on multiple projects, some local to them and others remote. In our world of constant distractions, there are so many different things trying to gain our attention, some work-related and others not. When I see people 'multitasking' in face-to-face meetings, I think how much more likely this is if they cannot be seen, say in conference calls.

There are solutions to these problems, though, which build on our own internal technology, our human brains. I have found several different ways to engage people, which include:

- visuals and graphics;
- faces;
- stories and narrative form.

We will consider the first of these in this chapter and touch on the second, as both involve the use of supporting technology. Chapters 5 will cover more about these and other ideas, focused on how to engage people in meetings.

Using visuals and graphics

Our brains are hardwired to think visually, as well as to listen to and remember stories. Inside human brains, hundreds of millions of neurons are devoted to visual processing, about 10 times those used for hearing. We take in huge amounts of information through our eyes, processing it in a split second, so our brains pick up an overview of visuals almost immediately. To read a written description of the same information would take much longer and it would not be remembered as accurately. Figure 4.1 on page 90 shows a high-level mind-map of this chapter. Look at it again and notice how quickly you gain a feel for the structure of the chapter. If you had needed to work out this structure from scratch, it would have taken much longer, even though you have just read most of the chapter. Our ancestors, just as they passed down stories, used pictures to communicate, starting with cave paintings – and we use pictures, maps, diagrams, graphs and more to share information. This works very well virtually.

When people cannot be together face to face, sharing information visually can be a very effective way to keep people focused on a topic. For virtual meetings where you cannot see each other, it gives people something to look at, which helps to keep them focused.

Mind-maps work very well here as a visual tool to structure and organize information or ideas. Each map has a central theme or idea, with branches radiating out of it. Each branch represents a different idea or concept that relates to the central theme. Each branch can then divide into sub-branches. This is a really powerful way of showing hierarchy. Mind-maps are helpful when you want to analyse, synthesize, understand, remember and even generate new ideas. I use them for planning projects, planning what I need to take on holiday and even for structuring every chapter of this book! While mind-maps can be drawn on paper, in a virtual setting it is much easier to use a mind-mapping tool on a shared screen. In this situation, remote colleagues can see changes that you make in the tool in real time.

My experience shows that while all visuals are powerful, visuals that evolve and change throughout a meeting are like still pictures on steroids! I draw live on shared screens in my virtual meetings and find that people keep focused as they can see the changes in front of their eyes while I talk.

I ran a webinar for the Association for Project Management (APM) on virtual leadership in 2015. I used a graphics tablet to draw live on my shared slides, building up information as I spoke. When I asked for feedback, I found that I had been the first presenter to draw live during an APM webinar. 'What difference did this make?' I asked. The organizer told me how numbers attending APM webinars usually peaked a short way into the webinar and then usually fell sharply as people left well before the end. In my webinar, with live drawing, the number of attendees increased to a peak, but then almost everyone stayed right to the end. This webinar is available as a recording in case you would like to see how engaging you find this drawing yourself (Pullan, 2015).

How can you create visuals live in your virtual meetings and then share them afterwards with attendees and others? As I am comfortable drawing in front of other people, I use a graphics tablet that plugs into my computer, in place of a mouse or trackpad. It comes with a pen that I use to draw with on the tablet and the drawing appears on my computer screen. As long as I have shared my screen with others, they can see everything I draw. Most presentation software incorporates pens that you can use to draw on your slides. As an alternative to a graphics tablet, you could use a touchscreen, which allows you to draw directly with a finger or a stylus.

So far, I have only described where only one person in the team can create visuals. Another alternative is to use an application that allows many people to draw on and view a shared screen, even though they are remote from each other. Everyone owns the shared output as they have all contributed to

Figure 4.6 The set-up I use for live drawing in virtual meetings

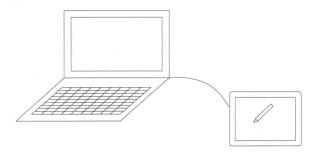

it. Another option is to use smart whiteboards, one in each location, which connect to each other and display whatever is drawn on all the others. This is very clever and rather fun to use! Of course, this requires considerable investment to provide a smart whiteboard for each location.

Using faces to engage people

Newborn babies love to look at anything that resembles a face, whether a person, toy or even an electrical socket. This seems to be hard-wired into humans to encourage babies to bond with their caregivers early on. It seems that some of this may persist into adulthood. Facebook, founded in 2004, had 1 billion members online in a single day in 2015. I wonder if their use of photos of friends' faces encourages people to keep returning?

I have noticed how virtual teams engage with each other better if they are able to see each other's faces, or simply just headshots of each person in the team. I like to create a picture of the team as a whole, using a map showing the whole world as a base, or the area over which the team has been spread, whichever is smaller. Then I add headshots of each team member, with their permission of course, close to their geographic location. I add each person's name and contact details. Then I print these out, laminate them and send one to each team member's location. People tell me that they find these useful and that it is good to have something tactile to touch and look at to remind them of the other team members. You can see an example of a team map in Chapter 3 (Figure 3.9).

Going beyond what is possible in the face-to-face world

It is easy to use our knowledge of the physical world to limit what we do virtually. But people are no longer limited by distance in the same way and all sorts of new possibilities open up. Let's look at some business examples of this. Imagine just how much time it would take to summon a translator to join a face-to-face meeting. Unless you had a translator waiting outside, just in case, it would probably take hours if not days to organize one to join you. In a conference call, some providers allow you to add a translator to your meeting in under 60 seconds in any of the top 100 languages in the world (for an added fee, of course). Amazing!

When you read the story about the QUBE virtual world earlier in this chapter, you could see several ways I could do things that would not be possible in the real world. I was able to jump instantly from the entrance hall to Professor Eddie Obeng's qubicle (office) by clicking a link. When Dr Watchorn wanted us to come back together after working in small groups, she was able to pull us back into a circle immediately. Eddie even floated us into the air, which was when I felt a bit sick!

I attended a conference when writing this chapter. It was held in Phoenix, Arizona in the United States. I had to travel to London and take a 10-hour flight from Heathrow Airport. During the conference, I sat in a huge room with over 1,000 other people for three days to attend the sessions. It was a good conference with lots of really useful content; however, there was considerable time and expense involved and the ensuing jetlag took its toll on me afterwards. Contrast this with my own yearly virtual working summit, which I ran a few days later from my home office. We had over 2,000 participants from all over the world. When designing this virtual conference, I could have run each keynote live, as in traditional conferences. Instead, with participants from 62 countries and a wide range of time zones, it made much more sense to pre-record each session and allow people to listen in at the best time for them within each day of the summit.

I have shared these examples to inspire you not to let the limits that you are used to in the real world constrain your thinking in the virtual world. You may well be able to be much quicker and more effective in some ways that you had never thought of before.

A day in the life: Rachel Smith

Rachel is a digital graphical facilitator, working both face to face and virtually. Whatever Rachel does, she works with visuals to help people 'see what they mean' and she seems to be comfortable pushing technology to its limits to serve groups. You may enjoy her video on visual virtual meetings with me and David Sibbet (Smith, Sibbet and Pullan, 2011). This is the story of one of her consulting days, mixing face-to-face and virtual work using a range of technology (for those who have not come across a World Café, it is a method for hosting large group discussions):

It's a Tuesday. I wake at 6 am and take a moment to remember which hotel this is, and which city I'm in. I'm dressed, breakfasted and out the door in time to get to the meeting room by 7.45 am.

▶

Today is split between two clients: a face-to-face meeting of a senior leadership team setting their vision and strategy lasting until mid-afternoon, and a remote graphic recording of an online World Café session from 4.30 pm to 7.30 pm. Typical? Not quite, but it's becoming more common for me.

The face-to-face session is the second of two days, so we're finalizing the vision and developing the strategy. The 11 people work together, sometimes as a whole group, sometimes in breakouts, as we narrow down what they want to commit to. I'm supporting the meeting visually using large paper templates and markers, and they're capturing ideas on sticky notes and posting them onto the templates to be finalized once they all agree. By 3.30 pm the vision, strategy and action plans are complete and they are ready to get to work making it happen.

At 3.45 pm I make my way back to the hotel, where I've already set up my laptop, tablet and premium-level internet connection. After changing into more comfortable, virtual-work clothes, I order dinner to eat while the World Café gets going. I join the meeting twice: once on my laptop, where I have the web conference, the Google document, and a Skype call open; and once on my tablet, where I'm ready to share my screen so that everyone in the Café can see my visual summary while I draw it.

I spend most of the two-hour conversation listening to breakout groups as the World Café technical support person moves me from group to group. I'm listening for patterns and themes, which I jot down on notepaper. Meanwhile, I'm creating the visual structure for my final document. When it's time, I share my screen so the group can see it, and, as people speak, I capture what they are saying in images and words.

The Café finishes at 7.30 pm. I spend half an hour making tweaks to the final document and send it off. After that, I video-call home to talk with my family for a few minutes. Afterwards, I consider watching a movie, but end up collapsing into bed before 10.00 pm.

Summary

This chapter has looked at how technology underpins virtual working. It considered the range of different types of technology for virtual working, including what works best in different situations. We also covered a range of ways to play to the strengths of human brains.

Whatever technology you choose to use, don't rely on it working absolutely all of the time. It makes sense to have a fallback and, generally speaking, the simpler the technology, the more reliable it is.

Questions for reflection

Here are some questions to help you choose the best technology for your situation:

1 What do you need to accomplish virtually?

2 What type of virtual meetings and collaboration tools will you be using? What do you already have in terms of synchronous and asynchronous technology? What extra do you need? What would the costs and benefits of this be?

3 If you need new technology, how long will it take to install? Many virtual technologies are available via the cloud, so can be used quickly. What about your organization's technical infrastructure requirements and security? How much will it cost? What are the benefits and risks, and what will be the return on your investment?

4 How straightforward are the tools that you will be using? How consistent are they with each other and with those that people are already familiar with? How will you overcome the barriers set out in this chapter?

5 How will you ensure a level playing field so that all have equal access?

6 What level of social connection will your chosen set of tools provide? How rich is the level of interaction? How will people know what technology to use when?

7 How will your people work with your chosen technologies? Are they already competent in all of them? What training will be needed, for whom and how much?

8 How will you use the different aspects of the human brain to keep people engaged when they are using virtual working technology?

References and further reading

Buzan, T (2003) *Use Your Memory: Understand your mind to improve your memory and mental power*, BBC Worldwide, London

Dirksen, J (2012) *Design for How People Learn*, New Riders, Berkeley

Fried, J and Hansson, D (2013) *Remote: Office not required*, Random House Inc, New York

Hall, K (2007) *Speed Lead: Faster, simpler ways to manage people, projects and teams in complex companies*, Nicholas Brealey Publishing, London

Harrin, E (2016) *Collaboration Tools for Project Managers*, Project Management Institute, Newtown Square

Johansen, R (1988) *Groupware: Computer support for business teams*, The Free Press, New York

Lipnack, J and Stamps, J (2000) *Virtual Teams: People working across boundaries with technology*, John Wiley and Sons, New York

Lipnack, J and Stamps, J (2010) *Leading Virtual Teams: Empower members, understand the technology, build team identity*, Harvard Business Press, Boston

Pullan, P (2015) [accessed 11 September 2015] Leading Virtual Project Work, *Association for Project Management*, 10/7 [Online] https://www.apm.org.uk/news/webinar-recording-penny-pullan-talks-through-leading-virtual-projects

Smith, R, Sibbet, D and Pullan, P (2011) [accessed 2 March 2016] Visual Virtual Meetings [Online] https://www.youtube.com/watch?v=pLqxQKeoAFA

Leading virtual meetings   05

This chapter explores how to lead virtual meetings. It considers live meetings where people meet at the same time, although they are dispersed geographically. To meet like this requires the support of synchronous technologies, such as audio and/or video, or even a virtual world! This chapter discusses how to prepare for virtual meetings, how to run effective meetings where people are engaged and involved in the topic, and how to make sure that actions happen afterwards. I will look at situations where you can make a positive difference even if you are not in charge of running the meeting. I discuss how to deal with meetings where some people are face to face and others are remote. As always, I will share how best to make meetings work for human beings.

Of course, virtual leadership is not only achieved through meetings, but also in between meetings. This chapter focuses on meetings and the next chapter focuses on working together outside of meetings.

By the time you have finished this chapter, you will:

- Have a clear understanding of how best to prepare for virtual meetings.
- Be able to choose strategies to engage people during your virtual meetings.
- Know how to encourage people to take action after your meetings.
- Have a range of ideas to apply when you are not in charge.
- Know how to run meetings with both face-to-face participants and remote participants.
- Be able to design your meetings for human beings.

My hope for you is that, after reading this chapter, your future virtual meetings are effective, productive and enjoyable for everyone concerned, yourself included!

Figure 5.1 Mind-map of this chapter

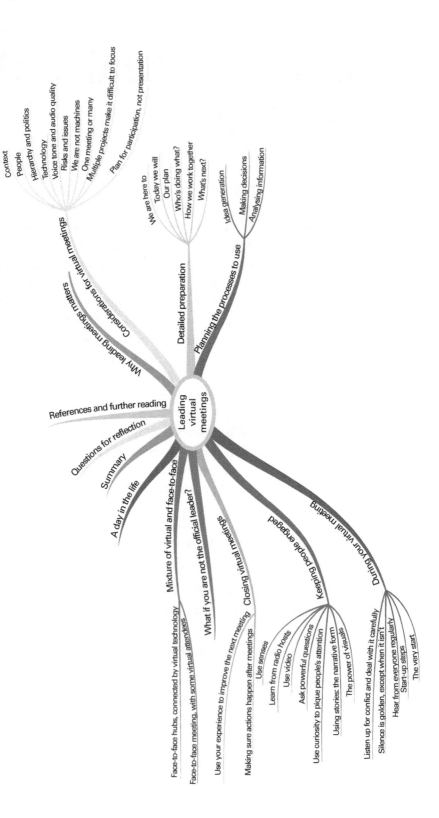

Leading virtual meetings

Why leading meetings matters

Considerations for virtual meetings
- Context
- People
- Hierarchy and politics
- Technology
- Voice tone and audio quality
- Risks and issues
- We are not machines
- One meeting or many
- Multiple projects make it difficult to focus
- Plan for participation, not presentation

Detailed preparation
- We are here to
- Today we will
- Our plan
- Who's doing what?
- How we work together
- What's next?

Planning the processes to use
- Idea generation
- Making decisions
- Analysing information

References and further reading

Questions for reflection

Summary

A day in the life

Mixture of virtual and face-to-face
- Face-to-face hubs, connected by virtual technology
- Face-to-face meeting, with some virtual attendees

What if you are not the official leader?

Closing virtual meetings
- Use your experience to improve the next meeting
- Making sure actions happen after meetings

Keeping people engaged
- Use senses
- Learn from radio hosts
- Use video
- Ask powerful questions
- Use curiosity to pique people's attention
- Using stories: the narrative form
- The power of visuals

During your virtual meeting
- Listen up for conflict and deal with it carefully
- Silence is golden, except when it isn't
- Hear from everyone regularly
- Start-up steps
- The very start

Why leading meetings matters

In this chapter, we explore leading virtual meetings. This means facilitating groups of people who are not together in the same room. They are likely to be diverse in several ways: from the cultures of their different countries to the different roles they play, from their mother tongues to the different generations represented.

While many people try to chair virtual meetings in a traditional way, command-and-control does not work that well remotely. People tend to mentally check out of meetings that are led in this way: they might still be on the phone line or connected to the technology but their minds will be anywhere other than the meeting. It takes a new style of facilitative leadership – inspiring people and engaging their interest – to keep them paying attention in virtual meetings.

By acting as a facilitator, the leader aims to make things as easy as possible for participants, allowing them to achieve their goals as effectively as they can. Indeed, the Latin origins of the word facilitate mean 'to make easy'. David Sibbet describes facilitation as 'the art of leading people through processes towards agreed-upon objectives in a manner that encourages participation, ownership and creativity from all involved' (Sibbet, 2003). Participation, ownership and, dare I say it, creativity are all too lacking from most virtual meetings! A facilitative leadership style is the most effective way I know to run virtual meetings. Done well, participation, ownership and creativity will follow. I will explore this style of working throughout this chapter.

While facilitation is easiest when the facilitator is neutral, a virtual leader is highly unlikely to be neutral! They will have their own views as both leader and a member of the team, as well as wanting the group to be effective and come to their own decisions. This means that a leader will need to manage a couple of 'hats' when working with virtual groups: their 'hat' as the neutral facilitator of the group plus their 'hat' as a valuable team member, and leader.

It is best to wear one 'hat' at any one time, being clear at each moment whether you are playing a neutral facilitator or the team leader with valuable information to share. This complex role mixing is often known as facilitative leadership.

While much of what I present will give you good ideas as to how to manage virtual meetings, it is leadership that makes the difference between mediocre meetings and great ones, with the leader sharing the vision and modelling the way for others.

Considerations for virtual meetings

In this section, I highlight key areas that make a difference to virtual meetings. You will want to consider each of these in turn to make any forthcoming meeting a success.

Context

The first thing to check is whether a meeting is appropriate and necessary. Most virtual work is carried out between meetings using the support of collaboration tools, as we will see in the next chapter. Virtual meetings are complex, especially if you face the challenges of widely spaced time zones, a mixture of mother tongues, diverse cultures and a range of generations in the group. While meetings can be great for getting to know people and for interacting in real time, they are not necessary for every type of work. For example, many people use virtual meetings to share information on PowerPoint slides – this does not need real-time interaction and could have been done separately. Other people use virtual meetings exclusively and do not consider supplementary ways of working. So a good question is, 'Why do you want a virtual meeting and is a meeting necessary to achieve your outcomes?'

People

Once you have chosen to hold a meeting and why, then consider the people who will participate. Why is each coming? What role will they play? What will they bring to the meeting? What resources do they need to take part (perhaps access to particular technology or a running translation)? We covered the aspects of working with others in Chapter 3 and you might find it useful to refer back there to consider your team culture, identity, levels of trust and more. What complexities will they introduce that you will need to handle? See Chapter 7 for more on dealing with culture, language, generation and wide time zones.

Hierarchy and politics

Once you have identified the participants for your virtual meeting, consider the mix. Will there be people from different levels in your organization? If so, could hierarchy interfere? Consider allowing anonymous input, where the group give ideas without identifying who has contributed each idea. You can organize this with a neutral person collecting everyone's input and then posting these onto a shared screen. This neutral person needs to be trusted by everyone or the flow of ideas will stop. Alternatively, arrange for people to contribute their ideas ahead of time anonymously. Remember that they might feel that their contributions can be traced back if given in electronic form, which can hinder participation. Anonymous input can also be useful in cases where office politics might affect the outcomes of your meeting.

If an upcoming meeting is particularly important or contentious, then it helps if the virtual leader talks on the phone with each participant one-to-one beforehand. This can surface any concerns, particular viewpoints and sticking points as you design your meeting. While it is tempting to limit these discussions to just a few senior participants, this can sow the seeds for future problems, so it is best to speak to everyone.

Technology

Virtual meetings need the support of technology that allows people in different places to communicate at the same time. You can find out more about the technology side in Chapter 4. Here are some of the possible synchronous technologies discussed there: chat, audio, shared screens with audio and/or video, smart whiteboards with audio and/or video, co-creation tools, live video, telepresence quality video rooms and virtual worlds.

As a virtual leader, make sure that all of the participants can access the technology and to the same quality.

In the 2000s, I was involved in a programme of work across governments in West Africa, chocolate companies and non-governmental organizations. Together we were working to ensure that chocolate from West Africa was produced free from the worst forms of child labour, standards set by the International Labour Organization of the United Nations and including children working rather than going to school, using machetes or spraying pesticides.

I joined the group as programme manager to set up a pilot certification programme. Staff visited a selection of independently owned cocoa farms to check that they were not using any of the worst forms of child labour. With over 3 million such farms in West Africa, this was a large undertaking!

▶

The virtual team met face to face for an hour or two every six months, usually in Brussels or Geneva when the participants were attending other meetings. In between, we kept in touch with conference calls and e-mails. Members of the team were based in various locations, from the west coast of the United States to Ghana, Ivory Coast and various European countries. Audio and e-mail alone were not ideal, but with participants joining meetings from remote cocoa areas, it was not practical to use video or screen sharing. Reliable broadband internet was not available from many remote areas, but mobile phones worked well and e-mail was easy to access. With each team member employed by a different organization and before the days of cloud storage, we were not able to access a shared space to work and collaborate in between meetings.

I wonder how different the project would be now, just a decade later, with much more widespread mobile broadband and access to cloud collaboration tools? I suspect that we could have used shared screens and showed people visuals to elaborate our ideas. We could also have kept discussions out of individuals' e-mail inboxes and instead where everyone could see the thread of the arguments. It certainly would have helped us to make sure that everyone had the latest version of each project document! The things that worked well for us then were good-quality audio, well-structured meetings and communications, plus a very strong sense of team, with good relationships and levels of trust across the board.

Voice tone and audio quality

There are three ways of communicating when a person speaks. These include the words themselves, the tone of their voice and their body language. If you cut out body language and rely on voices alone, as on conference calls, then it is really important that people can hear both the individual words spoken and the tone of voice used. I suggest that virtual leaders ensure that the audio quality will be as high as possible for their virtual meetings, whichever technology they choose.

In November 2015, I ran my annual virtual summit on the topic of 'Virtual Working in a Changing World'. Mark and John spoke, both of whom work as business analysts for a major multinational insurance company. They had a great story to share. Both Mark and John work with agile projects, which run in a series of short iterations rather than going through requirements, planning, design, build and testing as traditional 'waterfall' projects do. After years of grappling with running agile projects remotely, with their teams dispersed around the world, they had developed the experience and confidence to be able to run projects just as well remotely as face to face.

On the day of our interview, I was ready and had a large number of questions to ask Mark and John, sent in by participants who were keen to hear the details of how they could make remote agile projects work. I joined the conference bridge, eager to get going, only to hear a muffled voice in the distance, 'Hi Penny, it's John here. Mark is with me. We have booked a room and the phone is a special conference phone.' The only trouble was that the phone was sitting in the middle of a large boardroom table. Because it was so far from both John and Mark, the quality of the audio was very poor indeed. On top of this, the phone line used the internet. I had problems understanding their answers, as their voices were muddy and distorted. This didn't bode well for the recording. We tried using our mobile phones, however the audio quality was still poor, with additional noises and hiss on the line.

In the end, we decided that it was worth postponing the recording session until both John and Mark could work from home and use their home landlines. Luckily our final audio recording had great-quality audio. John and Mark's session was well received by the summit participants. It made me wonder, though, how many organizations compromise on their audio quality and the effect this must have when people need to communicate through audio alone.

Risks and issues

What might go wrong? What might go better than planned in your meeting? Risk is uncertainty that matters. It can be both positive and negative, so consider what might happen and what you can do now to tackle these in advance. Perhaps other people can deal with some of the risks better than you can? Review your risks later to see what has changed and make any adjustments necessary.

I find that many of the risks in virtual meetings come from the people attending (or choosing not to) and technology. Most virtual meetings start a few minutes late due to some sort of technological hitch, even with the most experienced participants and the most reliable technology involved! Due to this, I plan for five minutes at the start to find out who is on the call and where they are. This allows a little time for any technological issues to be smoothed out before the core of the meeting starts.

What other known issues could affect your meeting? How will you deal with those?

We are not machines

When you are planning your virtual meetings, remember that we are human beings, not machines. This fact is often ignored or even forgotten. I wonder if you have attended a virtual meeting lasting for hours where people are expected to look at a screen without a break? I'm sure I am not alone in placing myself on mute to go off to the rest room during a virtual meeting. When I ask people if they have heard the unwelcome noise of a flushing lavatory over a conference call, most agree that they have.

Plan breaks to allow people to have a drink or biobreak and have something to eat. While a meeting might not extend over a mealtime in your time zone, it might well do so for others. They will be far more focused on your meeting if they are not hungry, thirsty or sitting cross-legged! I have a rule of thumb that keeps virtual meetings to an hour wherever possible and does not exceed 90 minutes without a break.

One meeting, or many?

With virtual meetings, it is good to ask if the meeting should be split into a series of shorter meetings, spread out over time, rather than having one long meeting, which is often counterproductive for virtual working.

I spoke to Tom, a design engineer at a UK-based company that supplied diesel engine components. He had been asked to join an all-day meeting in the United States with colleagues based over there. Tom was initially delighted that he could attend remotely, which meant that he didn't have to travel, suffer jetlag and miss days of work. In reality, though, the meeting was by conference call, which meant that he was sitting at his desk in the office on the phone from 2 pm UK time until 10 pm UK time. He was the only remote participant as everyone else was present in New York. He told me that they appeared to forget all about him for most of the meeting until a point came when they needed his input. By then, he had lost interest and, after a long day in the office, was falling asleep. They called his name and he join in the conversation. Was this a good use of his time? Absolutely not!

How could the Americans have gained more value from Tom's input? They could have designed the meeting differently, perhaps with a short meeting with Tom in the office at 3 pm and then another at 9 pm, when he could dial in from home to check if they needed anything else. This would have been easy and would have saved Tom many wasted hours. All it takes for a virtual leader to come up with much better meeting designs is to consider the perspective of each participant, especially those who are remote when everyone else is together in a room.

Multiple projects make it difficult to focus

Many virtual participants will be involved in multiple projects. Remember that your meeting is not their only focus and they are likely to be easily distracted. In my work with project managers, around two-thirds of them are involved in multiple virtual projects. Around 30 per cent have five or more projects on the go concurrently! With so many things to think about at once, it is easy for virtual projects to fade away and for local, face-to-face work to gain more attention. It is natural that local work would gain more commitment as team members can just walk over to see how things are going.

So, if the participants of your virtual meeting have multiple other things on their minds, you will need to work even harder to engage them during your meeting and to entice them to join in the first place. There is a whole section later in this chapter entitled 'keeping people engaged – the key challenge'.

Plan for participation, not presentation

Too often, virtual meetings are full of presentations. It does not take long for people to check out, especially if they are busy people with multiple things on the go. Team activity reviews seem to be particularly prone to this, where people present on their own work for far too long. Remember that people will not stay engaged without participation and that information like this could be shared asynchronously, without needing everyone present at the same time to listen to it. Kevan Hall suggests a better way of running activity reviews: he suggests three slides for each person with a maximum of five minutes (Hall, 2007). The three slides should include: an overview;

a summary of the implications of their work for others; something that they are proud of.

It can be useful for each person to include a list of what they would like from others (wants) and what they can offer to other team members (offers). Kevan also suggests keeping the number of people in review meetings to a minimum.

Detailed preparation for virtual meetings

Careful preparation makes virtual meetings run much more smoothly. Think about all the considerations listed above and then plan your meeting in detail. While it is possible to spend huge amounts of time in preparation, agonizing over all the ways that a virtual meeting could go wrong, it is better to focus on just a few things and get these right.

My six steps for starting up a meeting are illustrated in Figure 5.2. If you make sure these are clear as you prepare and you use them to introduce your

Figure 5.2 Steps to start up a meeting

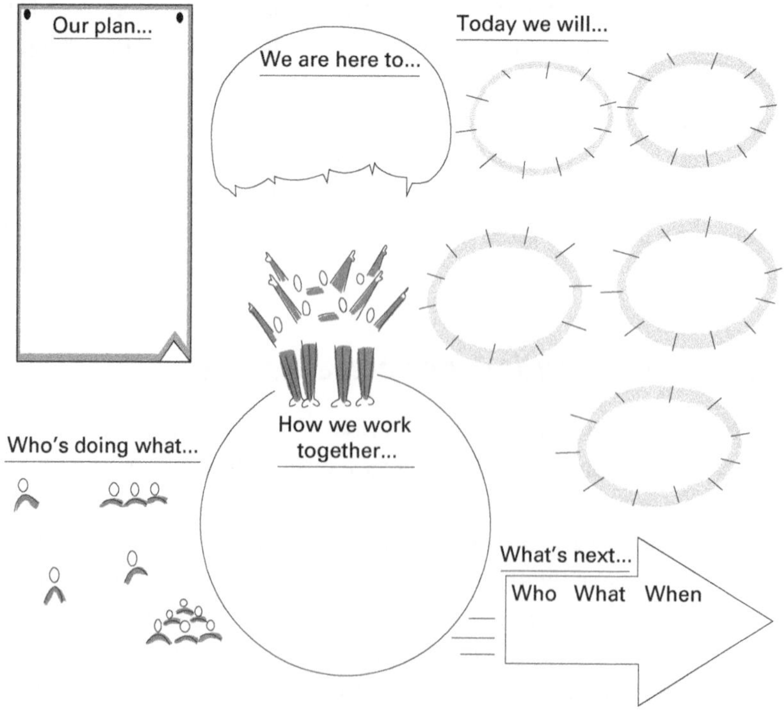

SOURCE: ©2007 Making Projects Work Ltd (used with permission)

virtual meeting, then your meeting will be set up for success. They bring the clarity that is so often lacking in meetings, both face-to-face and remote.

Let's go through these steps in turn below.

We are here to...

It is important to be clear about the point of the meeting. You should be able to state your meeting's purpose succinctly, say in 7–10 words. This should be an overview of the reason for having your meeting, rather than a list of all the things you would like to achieve! Without a clear purpose, a meeting is likely to lose focus and drift off course. A clear purpose will make it much easier to work out who should attend and to encourage them to do so. It will help people to stay focused. An example of a clear purpose is: 'We are here to agree this year's programme for our special interest group.'

Today we will...

In Figure 5.2 there is space for up to five objectives for the virtual meeting. Ensure that you know what your key objectives are and how you will know when you have achieved them. Four or five objectives are plenty for most virtual meetings. Any more will make it more likely that your meeting will overrun and/or lose focus, both of which would be disastrous: people would leave to join their next meeting or their attention would wane.

Here are some objectives from the same example:

- introduce everyone;
- recap on this year's focus of the special interest group;
- choose six potential speakers;
- choose six dates spread throughout the year;
- review actions and agree next steps.

Our plan...

Make the timing clear with an agenda showing what is going to happen when. What are the start and end times? When will you have breaks? Perhaps some people can join your virtual meeting just for a part, rather than attending throughout if they are not needed.

An example could be: 'We start this call at 6.30 pm and finish by 7.45 pm. Our president will join us until 6.50 pm to introduce herself and to explain this year's focus.'

When considering the plan for your meeting, check the length. How long does the meeting need to be? If it is likely to need longer than 60–90 minutes, then consider breaking it up into two or more shorter meetings, spaced out appropriately, to keep people focused.

Who's doing what...

The purpose will help you to work out what roles are needed for your virtual meeting. Typical roles include a timekeeper, a facilitator and a scribe, to record actions and decisions. The scribe should place actions and decisions on a shared screen or send them out by messaging people. The key is that everyone can see what has been agreed and highlight if they need any changes during the meeting, rather than waiting to make changes afterwards.

Some example roles could include: 'Penny – facilitator', 'Fred – keeping time', 'Liz – scribe for actions' and 'Everyone – participants'.

How we work together...

This is a crucial step for nipping problems in the bud by creating agreed ground rules for your virtual meeting. These rules explain how the group will work together. They work best when everyone present develops and agrees them at the start. It is useful to have some ready to suggest, so here are some that I use for the virtual meetings I run:

- *State your name at the start of any contribution you make* in order to prevent unidentified people taking actions or agreeing to proposals.
- *Mute if you are in a noisy environment* in order to stop noises such as announcements or dogs barking from disrupting your virtual meeting.
- *Only one person speaking at any one time* in order to make sure that your call does not descend into chaos!
- *Expect to be asked for your input every 10–15 minutes* in order to make sure that people are aware that they will be asked for contributions. Polling people like this works well. It means that you run through the list of attendees asking for input from each person in turn.

Other useful topics to consider for ground rules cover areas such as:

- how your group will deal with confidentiality issues, especially when you are working across different organizations;
- respect for one another, a good example of which is to agree to listen to other people's contributions.

By anticipating problems upfront and agreeing ground rules as a group, it is possible to avoid much conflict later on.

I like to include a ground rule: 'Spellling dusn't mater', which allows those with dyslexia or anxiety to take part fully when people are sharing written input, and it generally raises a laugh once I have explained why my spelling has temporarily gone awry.

One last tip on this point: don't call them ground rules! Instead, talk about 'how we work together'. The word 'rules' has connotations of authority and hierarchy, both of which detract from the facilitative, participative environment that works best with virtual meetings.

What's next...

At the start of your virtual meeting, consider what will happen afterwards. Who is going to do what by when? How will you capture actions during your meeting, plus how will you share these during the meeting and afterwards? Who will follow these up and how?

Planning the processes to use

You will need to plan processes into your virtual meetings: how will you come up with ideas from your virtual group? How will you come to a decision? With thought, many processes can be brought across from face-to-face meetings. Some aspects might improve in a well-run virtual session, especially where asynchronous discussion and collaboration can be included. In this section I highlight key things to consider about processes when you are planning your virtual session.

Idea generation

Of the meeting tools used in business today, brainstorming is one of the most popular. It is often used poorly face to face. Dominant people can monopolize meetings and, as the number of people in the room increases, it becomes harder for everybody's ideas to be heard. In a room, it is possible to see who is contributing which ideas and this can hinder creativity as politics and hierarchy can get in the way of good ideas.

On the other hand, results can be better in well-run virtual brainstorming sessions (Chamorro-Premuzic, 2015). When participants write down their ideas, rather than shouting them out, all ideas are captured, no matter how many people join in. If these ideas can be shared anonymously, or are sent to a trusted, neutral person to collate and share, then the ideas will be judged on their own merits rather than associated with any particular participant. There are tools available that are designed to support this type of virtual brainstorming and allow anonymous sharing.

Idea-generation works much better with time for individuals to think up ideas on their own, followed by time to work together, building on each other's ideas. In virtual brainstorming, it makes sense to have an initial session where you brief the problem to be solved and make sure that people understand the issues and constraints. Afterwards, encourage participants to think of ideas on their own and write these down, then send them through. During a second session, display all the ideas for people to read and build on. If you wanted to, you could also do much of this asynchronously.

Making decisions

Many factors apply here, just as they do in face-to-face decision making. These include ensuring a shared understanding of the decision to be made, hearing from all sides and discussing the options, sharing good information and answering questions.

You will find that cultural differences apply to decision making: some cultures value speed almost above all, whereas others require plenty of time to ensure that the right decision is made and that all the ramifications are understood. We cover more on these differences in Chapter 7.

It is important to make clear how decisions are to be made. Is the group making a shared decision that everyone will stick to or are they merely making a recommendation to an outside party or the group leader? Are some group members decision makers and the others only advisors? As a leader, be clear what you are asking for.

In face-to-face meetings, the default decision-making option is often a vote by show of hands. It is probably a good thing that this is not quite as easy virtually, as those who didn't vote for something feel little buy-in for a decision. Use voting merely to see how people feel. If everyone votes for an agreement, then you have unanimity and the decision is made. If there is a mixture of opinions, as is far more likely, then there is more work to do.

I have seen cases where groups use the 'consensus of silence' technique (Robson, 2002). It is not recommended and is really a form of manipulation rather than leadership, but happens a lot in virtual teams! The leader asks a question such as, 'Would anyone have an objection if we did this?' or, 'Can anyone think of reasons why we should not do that?' or, 'Are there any alternative suggestions?' When no one in the group says anything, which is highly likely in a virtual group, people assume that everyone agreed. Good leaders know that silence does not imply agreement. People were probably wondering what to say, or were bored, or reading their e-mail. A similarly unhelpful way of deciding is 'the loudest voice wins'. Design your decision-making process so that everyone has an equal chance of being heard.

If a decision is important and not particularly urgent, then it is worth going for consensus amongst the group. This means that group members aim for the best decision for the group overall, rather than their personal point of view. It means developing a decision that everyone can live with and will be happy to support afterwards, even though it might not be the ideal decision for them. Consensus means:

- Everyone is fully involved throughout.
- Everyone listens to others and is listened to.
- There is substantial agreement.
- Everyone is committed to support the final decision.

A virtual process for coming to consensus is likely to involve a mixture of meeting time and asynchronous collaboration. There are some helpful ground rules to use:

- Think of the best for the group as a whole.
- Only support ideas you can live with in the future.
- See differences of opinion as helpful.

Consensus can take a lot of time to reach, so asynchronous discussions are helpful in the run-up to the final decision.

Analysing information as a virtual group

When exploring information virtually, it is far better to do detailed analysis outside meetings. Let individuals or small groups collaborate on the analysis and bring their results along to a full group meeting. As a virtual leader, notice when people begin to dive into analysis in meetings and encourage them to take the information away, and present their results at a later meeting. Analysis paralysis brings virtual teams to a halt, even more than it does face-to-face.

During your virtual meeting

In this section, I cover how to start a virtual meeting successfully and how to use your time effectively by engaging people.

The very start

It would be incredible if every virtual meeting started on time, with each participant fully prepared and ready to go. In reality, this does not often happen! As people join the call, welcome each participant positively and check that their technology is working well. I tend to allow about five minutes of the agenda for this part with up to 10 participants. Allow a bit longer if there are more people involved.

Some people advocate starting exactly at the advertised time, so that anyone who arrives late will be shamed into coming on time next time. While this might work for face-to-face meetings, I find that it doesn't for virtual meetings – when people are remote from one another, it becomes much more important, and much more difficult, to engage participants in the meeting. There are often technological hurdles for people joining virtual meetings – even logging into a shared screen or conference bridge takes a few minutes.

One way to make the start of your virtual meetings much more enticing for participants is to share information on what is happening around the organization as people join. While some see this as sharing idle gossip, it can be an effective way for remote team members to tap into things they would not hear otherwise. Some of my clients have found that people join early just to keep up with this news.

Start-up steps

Use the start-up steps from Figure 5.2 when you start the core part of your meeting:

- *We are here to...*: make sure that the purpose is clear and that everyone knows what your meeting is for. When this is displayed for all to see, it helps people to focus, so use a space in your shared screen to keep this visible. Remember that if you display the purpose on a slide, then once you move to the next slide, it will disappear.
- *Today we will...*: state the objectives that you need to accomplish during your meeting today. Four or five objectives are almost always enough.

If new ones are added, agree what you will leave out of this meeting to ensure that your timescales are still realistic.

- *Our plan...*: this makes sure that participants are clear on timings, especially the finish time. It is usually a good idea to find out whether anyone needs to finish early, as you might need to change the order in which you tackle the objectives. Be clear if anyone will only be joining part of the meeting.

- *Who's doing what...*: by giving people in your meeting roles to play, they are more likely to stay involved in the meeting and less likely to check out. Appoint a facilitator, a scribe and a timekeeper. Ask the scribe to capture key decisions taken and actions agreed: **who** will do **what**, by **when**. In my meetings, I ask the timekeeper to let me know on the hour, half hour and at quarter to and quarter past the hour. Whatever the actual time for all the people on the call, these elements of time are usually the same, but not always! I ask for a five-minute warning before the end of the call. I suggest that the other meeting attendees play the role of active participants.

- *How we work together...*: these 'ground rules' are often what makes the difference between a mediocre and a successful call. Remember to model the rules. If you start the meeting by stating your name clearly at the start of every contribution, then you have modelled the rule 'state your name at the start of any contribution'. If you listen carefully and make sure you don't talk over anyone else, then you are modelling the rule to 'only have one person speaking at any one time'. By letting people know that you will poll them throughout the call, you have introduced the idea that everyone will be asked for input.

  Ask for contributions and ideas from participants, especially around tricky subjects such as confidentiality. One way of handling confidentiality is to use the 'Chatham House rule', where the contents of the conversation can be shared, but not the names of the people. This encourages openness and the sharing of information in a way that provides anonymity to the speaker (Chatham House, 2016). Other ways of handling confidentiality include allowing everything to be reported openly or, alternatively, keeping everything only within the group. It depends on the needs of your particular meeting and group.

  Agreed ground rules can help to reduce the likelihood of and even prevent conflict. They certainly help the facilitator to deal with conflict should it arise. All of the participants have agreed to behave in accordance with these rules and so, if and when they break the rules, the facilitator can point this out and ask them to follow the rules.

Hear from everyone regularly

It is very easy for a virtual meeting to turn into a monologue – one person talks and the others are quiet. Perhaps they are listening? Perhaps they are dealing with their e-mail? As a virtual leader, you cannot just glance around the room to see how people are responding, so it is important to replicate this by polling the group. This means going around the group, checking once with each person, asking for their input or agreement or 'pass' if they have nothing to add. Keep the responses short and do this every 15 minutes at least so that everyone is expecting to hear their name and is ready to respond.

Clients tell me that in meetings where polling has not been agreed, participants often drift off into doing something else until they hear their name. As they were not concentrating and not expecting direct questions, they have no idea what they have just been asked. The usual response is, 'Could you repeat that please?'

Polling the group like this does not need to be solely about the content of the meeting. It is a good idea to check things such as the quality of the audio and video links that each person is experiencing.

Silence is golden, except when it isn't

It is easy to make the mistake that silence means that people assent or agree with whatever is being said. The argument goes that, because they are not speaking up, they agree. But that is not necessarily so! Silence *might* mean assent. It *might* mean that they have gone to sleep! They *might* be furious and silently seething. They *might* have checked out of the meeting in frustration. Without good body language, you cannot assume which of these are true.

It is important to monitor people's participation throughout your virtual meetings. I do this by writing down the names of participants and ticking against each name whenever the person speaks up. This way, I can draw in those who are not participating and, hopefully, help to keep them focused on the meeting. In a face-to-face meeting this monitoring happens almost automatically just by watching the room, but it needs to be made more formal in virtual meetings.

Listen for conflict and deal with it carefully

In a face-to-face meeting, there are many visual clues to conflict. I have seen someone stabbing paper repeatedly with a pencil, or seen the expression on a participant's face darken until he looked like thunder. In a room together, the other participants are likely to know the person showing signs of conflict, understand their context and realize what is causing them issues. If the leader handles the situation well, it will be picked up and dealt with appropriately.

In a virtual meeting, on the other hand, it is much, much more difficult. Visual clues are completely lost to those on conference calls and might not be clear to those using video. Even if visual clues of conflict are picked up, others in the meeting are unlikely to know what they mean.

Remember from Chapter 3 that the main types of conflict are task, process and relationship related. Task and process conflicts often help people to find better ways of doing things and can be straightforward to solve. Relationship conflicts, on the other hand, are much more difficult to resolve. In a virtual meeting, conflict is as likely to arise as in a face-to-face meeting. Disputes over tasks can develop into relationship conflict more quickly, though, as there is often less understanding, empathy and trust between people and you cannot sort things out over a cup of coffee together. A simple disagreement on how to do a task can end up with people taking things personally, reacting emotionally and, before you know it, the conflict has escalated beyond a simple disagreement about how to tackle a task to a full-on, aggressive argument! Task conflict, as this started out, can be helpful. The emotionally charged, personal argument that it turned into is definitely not helpful. Conflict like this spreads and will impact team performance.

The key is to listen out very carefully for conflict and deal with it quickly, before it escalates out of control. Conflict is likely to show up very subtly at the start, through prolonged silence from individuals, subtle changes in voice tone and words used, as well as visual signs.

The best way to keep conflict low is to build a trusting team, who understand each other and each other's contexts. Explore Chapter 3 to find out more about building trust and preventing conflict in your virtual team. Lindred Greer, who researches conflict and power in virtual teams, suggests that giving team members a few days together face to face builds up invaluable personal connections (Greer, 2014). My survey backs this up, as respondents said that they were very keen to have face-to-face time together at the start of projects. This is not always possible, so consider other ways of building trust and understanding.

What can you do if you detect conflict in the middle of a virtual meeting? The worst thing is to ignore it! It won't go away on its own – it tends to fester and grow until it can completely derail virtual teams.

Here are some ideas to deal with conflicts that break out during meetings:

- You could reflect back exactly what you noticed in a non-judgemental way, point out how it infringes the ground rules you agreed and ask what you should do next. Here is an example: 'I noticed that Greg just starting talking while Anna was finishing her explanation. Greg, we agreed to have one person speaking at any one time. What would you like to do next?' In most cases, Greg would say something along the lines of: 'I'm sorry, I didn't mean to interrupt; I was just excited by your ideas. Go ahead Anna!' and the whole incident is over.

- If the conflict is between two people in your group, it can be a good idea to ask the other people to take a five-minute break. (I find that most people are very happy to take a five-minute break!) Ask everyone to leave the technology connected, but to walk away and have a break, otherwise it might take a long time for everyone to reconnect. Then talk with the protagonists, asking each one for their point of view. It might be helpful to talk with each individually alone and then with both together.

Outside of meetings, it can be helpful to have an online discussion area where problems can be raised and people can discuss issues transparently and sort them out.

When dealing with conflict, keep your focus on serving the group, rather than how you are coming across yourself as a leader. Keeping metaphorical – your 'spotlight' on the group makes it easier to be transparent about problems your group encounters rather than just ignoring them. Make sure you stay away from inferring why things are happening and just state what you observe. An example might be: someone has been speaking without pause for 10 minutes and you have heard others try to start to make points, but give up. In this case, it is tempting just to call for a new speaker, label the speaker as dominating the conversation or even just ask them to be quiet. Instead, it is more helpful to reflect what you heard: 'I've noticed that Greg has been speaking for 10 minutes and others have started to say things and then backed down, sometimes several times. What shall we do about that?' In this case, most speakers will back down, having not realized that they had been speaking for so long! This reply has kept the focus on the group and also avoided labelling motivations for the speaker's actions.

When I have suggested this tip to clients, they find that it takes courage to reflect back like this. They are concerned that 'Greg' might come back with negative feelings or a passive-aggressive answer and they feel far out of their comfort zone. It *does* take courage – I don't offer an easy life! Remember, though, that this intervention is in the context of clear and agreed ground rules set up at the start of the meeting. With these in place, by reflecting back to 'Greg', you are not picking a fight with him. You are reminding him of what he agreed at the start. Keep your voice tone calm and unthreatening, so that Greg doesn't hear blame in your voice.

A useful tool is the Ladder of Inference shown in Figure 5.3, which is adapted from Schwarz (2002) and others. In a possible conflict situation, check that your intervention is based on the data that you observe, without labelling, evaluating or explaining it. Stay down the ladder and, if you notice that you have moved up the ladder, come back down again as soon as you can! In Greg's case, I did not label what happened, for example, 'Greg won't stop talking.' I didn't evaluate what he was doing: 'Greg is dominating the conversation.' I didn't explain what he was doing: 'Greg is annoyed that we ignored him in the last meeting and now he's taking his time.' I merely presented what I saw in front of my eyes: 'Greg has been speaking for 10 minutes and others have been trying to speak but have then backed down.'

Figure 5.3 Ladder of Inference

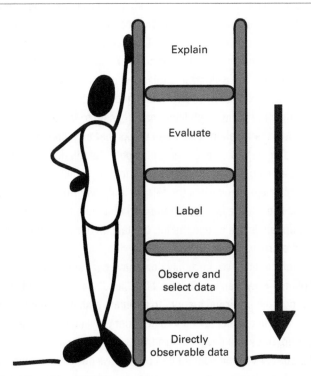

SOURCE: Adapted from Schwarz (2002) and others

Conflict – reframing conflict

Years ago, I used to feel that conflict was a very bad thing. I would be fearful of conflict raising its ugly head in virtual meetings, leading to all sorts of awful consequences. It was not until I read the book *Death by Meeting* (Lencioni, 2004) that I began to shift my understanding of conflict to something positive. Lencioni talks about meetings in organizations as deadly boring, hence the title of his book. He says that meetings about your work should be far more exciting and interesting than sitting in a darkened room watching projected images of someone else's story. Most meetings are far less interesting than watching a film! His remedy is to 'mine for conflict'. He says that conflict indicates that people are passionate and care about their point of view. While I would not go as far as Lencioni in advocating that you seek out and stir up conflict, especially with remote participants, this story certainly changed my view. Instead of being something to avoid like the plague, I'm now happy to deal with conflict and view it as a standard part of working with groups. I know now that most conflict only arises because people care so much about the outcomes of the work, and their own perspective. This is true for virtual groups too, so virtual leaders must be keep alert to conflict and work with it effectively.

A parable from India illustrates this view of conflict well. In this ancient story, there are six blind men, who know nothing about elephants. There is an elephant in the room. Each blind man goes up to the elephant in turn. The first feels the elephant's side and thinks that an elephant is like a wall. The second thinks the elephant is like a spear (he felt the tusk), the third thinks that an elephant is like a snake (he felt the trunk), the fourth thinks an elephant is like a tree trunk (he felt the leg), the fifth thinks that an elephant is like a large fan (he felt the ear) and the final blind man thinks that an elephant is like a rope (he felt the tail). In the story, they argue for the rest of eternity.

In virtual meetings we certainly don't have the rest of eternity to sort out problems! However, we do have both 'blind' men and 'blind' women. It is part of our role as virtual leaders to facilitate a shared understanding of whatever we need to do, taking into account the views of all the members of the group. Once you have a shared view, agreed by all, everyone has the full picture. Avoiding conflict completely will not get you there. Skilfully dealing with conflict by acknowledging it, listening to everyone and building up a shared view will use conflict effectively.

Keeping people engaged – the key challenge

Remote participants need to be engaged and involved in meetings so that they stay focused and participate. Whenever I ask people about their top virtual meeting challenges, keeping remote participants engaged comes out on top! This section will explore how to do so.

The power of visuals

Add in visuals to make your communication richer in virtual meetings. Try adding in video to share body language. You could use an immersive virtual world, adding visuals plus a sense of space. You can include pictures, tables, graphics and maps in your virtual meetings. Pictures of people's faces are very engaging, as we explored in the last chapter. As people suggest ideas, include them in a mind-map on your shared screen. This shows how you have listened to participants' ideas and it will help them (and you) to see the bigger picture as it emerges. When using a shared screen, it is useful to have visuals that change and develop throughout the meeting – even adding small ticks and simple drawings to the screen will keep people watching to see what else will change. Visuals are very powerful at engaging people. There are ideas in Chapter 4 explaining how to use technology to include visuals virtually.

Using stories: the narrative form

Have you noticed how the stories in this book help to bring the content to life for you? They are easier to remember than pure facts alone. This comes from the way our human brains have evolved. For thousands of years, before the written word, knowledge was spread from generation to generation orally through stories. Our brains are hard-wired to remember these over plain lists of facts. Stories are organized in sequence, with all the different events connected to each other in an order that help us to remember. We are used to stories from early childhood onwards, so we know to expect a beginning, middle and end. I have noticed that people stay attentive throughout a story, wanting to hear the final ending. Stories have characters, and we have a lot of background information about people and expectations about how they will behave. If the characters behave in ways that conflict with our assumptions, then that is surprising, which makes the story even more memorable. Stories that contain emotion, humour and exaggeration are more powerful than those that do not (Buzan, 2003). Stories can engage people's emotions, imaginations, value systems, motives and memories as well as their hopes and fears.

You can use stories to good effect in your virtual working. I was part of a global research group that explored how storytelling helped online groups to work effectively (Thorpe, 2008). One of the exercises was to find out how effective online introductions were when meeting new remote people. Each researcher told the story of how they had become interested in virtual groups. We then looked at their factual, written introductions online and explored how much we remembered from: 1) the story; and 2) the written introduction. We remembered much more from the stories. In fact, even after almost a decade, I can still remember some of the stories, especially those that stood out by being different.

So how can you apply this in practice in your virtual working? I don't advise turning your virtual meetings into storytelling sessions starting with: 'Once upon a time...' Instead, think about how you can relay information in a narrative form. Ensure that your story flows in a logical sequence. Have a beginning, middle and end. Introduce characters, perhaps members of your team or other stakeholders. For example, when you introduce new team members, rather than just giving their name and role, try asking them to tell the team the story of how they came to join you. When updating people, try linking the parts together as a story, including the characters involved, rather than just giving a whole series of facts. You will find that people listen in carefully, remember the flow and stay attentive to the end.

Should you use emotion, humour and exaggeration to make your stories even more powerful? Maybe you should, if it will help and if it makes sense. You do need to be aware of cultural, language and generational differences, though, as other people might not find your humour funny or your use of exaggeration appropriate. Remember that humour is very subjective and does not work across all cultures.

Use curiosity to pique people's attention

When you incite curiosity, you hook the automatic, emotional part of the brain (Collins, 2016). Ask interesting questions that require people to think and search for answers, rather than being able to answer instantly without thinking. Leave things out – leave gaps in your presentation that people need to fill in. Use visuals that are not immediately obvious, and explain how the picture links into the flow after showing it. Make sure that people are clear, though, before moving on.

If I had an important announcement to make to a virtual team, which I wanted them to remember for a long time, I might start by asking the group what they thought the answer would be, before sharing it. 'Who do you think will be joining our team and why?' This arouses a state of curiosity in people that will pique their attention. I would then tell part of the story, rather than giving the name of the new team member immediately. The level of curiosity they reached will help them to remember the answer.

It seems that, when people are curious, they are more willing to put effort into finding answers and more likely to remember them afterwards. Make sure, though, that this does not backfire – if you leave too much unknown, people might well feel frustrated and stressed rather than curious, especially in virtual teams where you have barriers of language, culture and generation. Check with your virtual groups to make sure that you are getting the right balance of curiosity, engagement and clarity.

Ask powerful questions

While questions can increase curiosity, they can also direct people's attention and energy. Wouldn't it be great to take people from bored and unmotivated in your meetings, to productive, ready to work and eager to solve problems? Of course, there is a catch: people do have to be listening and to hear your question in order for this to work!

While I was writing this book, I interviewed Judy Rees, a former news journalist, who is fascinated by questions (Rees, 2015). She reminded me that TV news reporters ask questions to provoke powerful, emotional reactions on screen. Virtual leaders could use this too, asking questions to direct people's attention and change their emotional state in virtual meetings. Judy thinks that the use of questions is a powerful tool at our disposal and is too often neglected by virtual leaders.

So how can you use questions with a virtual team? Go beyond asking questions for information. Use questions to bring the group together at the start. Judy suggests that we use questions that help the group to understand how different they are from one another and to provoke curiosity. When people get curious about each other, it helps them to ask better questions and to open up to each other, both of which help to build trust and authenticity. Judy suggests questions such as 'What would you like to happen as a result of our working together?' and to find out what the range of answers are. Another favourite question is: 'When you are working at your best, what are you like?' – this invites people to give a metaphor for when they are working at their best. Answers vary hugely and might include anything from a Formula 1 racing driver to a butterfly or a chef! Questions like these are powerful because they encourage people to think and answer for themselves. Questioning, listening and speaking up are the three key collaboration skills (Hill *et al*, 2014) and, through your own use of questions, you can model and encourage all three as a virtual leader.

Use video

As humans, we are able to process huge amounts of visual information in real time and, when we choose to use audio-only virtual meetings, we cut out a great deal of information. I encourage people to use video where they can. Video allows instant feedback, sharing participants' body language as well as their words and voice tone. It reminds people that the other participants are real human beings, with visible faces.

The trouble with video is that many people feel distinctly uncomfortable with a camera recording in front of them! Talking to a machine is not a natural thing to do and, for some, it fills them with dread, robbing them of their confidence and reducing their brains to mush. Worse still, the machine then exposes these flaws, worries and nerves out to the world!

It is important to realize that no one will expect you to look immaculate, they will just expect you to look as if you were at work in an office. In fact, you can get away with being smart on the top half – I have presented to thousands of people looking very presentable on the top half while wearing comfy leggings. Just remember not to stand up if that's the case!

Some members of your team will dislike video. It helps to introduce one-to-one video calls and model being informal and relaxed yourself. Explain the purpose of using video, which is to make it easier for people to engage and see each other as real human beings. At the end of each call using video, thank people for their commitment and for the extra connection that it enabled with their colleagues. Ask them for their feedback. What went well? What would make next time even better? I find that the more people use video and speak in front of a camera, the less of an issue it becomes.

Lisa and I chatted about how video cameras are not always welcome in virtual meetings. Lisa, a manager in an insurance company, said, 'Yes, I've noticed that sometimes people don't like video. It does seem to be women more than men! Perhaps the picture doesn't look very flattering or people are having a bad hair day? I know that when I work from home it is nice to be able to relax and be a bit dishevelled compared to what I look like when I'm at work in the office. Years ago, I chaired a conference call from home while wearing a full face-mask. You couldn't do that on a video call!' Lisa takes the attitude not to force video on people but to let them build up their confidence. When bringing new people onto virtual working tools, she suggests helping them get things working. With her own teams, she has offered test runs and some 'playground' meetings to try out the tools and to build confidence.

Learn from radio hosts

Presenters of radio programmes are great at communicating and engaging listeners. Unlike virtual leaders, presenters do not know the listeners personally and have no way of interacting with them in real time. Despite this, presenters design their programmes so that it is quite difficult to stop listening. They let you know what's coming up, perhaps even playing short snippets, piquing your curiosity, so that you want to keep listening even if ad breaks intrude. The pace varies, as does the presenter's voice tone. The next time you listen to a radio programme, notice how the presenter hooks your interest.

Create a sense of urgency

People usually attend to things that are urgent, rather than those that are important. When people work virtually, their good intentions to focus and pay attention to a meeting can be dropped immediately when they receive something urgent, even if it is not important – a notification or a new e-mail. If you need to bring people back, then urgency can help. To do so, focus on something that is happening right now that might affect people. Beware, though, as urgency can gain attention quickly but will not necessarily maintain attention for long. There is always something new and more urgent coming along. Ideally, it would be better to help the team to develop behaviours that support important work, rather than urgent interruptions. Perhaps a first step could be for everyone in the team to agree to turn off all notifications?

Use senses

As human beings, in face-to-face meetings, we engage all of our senses. We can look around us at the people in the room and at whatever is happening through the windows. We can smell our surroundings; perhaps stuffy meeting rooms or peppermint tea? We can taste whatever we have just eaten or the fruit or biscuits provided. We can hear people speaking, plus the hum of a projector or even air-conditioning. We can feel the table.

In virtual meetings, we tend to engage only one or two senses: hearing, plus sight if we are using video and/or shared screens. To engage people better, think about how you could add in stimuli that use the other senses in a way that is relevant to the meeting. I find it useful to create a team map in colour, with a headshot of everyone in the virtual team superimposed on a world map (see Figure 3.9 on page 80). It is good to share this with everyone in the team. Send a laminated copy that team members can prop up on their desk and use during virtual meetings. This adds the sense of sight to audio-only meetings and brings in a spatial element, plus the sense of touch. It makes a big difference to my own ability to focus – try it and see how it works for you.

What about the senses of taste and smell? These are probably not used often, but can be powerful for a special occasion. I can remember a global meeting with people on four continents, where we arranged for a box of chocolates to be available in each video room. Once we even supplied the same type of pizza at the same time!

Build rapport and relationships

With a sense of rapport, belonging and trust, people will want to come together and meet their colleagues. It is engaging! Design your meetings for interaction and bring in elements that help people to get to know each another.

John Stuart Clarke, who is a business analyst for Aviva, has worked on projects with virtual teams located in many sites across the UK and India. I interviewed him about building rapport across boundaries. He says:

Building rapport is interesting, because trying to make your work fun or engaging when some aspects of communication are denied you is a challenge. I'll give a simple example of how you might overcome this.

In one of the teams where I was a Scrum Master a couple of years ago, we had a test resource based offshore in Chennai in India. Obviously, I happen to know it's quite warm in India – certainly warmer than the UK. We also know that British people tend to be unhealthily obsessed with the weather, probably because our weather isn't particularly great! I got into the habit of asking one of my colleagues in India what the temperature was in Chennai that day and she would always tell us. Of course, there would be groans and other comments from people in the room in the UK who were jealous. Perhaps they had just got back from holiday and were wishing they were back out there again where it was nice and warm instead of in cold Britain! It was a very small thing, but I kept on at it over a period of time and it became a topic of humour. It also became something that people anticipated as part of the daily stand-up meeting; it became part of the rhythm of the team.

There are little things like this that you can do to help bring remote colleagues into the conversation and make them really feel part of the team. The reaction of everyone else means that you will bring other people in as well, not just the person who is offshore and telling you how hot and sunny and lovely it is in their location.

At the end of the day, it's about just treating people as human beings. Treat your remote colleagues as human beings and involve them in the same sort of banter and conversations that you would have if you were all standing in front of each other.

Closing virtual meetings

The quality of your virtual meetings does not just come from the content of your meetings. How you end your meetings can make a huge difference to whether anything happens as a result and whether your future meetings improve.

Making sure actions happen after meetings

Too many virtual meetings result in no action. Sometimes this might be a deliberate choice but often actions are planned, but don't happen. I wonder why? Perhaps the actions were unclear? Perhaps people did not take notes of their actions and were not reminded? Perhaps they had no intention of taking action? Perhaps people intended to take action when they were in the meeting, but then returned to their work and found everything else took precedence? Perhaps no one followed up on the actions? I'm sure that some of these are true for most virtual meetings!

To ensure that actions happen as a result of your meetings, there are a few steps to take:

- Write down actions publicly during your meeting on a shared screen or group chat.
- Ensure that actions are clear and unambiguous, clearly stating who will do what by when.
- Gain agreement on the actions before people leave, rather than sending them out afterwards.
- Ensure that everyone has a copy of the actions as quickly as possible after the meeting.
- Follow up to check that actions are completed.

You might like to try out an intentionality check at the end of your meeting. This asks participants how sure they are that they will be able to carry out their actions. You can ask this publicly if your group is able to be open and honest with each other, or you can ask people to consider this on their own. I find a scale from 1 (unlikely to do any of my actions) to 10 (certain I will do my actions) works well. If people's intent is lower than 10, why not amend the action to make it more likely to happen? Surely it is better to have an imperfect action carried out than a perfect action that never happens.

Use your experience to improve the next meeting

Use the last five minutes of your virtual meetings to review. It doesn't take long and it's easy. There are two questions to ask your group. Gather answers publicly or privately, whichever works best. Here are the questions: 1) What went well for us today? 2) What do you wish we could do differently next time?

Take these questions in turn, starting with the positive 'what went well' question. You will find answers from this question that you should make sure happen again next time. Recap them at the start of your next meeting.

With the question about what could be better next time, make sure to keep the answers positive. So rather than, 'We didn't do any preparation, which meant that we didn't know enough about the case', frame this answer as, 'Next time, let's all prepare properly, so we will all know enough about the case.' This keeps the tone positive and avoids blame and the negative spiral of a whine fest. When you review, every meeting will improve, gradually evolving your meeting practices and increasing people's participation and enjoyment.

What if you are not the official leader of the meeting?

It is easy to make changes to virtual meetings if you are the leader, but you can make a difference, whatever your position.

Before the meeting, ask the official leader about the start-up steps to ensure that all these elements have been thought through:

- what we are here to do;
- today we will...;
- our plan;
- who's doing what;
- how we work together.

You can suggest ground rules that have worked for you in the past. You can offer to play the role of timekeeper or scribe, to help the leader. You could suggest running a review at the end of the session.

During the meeting, you can show virtual leadership by modelling useful behaviours, such as asking questions, stating your name at the start of anything you say and drawing out answers from people who are holding back. In a positive way, you can reflect back to the group when you notice things that are not working well.

At the end of the meeting, suggest that the leader review the actions before people leave, to make sure that they are correct and that everyone has agreed them. You could run a review. Another option is to give the official leader a copy of this book or to share your thoughts as you read it.

When your meeting is a mixture of virtual and face-to-face

The advice in this chapter should work for you if your meetings are a mixture of remote participants and others who are face to face. Below we look at two different situations: first, a face-to-face meeting joined by people remote from one another geographically; second, a meeting where there are several face-to-face groups connected to each other using virtual technology.

Face-to-face meeting, with some virtual attendees

Figure 5.4 A face-to-face meeting with three virtual attendees

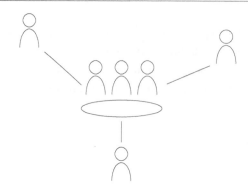

In this case, a core group is in the same room with other participants attending remotely via audio and video links (Figure 5.4).

There is an important principle to apply: ensure a level playing field. Far too often, these types of meetings are designed for the face-to-face participants, with the remote people added in as an afterthought. For a particularly bad example of this, see Tom's story earlier in this chapter, page 130. It is far too easy to forget about the people you cannot see and for the remote people to end up forgotten about and not involved.

How can you create a level playing field? How can you design for everyone to participate fully? Consider the virtual participants first. They have the poorest connection to the core group. Do they need to be present all the time? Could the meeting run face to face and then give the virtual people a briefing and gain their input instead? I did this once with a full-day meeting in Copenhagen with a pharmaceutical company. Let's use this as an example. People had travelled from all over the world to learn how to run virtual teams effectively. We spent the whole day making the most of our face-to-face time to engage with each other and learn together. We ran powerful exercises with blackout goggles, to mimic the uncertainty that comes from a lack of visual clues. There was one person who couldn't make it to Copenhagen and who was stuck in the United States. The team leader was keen for him to join us all day by video, which would have meant skipping the exercises. Instead, I suggested that the people who were in Copenhagen built up a summary of everything that they had learnt. They presented the remote attendee with a summary, designed for him, showing what they had learned in a fun, engaging way. It only took 45 minutes, but he was fully engaged throughout and thanked me afterwards. The summary was useful for those in the room too, as it reinforced their learning.

What if you do need to be together throughout the meeting? What often happens is that people sit around a board table with a speakerphone in the centre of the table. Those present in the room have a normal discussion, while the virtual attendees do not know who is talking and cannot hear many of the words due to poor quality audio, especially when speakers are a long way from the microphone.

In this case, use the lowest common denominator: design for virtual. Use ground rules that work in a purely virtual meeting. For example, ask everyone to state his or her name before any input. While this seems nonsensical to those in the room, it makes a huge difference to those who are virtual. Use video where you can, as it helps the remote people to see what is happening. Ask them about the quality of the audio that they are hearing. It often helps to move speakerphones around the room so that the microphone is closest to whoever is speaking at the time.

Keep meetings short! While those in the room together may feel able to keep working for hours, the virtual participants are likely to flag after 60–90 minutes. Plan in breaks. It can be useful for remote people to have an 'in-the-room buddy', who can get in touch during the breaks and answer any questions they have. Remember that remote participants need their breaks too, though!

Face-to-face hubs, connected by virtual technology

In these meetings, there are several face-to-face hubs, each with people in the room (Figure 5.5). These hubs are connected together virtually, via audio and/or video links. This is a very different case. Design for face-to-face sessions to run at each hub, with short virtual sessions to connect the hubs and to draw together the work that they are doing. This can be a very good way to get things done virtually, especially with teams on various sites on different continents or with wide time-zone differences. It can be useful to have a central facilitator overall, able to field questions from any hub, plus a local facilitator at each hub running their part of the meeting.

Figure 5.5 A virtual meeting with three face-to-face hubs

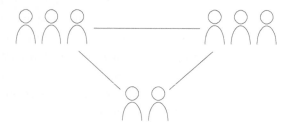

A day in the life: Liz

Liz works on projects in the pharmaceutical industry in the UK, sometimes in the office and sometimes from her home office. We will hear about a day when she is working from her home office, peppered with meetings with people around the world.

8.15 am Liz goes up to her home office with a large cup of coffee. Over the next 45 minutes, she checks what has happened since she finished work yesterday. Are there any emergencies that she needs to deal with? Is there anything else she needs to be aware of? Liz reviews the project collaboration tool and collects her thoughts before the morning meeting.

9.00 am Liz joins her project's 15-minute daily meeting with her Indian colleagues, who are drawing near the end of their working day. This daily stand-up meeting is short and sharp, designed to keep everyone up to date.

9.15 am For the next couple of hours, before people in India go home, Liz works with them on problem solving and sorting out issues, either one-to-one or in small groups. Screen-sharing technology really helps her as this allows everyone to see what each other is looking at while have a conversation.

11.00 am By now, things are quieter. Liz has a lull where she gets to catch up with her own work. It is also a good time for one-to-one meetings with people in the same time zone.

1.00 pm Colleagues from the east coast of the United States are now starting to come online. This is the time when many of the countries that Liz works with are in the office, so big group meetings tend to happen now. Today Liz joins her community of practice for a virtual get-together.

5.00 pm This time coincides with most of Liz's US colleagues taking their lunch, so big meetings have finished. She reviews the day and completes any extra work before packing up and going downstairs.

8.00 pm Around twice a month, Liz has one-to-one meetings with US-based experts in the evening. These are people who are in demand and whose calendars are booked up well in advance. Once Liz has been unable to find any slots in their calendars online during her working hours, it is usually much easier to find a time slot for a conversation in her evening.

Summary

This chapter looked at how to lead virtual meetings, where people meet at the same time using synchronous technologies although dispersed geographically. I covered how to prepare for virtual meetings, how to run effective virtual meetings where people are engaged and involved in the topic and how to make sure that actions happen afterwards. We looked at continuous improvement, virtual leadership when you are not in charge of a meeting and how to handle meetings with face-to-face and remote participants.

Questions for reflection

1 What types of virtual meetings do you lead and/or attend?

2 From the 'considerations for virtual meetings' section, which areas do you already plan for? Which areas need further work? What will you do differently in the future?

3 What do you think of the start-up visual and steps? How could you use these in your own meetings?

4 Which ideas from this chapter do you already use in your meetings? What else do you plan to add now that you have read it?

5 How engaged are people in your virtual meetings? What are you going to do differently to improve this?

6 How do you close your meetings now? What will you do differently in terms of actions and reviewing the meeting?

7 Do you attend meetings where you are not the official leader? How do they go? What will you do differently now you have read this chapter?

8 Mixing face-to-face and virtual participants – is this something you have experienced much of? If so, what do you do now and what will change?

9 What will you take from Liz's 'day in the life'?

References and further reading

Buzan, T (2003) *Use Your Memory: Understand your mind to improve your memory and mental power*, BBC Worldwide, London

Chamorro-Premuzic, T (2015) [accessed 21 December 2015] Why Brainstorming Works Better Online, *Harvard Business Review*, April 2015 [Online] https://hbr.org/2015/04/why-brainstorming-works-better-online

Chatham House (2016) [accessed 28 February 2016] Chatham House Rule [Online] https://www.chathamhouse.org/about/chatham-house-rule

Collins, S (2016) *Neuroscience for Learning and Development: How to apply neuroscience and psychology for improved learning and training*, Kogan Page, London

Greer, L (2014) [accessed 18 December 2015] Why Virtual Teams Have More Conflict: Insights by Stanford Business, *Stanford*, November 2014 [Online] https://www.gsb.stanford.edu/insights/lindred-greer-why-virtual-teams-have-more-conflict

Hall, K (2007) *Speed Lead: Faster, simpler ways to manage people, projects and teams in complex companies*, Nicholas Brealey Publishing, London

Hill, L, Brandeau, G, Truelove, E and Lineback, K (2014) *Collective Genius: The art and practice of leading innovation*, Harvard Business Review Press, Boston

Hunter, D (2007) *The Art of Facilitation: The essentials for leading great meetings and creating group synergy*, 2nd edn, Random House, Auckland

Lencioni, P (2004) *Death by Meeting: A leadership fable about solving the most painful problem in business*, Jossey-Bass, San Francisco

Rees, J (2015) Asking Powerful Questions. Interview recorded as part of the Virtual Working Summit 2015, Loughborough [Online] www.virtualworkingsummit.com

Robson, M (2002) *Problem Solving in Groups*, 3rd edn, Gower, Aldershot

Settle Murphy, N (2013) *Leading Effective Virtual Teams: Overcoming time and distance to achieve exceptional results*, CRC Press, Boca Raton

Sibbet, D (2003) *Principles of Facilitation*, The Grove Consultants International, San Francisco

Thorpe, S (2008) Enhancing the Effectiveness of Online Groups: An investigation of storytelling in the facilitation of online groups, Auckland University of Technology, PhD thesis, Auckland

Virtual working in between meetings 06

While virtual meetings are important, most work happens in between meetings. In this chapter, I discuss why it is so important to have effective ways of getting things done outside of meetings and how to use this in practice. We review communication, relationships, conflict and engagement, before focusing on productivity and effectiveness, delivery, performance and the virtual working environment.

By reading this chapter, you will:

- Learn why most virtual work happens outside meetings.
- Review communications, relationships, conflict and engagement for virtual teams.
- Know how you can be productive as a virtual worker, and how to help others to be more effective too.
- Be aware of challenges to delivery and how to overcome them.
- Understand the challenges of remote performance management and how to make it happen.
- Be more aware of your environment as a virtual worker.

Introduction

Many people think of virtual meetings when they think of virtual work and virtual teams. In reality most work is done outside of meetings. Consider your own working day. When do you get most done? Is it when you are on a call or in a meeting, or is it when you are back at base, ploughing through tasks and ticking off actions?

Figure 6.1 A mind-map of this chapter

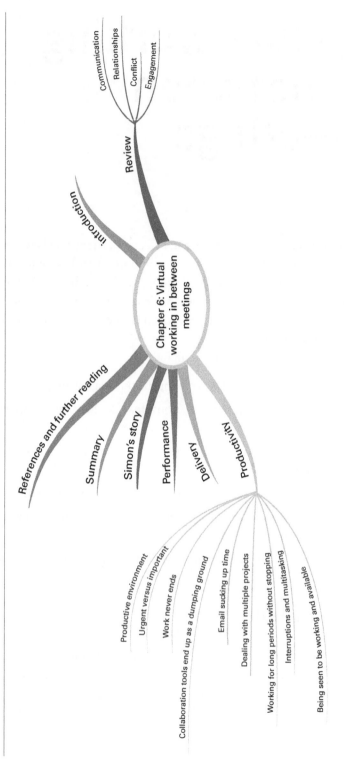

Figure 6.2 Don't forget the different time/different place quadrant

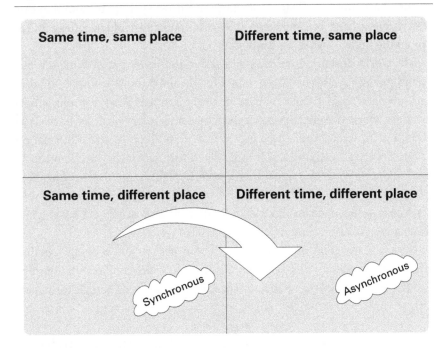

In this chapter, we look at virtual work away from team meetings. It is very easy to focus on the same time/different place quadrant shown in Figure 6.2 when the different time/different place quadrant gives many convenient options. I have noticed how people often try to pack everything into live meetings when they start working virtually. This makes virtual working much harder than it needs to be, especially if the team is spread across wide time zones and meets outside office hours. Instead, virtual teams can use asynchronous tools to collaborate effectively, with all information up to date and available in real time, meaning that inconvenient live meetings can be kept to a minimum. As well as tools, participants need cooperative attitudes, with good relationships and levels of trust, which keep work progressing even when meetings are spaced out. These prevent team members feeling isolated from one another.

Remember that this sort of collaboration with open sharing is the norm for new generations joining the workplace. They use social media to keep in touch with friends and expect to be able to do this at work, especially across virtual teams. On the other hand, some older generations will remember work without e-mail, where memos had to be typed up and the only way to get text to other parts of the world quickly was to send a telegram! We will cover more about generational differences in the next chapter. You might find younger colleagues an inspiration using tools to communicate asynchronously or you might be able to support those older colleagues for whom this style of working is not natural.

The world of work is moving at a faster and faster pace. While a typed memo might have been fast enough when I joined the workforce 30 years ago, now it would be out of date before it arrived! Weekly project team meetings worked well 10 years ago. Nowadays many projects have daily check-ins. To work at this pace means that we need up-to-date information at our fingertips. Collaboration tools allow this, when they are kept up to date and everyone has appropriate access. Figures quoted by Elizabeth Harrin show that project managers report time saved, reduced stress levels, a stronger sense of team morale and better control of project costs when using good collaboration tools (Harrin, 2016).

Now we are going to touch on different aspects of working together effectively outside of virtual meetings: communication, conflict, relationships and engagement, before we focus on productivity, delivery and performance.

Reviewing aspects of virtual work outside of meetings

Communication

Communication holds virtual teams together. It is about effective and timely flow of information, supporting the team as they work together. Good communication is not just one way, sending out information for people to absorb, but two way, with suggestions, queries and confirmation flowing back. It is more than just transferring information between people – it is a powerful way of building a sense of team amongst virtual colleagues. Plan your communications to build a sense of team outside of meetings, in addition to transferring information around.

We introduced communication in Chapter 3 and considered individual preferences. The Drexler/Sibbet Team Performance Model® shown in Figure 3.8 helps us to identify different communication needs at each stage of team development. The virtual team communications plan is a helpful tool. Review it regularly so that it stays current and meets the changing needs of your team.

Communication is best when it is appropriate for each person and personalized and tailored to their needs. Don't communicate everything to everyone, but allow people to be able to choose what they receive, so that they can receive what is best for them. An information hub works far better than sending out or copying in e-mails to far too many people!

When communicating, it is helpful to be honest and transparent, building trust and relationships by sharing with others. Of course, some things cannot be shared due to security or legal issues, but keep these to a minimum.

You need structure for your shared team storage

While writing this section, I had a conversation with a client. The company's virtual teams used two different systems for storing project documentation. Unfortunately no one knew where to put things and, as a result, it was very difficult to find anything. Document storage methods varied from project to project and from person to person. The only person who really knew how to find things in one of the systems had just resigned. What a nightmare! Finding a document was a challenge. Did it exist? If so, where was it? Answering these two questions could take many hours.

You might think this could never happen in your organization. It could. If you have someone who keeps things neat and tidy, they might leave. Would anyone else take over? If you don't have clear, agreed rules and principles governing how documents are stored and where, then everyone will come up with their own ideas and the result is all too predictable. To avoid chaos, agree a simple and clear structure for everyone to follow. Make it as easy as possible for people to find things. Allocate the role of curator to look after your collaboration tools and ensure that tools are kept tidy and up to date.

Relationships

Your team needs rapport, trust and commitment to get things done. Except for simple 'star' groups who only interact with the leader, virtual teams should work as a community, with a sense of belonging and trusting one another. Community comes from a shared vision, common objectives and the ability to interact and form relationships. Much of this will develop in team meetings (we considered this in the last chapter).

Individual relationships between team members are best built up one-to-one, outside of large virtual meetings. Plan in time to get to know one another. These informal, one-to-one sessions and communications with team members will help to keep connections alive and grow trust and empathy.

Lisa works for an insurance company in Norwich, England. She is a manager and part of her role is to be personable, as she needs to build relationships and trust with people quickly. Face to face, it is easy to read people but virtually this is much harder. Lisa finds instant messaging really useful, along with video calls and screen sharing. She says of instant messaging: 'It's a great way to have general conversations with people in the morning. On our system, we can see if they are active and then ping them a message. Perhaps it will say something like: 'You're in early today!' or 'How was your evening last night?' or just share some chit-chat in a friendly way. It's instant – so it's much easier than writing an e-mail. It helps to build bridges. People are now so used to sending messages in their private lives that it comes over easily into the work environment.'

I have noticed that those who are used to virtual working often get going more quickly than those new to it. With experience, it seems to be easier to assume trust with remote people than for people who have not done it before, for whom it seems very odd to trust someone you have never met face to face.

It is important as a virtual leader to monitor how people are in between meetings. If people are in danger of becoming invisible, you can explore what's wrong. There are many possibilities: perhaps someone who withdraws is introverted and prefers to think things through thoroughly before they commit their ideas; or perhaps they are suffering from a life event or illness that is affecting their work. Other signs might indicate that there is conflict in your virtual team and we will explore that aspect next.

Conflict

Conflict can be very difficult to detect remotely, as we discussed in Chapters 3 and 5. This is especially true when conflict arises outside of meetings. Perhaps someone doesn't share information that would be useful to colleagues elsewhere. Perhaps a team member doesn't pull their weight and lets actions slip past end dates without carrying them out. Little things can quickly spiral into bigger problems. My advice is to listen out carefully, keep in touch with team members one-to-one and ask them to tell you when conflict arises. Intervene quickly to sort things out. Review the discussion on conflict and how to prevent it in virtual teams as set out in Chapter 3.

While people might go quiet in a virtual team due to conflict, quite often they have checked out because they are not engaged. In the next section, we consider how to keep people engaged in between virtual meetings.

Engagement

We talked in the last chapter about how important it is to keep people engaged during virtual meetings. It is even easier for people to disconnect and check out between virtual meetings, so it is important for you to consider how to keep people engaged.

In meetings, you can engage people with the use of visuals, stories and the faces of people in the team. Outside of meetings, these can be powerful too. Use other senses to help make people connect with one another beyond virtual meetings. One example of this uses the team picture map shown in Figure 3.9 on page 80. You could print this out in colour, laminate it and send it to each team member. Then they can see each other and touch the map to remind themselves that the others in the team are real people, not just disembodied voices. Encourage people to share their stories in team online discussions and to talk about issues using the narrative form rather than as long lists. This will help people to remember each other's stories and keep people engaged to the end when reading through issues.

Another way to use visuals to connect people is with team metaphors. For example, a new project might suit a journey metaphor, with a long road ahead into the mountains, with bends in the road and unknown dangers, but ultimately leading to the destination you want to reach. An alternative team metaphor is a white-water rafting trip. This requires everyone in the team to pull together to survive across tricky rapids, while also providing quiet, still areas for reflection and recovery. What suits you and your team? What metaphor would help you to work together and engage people and their creativity? Remember that you need to choose carefully, as some metaphors will work well across cultures and others won't. Any team trying to engage me with a football metaphor would leave me cold. Other cultural issues can get in the way. I wouldn't use a white-water rafting metaphor with my colleagues in the Middle East as they are far more used to desert than to rapidly flowing rivers!

One last advantage of the use of images and metaphors is that they are easy to remember. Mind-maps are helpful too, as you have seen in this book – I hope they help you to engage with the content.

People disengage by focusing on other work, especially local, which means they don't carry out their actions. Ensure that someone follows up actions after meetings, so that team members remain focused and are reminded of what they have committed to do.

Productivity and effectiveness

How can we be productive and effective? This is a challenge in our fast-paced world, but especially for those of us who work virtually. The very tools that connect us to our colleagues around the world are liable to interrupt us and throw us off course. Our work is not completed by the end of a working day, as others elsewhere are likely to be still working. It can be tempting to join in. But working longer and longer hours will not make us more productive. Rising before sunrise to work with colleagues in the east and staying up way after sunset to deal with other colleagues further west is not the answer.

So what are some practical strategies for virtual leaders and their teams to employ? I interviewed Grace Marshall, who says that most productivity is about managing attention rather than managing time (Marshall, 2015). Below are some key ideas from this conversation, sparked by questions from virtual leaders from around the world.

Being seen to be working and available

Many virtual workers use tools that can indicate whether or not they are available. It is tempting for a virtual worker to show that they are available and present all the time, so that their colleagues and team leader can see that they are working. However, this has the disadvantage that people feel free to send messages and requests that interrupt the flow of work.

There are two issues here: 1) the need to be seen to be present; and 2) the level of interruptions. Let's tackle them in turn. Ask yourself why people might feel the need to be seen to be present. Are you asking for this as their virtual leader? Do you measure people on their availability, or on their results and the impact that they make? When leaders feel uncomfortable when they cannot see people, and want to know that they are working, this is harking back to old, outmoded forms of leadership. Remember command-and-control, which we discussed in Chapter 2? It does not usually work well when people are spread around the world.

As a leader, model the way. Let people know when you will be available and when you need to focus on getting work done. Let them know that you expect them to do the same. You are more interested in the results they obtain than the hours they are visibly available. Remember that what you do matters and setting expectations of yourself and others is important.

Interruptions and multitasking

A computer with many windows open appears to be multitasking but is only working on a single thing at once. It can switch from one program to another so quickly that it gives the appearance of executing everything concurrently. Human brains work in a similar way when we do things that require mental focus. Although we talk of multitasking, in reality what we are doing is serial 'monotasking': focusing on each thing in turn. Unlike computers, though, we humans are not very effective when switching between tasks. It slows us down.

Are you convinced? If not, here is an exercise to try. Take a sheet of paper. Draw a line down the centre to give you two columns. The left column is for letters and the right is for numbers. We are going to explore the effect that switching from the alphabet to numbers and back has on your speed of processing. You will be writing down the first 10 letters of the alphabet and the first 10 numbers. Sounds easy, doesn't it?

Figure 6.3 Setting out your multitasking exercise sheet

Letters	Numbers
A	I

Ask someone to record your speed when you complete this task twice, once on either side of the paper. The first time, write the first letter (A) in the left column, then the first number in the right column (1), then move to the second letter, second number, all the way through to the tenth letter (J) and the tenth number (10). Figure 6.3 shows what your piece of paper will look like after the first letter and number.

How long did that take you? It is usually 15 to 25 seconds with the groups I work with.

Now try it again. Ensure that the first attempt is not visible. This time, instead of switching between the letters and numbers, write all the letters in one column and then move across to write the numbers. Time it.

How long did that take? What was the difference? This task usually takes 7 to 20 seconds, with most people cutting 30 per cent off their initial time. Why? This time there was no need to switch mental focus from one series: A,B,C,D,E,F,G,H,I,J to another: 1,2,3,4,5,6,7,8,9,10.

If we lost time switching between two such simple series, how much time do we lose when switching out of deep concentration? It takes me around 15 to 20 minutes to regain focus on writing this book when I am interrupted, in line with studies by Microsoft and others. This is even if the interruption is very short – the doorbell ringing or someone saying, 'Penny, have you got a minute?' Unfortunately, even if I ignore the doorbell or say, 'No, I haven't got a minute now', then my flow is interrupted and it still takes me ages to get back into writing.

As an effective virtual leader, you want to be available for your colleagues. However, interruptions will slow you down, just as when you interrupt other people you will slow them down. So cut down on interruptions when you need to get things done efficiently and effectively. Remain available, just not *all* of the time. Agree specific times with your team when people can contact you directly by instant message or phone calls. Encourage them to do the same with their colleagues and with you. Agree as a team how you can flag to others when you are focused and do not want to be interrupted. You could send a message saying: 'I'm writing my chapter from 10 am to 2 pm UK time but will be available afterwards. Please don't disturb me now.' Setting expectations with others is key, so that people know when they can get hold of you.

Many interruptions come from your environment, rather than your remote colleagues. Try turning off alerts that appear on your computer, pings and other sounds made by devices. Set aside time to catch up on e-mail at specific times in your day. If you work from home, ensure that other people will not be able to interrupt you, except in an emergency, and turn off alarms and beeps from household equipment. Turn your phone ringer off or divert your phone elsewhere.

Sometimes interruptions come from within. For example, while I was writing this chapter, my mind kept thinking about booking a summer holiday. Perhaps the chilly English winter weather was prompting me? These thoughts didn't help me to focus on asynchronous virtual work! In the end, I wrote, 'Book summer holiday' on my home to-do list and then I could get on with my work.

It is easy to work for long periods without stopping for breaks

When you are remote from colleagues at work, or catching up with virtual colleagues at home in the evening, it is very easy to keep going for a long time without stopping. Some people might imagine that this is what a virtual leader would want – their people concentrating on work for hours and hours! However, we are human beings not machines and purely ploughing on through work is not very productive. We need breaks to recharge, refresh and recover. Grace Marshall puts it like this: 'Our tendency to work under pressure without any breaks is completely counterproductive' (Marshall, 2015). As humans, we are designed to have periods of high performance followed by periods of recovery. We sustain peak performance and health by this mixture of performance and recovery. Focus on attention, not time, and take a break to restore your focus and help you do your best work.

One way to do this is to apply the *pomodoro* technique of Francesco Cirillo (www.pomodorotechnique.com). He suggested working in 25-minute blocks, each block followed by a five-minute recharge before the next 25-minute block. This ensures that you stay focused and productive with regular breaks. You can use a kitchen timer, hence the pomodoro name, or just set an alarm.

Dealing with multiple projects

Virtual leaders, and workers too, often have multiple projects running concurrently. Grace suggests that, to be productive with so much going on, we need to separate out two ways of working:

- 'Boss' mode, when we are defining what to work on, what success looks like and deciding on goals and tasks.
- 'Worker' mode, when we are getting things done.

These two modes work far better separately: first choose what work to do and identify the outcomes and tasks needed. Then dive into worker mode and do the tasks. With multiple projects, in boss mode, work out what similar things needs to be done across projects and batch them up, such as making telephone calls. Then go into worker mode to do them.

E-mail sucking up time

E-mail is bound to come up in a chapter about asynchronous virtual working. It is a free, easy way to send out messages to people in different places that they can read at a different time. It is reliable and people are used to it in today's workplace.

However, e-mail can be a huge problem. It comes in at various times throughout the day, whether that suits the recipient or not. Some people expect answers to e-mails immediately, which means that their colleagues feel obliged to check for them all the time, just in case. Other people copy in far too many people, so that e-mail inboxes can be filled up with unnecessary mail!

As a virtual leader, take time to agree and set up the e-mail etiquette that you will be using as a virtual team. Who should be copied in on what? How quickly should people expect a response? When is e-mail best and when should other tools be used: the phone, a text or instant message or the team online collaboration tool? Make sure that you all know the communication preferences of each member.

Collaboration tools can end up as a dumping ground

Just like e-mail, other tools can be used poorly, reducing productivity for team members. Collaboration tools and shared storage areas can end up as virtual dumping grounds for stuff that is almost impossible to find. Everyone in the team wants access but finding volunteers to keep the shared space tidy tends to be nigh impossible!

As a virtual leader, make sure that the purpose of the shared space is clear, whatever collaboration tool you use. What goes where and what is the etiquette that governs how people can use it? Who will curate it? Grace suggests that you separate working documents from reference materials, which are finished and archived.

Work never ends

In a virtual team, there may be people working at any time of the day or night if work follows the sun as the day progresses. There is a temptation as a virtual leader to keep going alongside your team members. However, getting up at 4 am to work with your team in the east will not help you to be productive during your own working day. Neither will staying up until midnight to work alongside your team further west. Instead, be clear on what you want to achieve each day. What is your completion point? As an example, for me, my completion point when writing this part of the book was to finish this section and then to go off to an orchestra rehearsal. Don't just look forward, but celebrate what you have achieved. Encourage your team to celebrate successes. In the companies I work with, people often rush to start the next project rather than taking time to stop, reflect, learn lessons and celebrate and thank those involved at the end of a major piece of work. As a virtual leader, consider whom you should thank for their contributions. How can you celebrate as a team when you achieve a milestone or deliver a result?

Notice too that your team members may well be tempted to work for very long hours, just as you are. Encourage them to work sensible hours, avoid overload and to switch off. Of course they are much more likely to follow your example if you model this yourself!

Urgent versus important

People tend to focus on things that are urgent, over things that are more important. Over 50 years ago President Eisenhower quoted: 'I have two kinds of problems: the urgent and the important. The urgent are not important, and the important are never urgent.' Stephen Covey developed this idea into a two-by-two matrix, plotting urgent/non-urgent against important/not important (Covey, 1989). He suggested exploring our tasks in terms of four categories:

- *Important and urgent*: the things that happen anyway that we cannot ignore. They tend to be unforeseen or work that was left to the last minute.
- *Important and non-urgent*: the things we tend to neglect and where we should focus to become more effective. These help you to reach your goals and deliver.
- *Not important and urgent*: things that are not really necessary for our work but which other people would like us to attend to quickly.
- *Not important and not urgent*: things that really should be dropped or avoided completely as they offer little or no value.

You can see how Malcolm, a virtual leader, applied this in Figure 6.4. Try doing the same for your tasks. Free up time by avoiding the not important/ not urgent quadrant entirely and cut down your responses to things that are urgent for others but not important for you. Focus on important tasks before they become urgent. What are you neglecting now that would make a difference to your work – perhaps planning, learning and developing skills or building relationships?

A productive environment

Too many people drift into virtual working from home and end up spending hours each week in an unsatisfactory environment. It was true for me: I remember propping my laptop on my knees when I started working from

Figure 6.4 Important versus urgent grid for Malcolm, who leads a virtual team

	Urgent	Not Urgent
Important	*Emergencies, work you couldn't foresee or work that you left to the last minute.* Some calls regarding my work; Some 1:1 calls with my team; Some virtual meetings; Some tasks with a close deadline.	*Work that helps you to reach your goals and deliver on these.* Planning; Learning and developing my skills; Time developing relationships with my team and our clients; Some 1:1 calls with my team; Getting work done ahead of the deadlines.
Not Important	*Work that is important for others right now, but not for you.* Interruptions and distractions; Other calls, not directly relevant for me or my team; Most alerts from e-mail/messages; Virtual meetings to deal with other people's crises.	*This isn't important for you or other people, either right now or for your work in the future.* Most of the internet – for me, catching up with friends; Most e-mail that is unrelated to my goals, such as newsletters; Games I play on my phone.

home. Now I have a dedicated office at home, with a choice of standing or seated desk, good lighting, my laptop raised to eye height, a separate keyboard and tracker pad, an adjustable chair, an adjustable foot rest, a telephone headset for calls and an adjustable microphone to use with my computer. There is plenty of space on my desk for working away from my computer and bookshelves for my books. I have printers close by. I work alongside a south-facing window, letting in natural light and with a view of Victorian roof tiles and large horse chestnut trees.

Some people injure themselves with repetitive strain injury (RSI). In many countries there are legal requirements for keyboard use, so your organization may provide you with appropriate equipment to work virtually from home. It is worth investigating what is available for yourself and your team members so that you can work in productive environments.

Feng shui for your virtual working environment?

Sarah McAllister works with businesses around the world to make the most of their physical environment. She is a Master of feng shui, the ancient Chinese art of how our environment affects us. Her expertise is in how we can become more productive, healthier and happier through optimizing the layout of our space.

I asked Sarah for her tips for virtual workers. She usually works with a particular space in mind, but here are some general hints that she hopes will be useful as you consider your environment:

- If you live alone and work from home, it can be isolating. Adding a fish tank may bring some more vitality to your office.

- Avoid red and black together. While geometric patterns are fun on a feature wall, they can be overstimulating.

- Many virtual workers have far too many messy cables crisscrossing the floor and their desks. Instead, invest in a cable tidy to organize the leads. Label the plugs so you know which belongs to which device.

- If the space where you work is cluttered and confusing, it will encourage cluttered thinking.

- If you have a choice over your office location, facing east, south-east or south can be best for business.

Delivery

In virtual meetings, you can ask people how things are going. You might, or might not, find out what is happening though, as culture, language and generational factors can get in the way. In between meetings, it can be a real challenge for leaders to know how things are going.

So how can you ensure that work gets done? You cannot monitor by watching what people are doing, so, as a virtual leader, you will need to keep in touch to find out what is working and what people need your help with. You also need ways to monitor outputs and deliverables.

Be wary when a member of your team states that their piece of work is 'almost complete' (others say that a task is '90 per cent done'). What does that mean? Once a team member told me that something was 'almost complete'. The task stayed 'almost complete' for several weeks! I have noticed a tendency to underestimate the work still to be done. Another reason for overenthusiastic reporting can be cultural. In some cultures, it is important to avoid bad news, as it reflects badly on team members, and on you as leader; this is 'saving face'. We will explore this further in Chapter 7. I suggest avoiding '90 per cent done' and 'almost complete'. Ask people whether a task is not started yet, 50 per cent complete or finished entirely, and set up your collaboration and project management tools to do the same.

A key part of ensuring delivery in virtual teams is that team members feel accountable for their actions and responsible for their own performance and progress. Make sure that they understand what is expected of them, now and in the longer term.

It can be useful to implement a 'virtual open-door policy' where team members can ask for support, guidance, raise issues or ask for help. Nancy Settle-Murphy suggests setting aside times in your diary when people can approach you (Settle-Murphy, 2013). Make sure that this is available to all the members of your team within their usual working hours – you might need to run sessions at different times for this.

Clear documentation helps in virtual teams so that people can check back with one another. If you are doing work in highly regulated industries, such as pharmaceutical companies or financial services, this documentation might be needed for an audit trail. Choose the appropriate level of detail for your documents upfront: as much as you need but no more.

Years ago, someone was convinced that no one read his detailed documents. To test his theory, he added a paragraph from the novel *Moby-Dick* into his document. No one commented! A client of mine added 'Santa Claus says' into a document and no one noticed. Make sure your team are not wasting valuable time producing documentation that will never be used.

As your work progresses, encourage people to review what is working and how things could be better. Reviews like this highlight possible improvements and remind you to keep doing those things that work well. Get into the habit of running these regularly, gathering input from your team and making appropriate changes. It is not difficult and makes a big differnce. When I collect input I use the headings: 'What went well' and 'I wish that...'

Ensure that the workload is spread fairly around the team. In a face-to-face environment, you would be able to see at a glance who was working flat out all hours and who was taking things at a more leisurely pace. Set expectations upfront of the number of hours that you expect each person to be working. Gain commitment from people as they join the team as to these expectations. Remember that the team is working to a shared, agreed, common goal, so encourage everyone to hold each other, and you, accountable for doing what they have agreed to do.

To ensure that work is delivered to the right standard, you will want to observe what is happening through status reports, virtual meetings and the actual work produced. What you will not be able to see is *how* people are working. Are they struggling with aspects of their role? How do they work with other people? Are there areas where individual coaching might help? Could they be more effective and, if so, how? You will need to be alert to subtle clues that something is wrong, perhaps one-to-one meetings cancelled at the last minute, little or no input in meetings, delivery slipping or no response to e-mails and calls. We consider performance in the next section.

Performance

You need to develop your team members and manage their performance virtually. It takes careful thought to plan this: you are not going to bump into your direct reports in the corridor, so you need to make time for planned catch-up conversations. Take care not to let operational issues take up every minute of your one-to-one calls, leaving time for discussion about performance and professional development.

In a virtual team, don't try to find out all the information you need about people's performance yourself. Nancy Settle-Murphy recommends implementing a peer feedback process to gather feedback periodically on the performance of everyone in the team (Settle-Murphy, 2013). Include yourself too. Choose a method that works best for the particular group of people involved and their circumstances. Consistently apply this process with everyone. Make sure people know what you are intending to do with the results and that the data will be used to help everyone develop. If some of your team are employed by partner organizations, it makes sense to gather performance data for them too. Talk with each team member's own line manager so that you can support your learning and professional development together.

Listening is a key skill for virtual leaders, especially at times where there are performance issues. Use the richest communication medium you can: this is not a time for working asynchronously. It is time for a one-to-one meeting. You might find that meeting face to face is helpful for particularly difficult situations, but it is not always possible. A high-definition videoconferencing facility can be almost as good. Listen carefully, noticing all aspects of your team member: their body language, tone of voice and the words spoken. Aim to listen for the underlying need, not just surface symptoms of any problems. Ask for permission before giving advice or assistance. Nancy says that this can do wonders to help empower a team member and create greater self-sufficiency in the future!

Luckily, performance management is not just about solving issues, but also about celebrating success, both individual and team. While it is easy to feel isolated, invisible and unnoticed as virtual team members, it is easy to counter this by thanking individuals for their contributions and for taking time to celebrate successes as a whole team.

Simon's story

Simon has worked in a global telecommunications company for 12 years. His background used to be in internal IT until he moved into a global role five years ago. His typical day consists of a range of activities, including:

- pre-sales work to support his largest telecoms customers;
- business process modelling with customers;
- working out how to automate systems integration and creating a service operating model for clients;
- preparing documents and progressing projects.

Simon finds that he is working away from the office more and more, and that this works well for him. With project teams distributed around the world, he has never met most of his colleagues face to face. Good Wi-Fi is essential! While he sometimes works in coffee shops, the background noise gets in the way. With the growing use of personal web cameras in virtual meetings, he prefers a quiet place at home.

A typical day for Simon starts in the gym, followed by updating his status and starting calls at around 9 am. He plans each day and prepares for calls in advance – even more important for a virtual meeting. On the day we spoke, Simon had four virtual meetings, which was a fairly light day. Often his days are filled with back-to-back meetings, with six or seven virtual meetings per day. During the week, he sometimes stays up until midnight to catch up with his colleagues in the United States.

Despite many years of working from home, I was surprised that Simon's usual workspace was the dining-room table. He is not officially a 'teleworker' and has a permanent desk in the office, which he rarely visits. On the day we spoke, Simon had to move out of the dining room as his wife was expecting guests, so he was working in the study instead. Other challenges include his son practising the piano after school while Simon is on conference calls!

Summary

In this chapter, we considered virtual working outside of meetings, reviewed communication, relationships, conflict and engagement and covered how to be productive, how to deliver as a team and managing performance virtually.

Questions for reflection

Before implementing the ideas in this chapter, it is helpful to have read and applied those in Chapter 3.

1 How do your communications support your virtual group? If you have some people co-located and others remote, is there a level playing field so that everyone has equal access and influence to you? If not, what will you do differently?

2 Who in your team feels isolated and why? What can you do to help them feel part of the team?

3 How are you building rapport, trust and empathy with individuals in your virtual team one-to-one? How are they doing this with one another?

4 How are you monitoring and listening out for conflict? What will you do when and if it erupts?

5 How do you engage your virtual team members now and what will you try in the future?

6 What ideas have you gained to help you with productivity? What already works for you and what will you do differently now? Consider: being always on, interruptions, multitasking, multiple projects, e-mail, your shared storage space and how it is curated (or not), focusing on what is important and the physical environment.

7 What about delivery? How will you use lessons learnt to improve delivery?

8 What do you feel about performance management in your virtual team? What works and what needs to change? Which ideas would you like to incorporate into your own practice?

9 How do you celebrate success virtually with your team? What new ideas might you use from now on?

10 How did Simon's story resonate for you – perhaps you also work from the dining-room table like Simon? What is your own virtual working environment? How can you improve it?

References and further reading

Covey, S (1989) *The Seven Habits of Highly Effective People*, Free Press, New York

Crenshaw, D (2008) *The Myth of Multitasking: How doing it all gets nothing done*, Jossey-Bass, San Francisco

Harrin, E (2016) *Online Collaboration Tools for Project Management*, PMI, Newton Square

Marshall, G (2015) *How to be Really Productive: Achieving clarity and getting results in a world where work never ends*, Pearson, Harlow

Settle-Murphy, N (2013) *Leading Effective Virtual Teams: Overcoming time and distance to achieve exceptional results*, CRC Press, Boca Raton

Virtual working complications: time zones, language, culture and generation

07

So far, this book has covered many aspects that make remote working different from working with co-located colleagues. There are a few things that we haven't touched on much that add whole new levels of complexity: wide time zones, language issues, cultural differences and cross-generational working. These aspects of remote working are the focus of this chapter. There is a chance that you might feel that you don't need this chapter at the moment, especially if you work with people of the same age and background, from the same profession, all with the same language as their mother tongue and from the same part of the world. However, most virtual teams are really quite diverse, so I hope that this chapter will be helpful as you explore these fascinating aspects that add complexity, but richness too.

By reading this chapter, you will understand:

- The effects of wide time zones in virtual teams, and four strategies to work with wide time zones more effectively.

- The ways that language can get in the way of virtual communication, from native English speakers, non-native English speakers and those who speak other languages.

- How you can use offshore English to improve understanding and model a helpful way to cope with language issues.

- Why culture matters for virtual leadership and how cultural differences play out.

Figure 7.1 A mind-map of this chapter

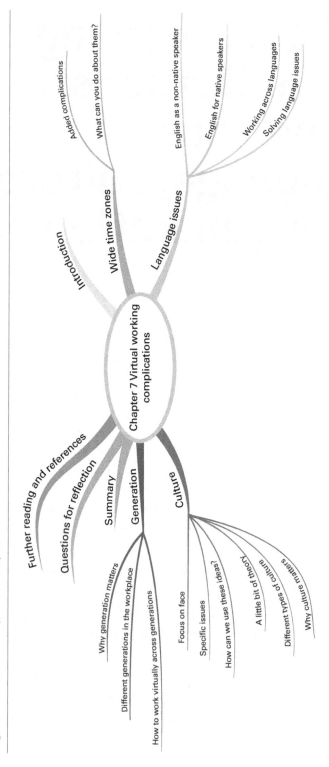

- How you can work effectively across cultures.

- Why generation is important for virtual workers and which generations you might find amongst your virtual colleagues.

- What works for different generations, and what does not.

Wide time zones

The added complications of wide time zones

What time zones do you work with? Adding wide time zones and multiple countries certainly adds to the complexity of virtual working! Let's explore an example and highlight the different aspects that make working together more complicated.

Looking back, I really was thrown in at the deep end when I started to work virtually. My team members were spread around the world, from the UK, France, USA and Australia. It wasn't an ideal start. Had I been able to choose the easiest way to ease into virtual working, I might have picked team members from just the UK and France, with only an hour's time difference between London and Paris, and normal office hours overlapping between 9 am and 4 pm UK time. Even the switch from winter to summer time happens in synch. That would have been easier, but it wasn't the case.

By adding New York to the mix, the overlapping office hours shrunk from seven hours each day to just two. With New York in the northern hemisphere, at least we were all on summer time at roughly the same time. However, there is often a gap of a few weeks when the time difference between the USA and Europe is out by an hour as the day the clocks change is different. This caught me out on several occasions when I turned up an hour early or, even worse, an hour late for meetings.

By adding in Canberra in Australia, we had no overlapping office hours at all! With Canberra in the southern hemisphere, the time difference changes the *opposite* way to the northern hemisphere. In Australia, the clocks go back March/April whereas they go forward in Europe and the USA. Of course, the Australian dates don't synch with either the USA or Europe, so once again, it's important to check what the time difference is when you're scheduling meetings, especially around March/April and October/November. But even once we understood the time differences, the bigger problem remained: we had no overlap of normal office hours (see Table 7.1).

Table 7.1 Wide time zones from my example – showing just how complex they are

	London, UK	Paris, France	New York, USA	Canberra, Australia
Time (in January)	9am	10am	4am	8pm
"	2pm	3pm	9am	1am
"	5pm	6pm	12 noon	4am
Summer/ winter time changes in 2016	27 March Forward one hour 30 October Back one hour	27 March Forward one hour 30 October Back one hour	13 March Forward one hour 6 November Back one hour	3 April Back one hour 2 October Forward one hour

In this first virtual team I was part of, at least there was one area of complexity that did not affect me. Imagine if my team had expanded to include Qatar in the Middle East! Their weekends are different from Europe, USA and Australia, as they work Sunday to Thursday as opposed to our Monday to Friday. Interestingly, Qatar doesn't have summer time, so the time difference with the UK changes from four hours in winter to three hours in the summer.

Something else that affected my team was the fact that, with so many different countries involved, there were different holidays that people were entitled to. In addition to the statutory holidays such as Eid or Christmas Day, there are also wide variations on the number of holidays that people can take. I remember that some of my colleagues in the USA were only entitled to two weeks' holiday a year, where some French colleagues had six weeks and routinely disappeared to the country for all of August! In addition, many countries have local holidays in some states, some of which are sacrosanct and some of which are not.

So let's sum up the issues that can arise from wide time zones: limited overlapping office hours; daylight savings changes out of synch and opposite for different hemispheres; weekends and holidays varying around the world.

What can you do about wide time zones?

Do you all need to meet together at the same time?

First of all, consider whether you need the entire group to work together as a whole. Could you split into groups with work following the sun around the world, passed from one team to another at short handover meetings at the end of shift? Alternatively, could you split into groups by time zone, with people only meeting synchronously with those in close time zones (like the Eco-Bishops story below) and keeping in touch asynchronously? Either of these options are worth considering.

You might not expect a religious organization such as the Anglican Communion to be modelling virtual leadership in the 21st century. It is a global network of churches all over the world, many of which have been in existence for hundreds of years. However, with huge global problems facing humanity, such as the serious impacts of climate change, the Anglican Communion needs to coordinate globally. It would be counterproductive and expensive to do this just by ferrying people around the world on planes!

I trained a group of facilitators from the Anglican Communion in Virtual Leadership five years ago and, since then, they have been sharing their knowledge and skills with networks of people within their organization. Terrie Robinson participated in my training, and I caught up with her in December 2015 to interview her for this book. Terrie told me that part of her job is to support networks working internationally. An example of these groups is the Anglican Bishops for Climate Justice Initiative, known colloquially as the 'Eco-Bishops'. These leaders come from all over the world, from areas already experiencing severe impacts of climate change, whether ravaged by drought, disappearing under the sea or suffering from increased natural disasters and storms. The Philippines, for example, are facing more frequent and more destructive typhoons, and changes to land in Northern Canada have made it much harder for indigenous peoples to live by traditional hunting and fishing. White beaches in Fiji are being washed away and hurricanes have even struck New York.

When I interviewed Terrie, the Eco-Bishops had been working together over a period of a couple of years. Their meetings were virtual, using shared screens, video and audio as they prepared for a major face-to-face consultation. In addition, they could share documents over e-mail and with an online stored space.

▶

The Eco-Bishops are in countries with wide time-zone differences. To work most effectively together, they split into three groups, created for those with the closest time zones. As bishops are not necessarily technologically savvy, each member of the group received training in the technology and practised it before the meetings began.

Through their three virtual groups and with information shared across all groups, the Eco-Bishops were able to get to know each other, listen to each other's stories and build up trust before their meeting in February 2015, the only meeting to happen face to face. This led to the group agreeing on a shared strategy, declaration and call to action on climate change, which was presented to the Anglican Communion as a whole. A few of the Eco-Bishops took it to Paris to the United Nations Conference on Climate Change in November 2015. At this summit 195 nations signed up to a landmark agreement to take action on climate change.

Terrie told me that part of her job is to support networks such as the Eco-Bishops working internationally. Virtual leadership is a key part of her role as she inspires people from very different parts of the world to work together. Of course, this can be a very challenging role with a wide variety of obstacles to tackle, from poor internet access for participants from conflict zones, to wide time zones and people grappling with new technology. However, when her coordination supports groups such as the Eco-Bishops, it makes it all worthwhile.

Create an overlap for live virtual meetings

If you all have to meet together at the same time, then you will need to find some overlap when you can. If you need frequent live meetings, then shifting the working day might be helpful. In my example earlier, if my colleague in Canberra, Australia had been happy to work nights, that would have created an overlap. However, it can be a huge imposition to ask someone to work different shifts, so I would avoid this where you can. In most situations, it works better if people are able to work flexibly, taking it in turns to join virtual meetings outside of office hours.

Make sure that the burden of joining meetings outside office hours is shared around the team in order to keep a level playing field. Remember that equal treatment is a key component of virtual trust when it comes to organizations, as we found in Chapter 3. Unfortunately, I hear all too often that the person with the least office hours overlap with the rest of the team is asked to join calls at inconvenient hours, often when they ought to be asleep. In my example, the person who was furthest away was Australian, with no office hours overlap with the rest of us. While life would have been easier for those of us from the United States, France and the UK if he had always got out of bed to join our meetings during our office hours, that would of course have been most unfair! Instead, we shared the pain and inconvenience and changed the time of the meetings to suit everyone in turn.

Remember, too, that working flexibly might be easier for some than for others. For example, some team members may have parenting or elder care responsibilities at home; others may contribute to the community, participate in sports, or have very active social lives. It is never safe to assume that people can drop everything to join your meetings. Take the time to understand the rhythm and flow of peoples' lives and the work hours that best suit them. Some may be very willing to meet late in the evening (their time) on occasion, while others will see this as unacceptable. Once again, it comes back to knowing your people and what is important to them.

Be very organized, with a clear calendar and time in each location visible to all

With wide time zones, it pays to be well organized! Have a shared calendar to keep track of working days in each location and each team members' holiday schedules. Make sure that you can all see the current time in each time zone represented in your team. A world clock on the wall is helpful for this, as are apps on devices. Ensure that all your team know precisely how daylight savings changes will change your time differences for meetings so that you can plan meetings ahead of time. Be particularly careful in the months of March, April, October and November, when these changes happen.

Make the most of asynchronous working

Challenge yourself as to whether you really need to work together in real time. When people need to work across wide time zones, it makes sense to use asynchronous technology, to support individuals working at times that suit them. Use the suggestions in Chapter 6 to help you. For example, you can have online conversations using virtual collaboration tools. You can also record conversations or presentations for later (using audio, video or both). Written transcriptions can be helpful too, as they allow people to catch up quickly by scanning without having to sit through an entire recording.

Language issues

Issues with English for non-native speakers

English is often used as the international language of business, so I will start by considering a few issues that arise when people are speaking English. Now, as you are reading this book and you are a long way into it, I can make the assumption that you are either a native English speaker or you are very good at English. As such, you might decide to skip this section and move on. Please don't! Read on, as many of the problems with the use of English when working virtually come from those of us who are native or fluent English speakers.

The trouble is that English is a language full of subtlety and nuance, and with roots in various languages, from Latin to German. English is full of metaphors and idioms. It contains sentence constructions that make perfect sense to native speakers, but make little sense to others! All of this can be very confusing to non-native speakers, even those who understand each individual word.

Let me give you some examples to show just how easy it is to confuse people. A few years ago I interviewed Richard Pooley for my Virtual Working Summit (Pooley and Pullan, 2012). I introduced him as a 'leading light' in the field of successful virtual communication in English. It's true. He is acknowledged as a leader in his field. However, someone for whom English is a second (or third or fourth) language might well have been confused by the metaphor 'a leading light' and lost the thread of the conversation. Looking back, I should have cut out the metaphor completely and simply said, 'Richard is acknowledged as a leader'. Idioms and metaphors like this can get in the way of people understanding what you mean.

Other ways that native English speech is harder for others to understand include the use of verbs instead of nouns. An example is, 'Who do you work for?' It would be much more straightforward to ask, 'What is your company?' Although it sounds a bit more formal: 'Please inform your manager' is much easier for non-native English speakers to understand than 'Please let your manager know...' Similarly, 'Collect me from the office at 5 pm' sounds more formal but is much easier than 'Pick me up from the office at 5 pm'. This last sentence contains a phrasal verb, 'to pick up', which apparently is a nightmare for many non-native speakers!

Keep in mind that the English words 'do' and 'get' have so many uses that they can easily cause confusion for someone trying to understand the intended meaning. It is far better to avoid vague terms and use more specific ones in their place. So instead of: 'I get what you mean', try 'I understand what you mean'. Or instead of: 'What do you do?', try 'What is your job (or role)?'

Individual words can cause problems too. You can find a long list of these 'false friends' in Carté and Fox's book *Bridging the Culture Gap* (2008). An example is the word 'formation'. To anyone who is Spanish, French, Italian or Portuguese, this word means 'training' in their own language, so they are likely to understand the English word the same way. To a native English speaker, though, it often means to create something. Richard shared a story illustrating this. He had heard a British reporter interviewing a French diplomat on the radio. The diplomat stated that the French 'formed the Iraqi police'. The reporter understood this as meaning that the French had created the Iraqi police from scratch – which was not true – and reacted correspondingly! Actually the diplomat meant that the French had trained the police, which was true and was far less controversial. Here is one more of these 'false friends' that can get us into trouble: the French word *'demander'* means to ask. Yet a native English speaker may see a simple request from a French colleague as a demand!

Issues with English for native speakers

There are pitfalls for native English speakers, too, as some English words mean different things to different people. I am English, but lived for several years in South Africa as a child, visited my aunt who lived in the United States and now I'm married to a New Zealander, so I know how different these four versions of English can be. For example, what would you think a South African meant if they said, 'I'll do that *just* now'? Most people would assume that they would start immediately. But if a South African is going to start something immediately, they would say something different: 'I'll do that *now* now.' Can you see how that could cause problems in a virtual team with some South African members? But it is not just South African English. Misunderstandings can happen between native English speakers from different places.

Issues when working across languages

Not all virtual teams work in English. There might be several different languages spoken. If people have to speak languages that are not their own mother tongue, they are likely to need a little more time to translate, think and respond.

As a virtual leader, ensure that people have the opportunity to speak and that the fluent speakers do not dominate the conversation. Remember, too, that speaking in another language is tiring. I remember attending a conference call in French for an hour. Although I was very quiet throughout, as my schoolgirl French was a bit rusty, I finished the call absolutely exhausted and with a pounding headache. It is all too easy for those of us who are fluent in the language of a virtual meeting to forget just how much extra work those who are working in a second or third language are having to do.

Solving language issues

So what can we do about these language issues as virtual leaders? Consider the people who participate in your virtual meetings and think about their needs. As usual, awareness of issues is a really important first step and allows you to let team members know that you understand their situation and to work together to craft solutions.

Are there any non-native speakers of English in your team and English is your shared language? If so, consider speaking a subset of English, known as global or offshore English, in your meetings. Apparently, this is what non-native English speakers use to speak with one another and they tend to find it easier to understand one another than people who have English as their mother tongue (Carté and Fox, 2008). Offshore English leaves out words and expressions that are tricky for non-native speakers. It leaves out metaphors and idioms, phrasal verbs and does not allow the use of verbs as nouns. While it comes across as rather plain and sometimes formal, it can help ease communication and create the level playing field that I often talk about in this book.

Make sure that you are aware of the words that mean different things in different languages and, when in doubt, ask for clarification as to exactly what people mean. Be as specific as you can be in your own speaking and encourage others to be too.

Enunciate your words and leave pauses at the end of phrases and sentences to allow people to catch up. Many people speak too quickly, so slow down a bit and make sure you finish your sentences. As an extra precaution, pause to rephrase what you (or someone else) just said to make sure everyone understands key points in the intended way.

Remember that those who are translating continuously during your virtual meeting are working extra hard. Where possible, provide written notes of key points and decisions alongside your audio, perhaps in the corner of a shared screen. Add in video where possible, as this adds body language to the words and voice tone, and can help people to understand.

When there are clusters of virtual team members participating in virtual meetings who speak different languages, consider building in translation and reflection time as part of your agenda. I heard of a French–American team who were frustrated with each other when the French would stop for a verbal huddle to ensure shared understanding on key points, as the Americans proceeded with their agenda. Once the Americans realized that their French colleagues needed this 'soak' time in their own language before tackling the next topic, the team decided to insert a period of one or two minutes between each agenda topic at every meeting.

If people would like to review everything, you might choose to record sessions and provide a transcription, perhaps with a translation into team members' own languages. Really clear, simple minutes can help people to get the gist of the conversation and summarize decisions and actions. Some conference bridge providers allow real translators to join your calls at the touch of a button, which can allow people to speak in their own tongue, although it does slow things down for everyone, and it can be costly. Make good use of asynchronous collaboration tools, as these allow for people to read and contribute in their own time and at their own speed, which is easier than listening.

What I recommend above all is that, rather than waiting until you have issues that need fixing, carefully consider your communications principles as a team at the outset, and involve team members in creating these principles. For example, what language will be used for team communication? (If English, which English?) How can team members make sure that everyone can understand their communications clearly? What should people do if they are struggling to understand? How can we design agendas and use technology best to encourage understanding by all?

Urge people to be clear and specific in their speaking and their writing, and encourage everyone to let others know if there is something that they cannot understand. As a virtual leader, it is very helpful to model this behaviour yourself by asking questions when you are not clear about someone's meaning, as it makes it much easier for others to do the same. I find it helpful to say at the start of meetings with a new group: 'There are times when I will say things that may not make sense – please help me by pointing them out.' You may find that with some cultures, people may not want to point things out immediately and prefer to wait until they can speak with you privately. At that point, it can be helpful to ask, 'How could I have been clearer?' Or, 'What can we do next time to make sure everyone understands things before moving on?' As a positive, open question, it is not putting the blame on anyone but myself, and it is a gentle invitation to help us improve our communications as a team.

Culture

Virtual leaders need to help their teams to work across cultural differences. Each individual team member's culture depends on the environment and context in which they have grown up. While stereotypes, especially when used to evaluate or judge others, can be dangerous, they can be helpful in allowing us to take our first best guess at how best to communicate effectively.

Why culture matters for virtual leadership

Our culture is our way of life – the ideas, customs and social behaviours that affect how we do things. The trouble is that our own culture is quite normal to us and so we tend not to notice it. Think of a goldfish swimming in a fish tank, completely unaware of the water around it. Culture is like the water – it's there, but not noticed.

As a virtual leader, though, your teams are likely to be culturally diverse, and when you experience a clash of cultures, suddenly culture becomes visible.

Here is an example of a culture clash that played out in front of me as I wrote this chapter on a train to London. Most of the people on the train were British apart from Jim, the person sitting opposite me. Jim came from the United States and was not aware of the British culture of dealing with strangers on trains. We tend to keep to ourselves and only interact if we feel we must apologize for something, such as standing on someone else's foot by mistake. (We often apologize even when other people are in the wrong!) I watched in amusement as Jim introduced himself and tried to start a conversation with a complete stranger sitting across the carriage. There was a very uncomfortable feeling emanating from most of the British people near me and even the odd stare! I noticed myself joining in automatically until I broke out of it and joined in the conversation with Jim, ending the awkward silence. We had a very interesting discussion about the differences between people from the UK and the United States. I wonder when you have noticed cultural clashes like this?

Cultural clashes can cause huge problems in interpersonal relationships, too, with people coming across as thoughtless and uncaring when their intentions are completely the opposite. And that is when people can see each other, as in my example! This is an area that can cause even more havoc for virtual leaders and team members. When we meet face to face with people from different cultures, we are constantly reminded of our different cultures, since we can see their body language, gestures and other visual cues. When we can see difference, we are more likely to understand and adapt.

However, in virtual meetings, it can be easy to forget that we are dealing with different cultures and we tend to look from our own cultural lenses in how we treat others. This is a recipe for disaster! Problems arise due to our cultural differences and, as a virtual leader, you do not have the option to walk over to people and see what is playing out. Instead, you have to listen carefully to discern when cultural differences are getting in the way of collaboration. When this happens, you need to intervene, quickly and diplomatically.

In my survey of virtual working challenges for this book, over half of respondents picked cultural differences as a key challenge of virtual working. At 56 per cent, this came out very slightly higher than working across time zones and quite a bit higher than working across different languages.

Different types of cultures at play

Each of us belongs to different cultures, any one of which may affect our working relationships. First, let's focus on **national** culture. Where are you from? Where do you live now? What is your defining country culture? Mine is British, although I was born in Malaysia and spent some time in South Africa as a child and have lived in New Zealand. If you, too, have moved around or your parents were from different countries, you may have within you the cultures of several countries.

Second, what **profession** or organizational function do you come from? People with different training may have very different professional orientations. Take artists and engineers, for example, who may have very different ideas around the need for detail or the importance of time. I have often noticed more of a difference between actuaries and sales people inside many companies, than between people from different countries. Perhaps you have, too? In my experience, it is really helpful to understand where people are coming from in terms of their professional and/or functional background as well as their national culture.

Third, if you belong to a large organization, you might have found that attitudes are expressed in a certain way, showing your **corporate** culture. As I work with a range of organizations across countries, I notice how things vary from one firm to another. I notice that certain ways of doing things are considered normal in one place and unusual elsewhere. Some organizations are very formal and hierarchical, which affects how freely (or not) information is shared. Some organizations value and reward teamwork, while others tend to promote individual contributors, which can have a profound impact on how people work as a team. Some organizations are formal and others are more informal. One company that I worked with had 'five principles' that governed how people work together and I can still remember them over a decade later! They were an integral part of that company's corporate culture: how people did things.

A little bit of theory

Each national culture tends to have shared, specific ways to solve problems:

- in relationships with other people;
- in terms of the passage of time;
- that relate to the environment.

There are useful theories about the dimensions along which differences between national cultures lie.

Trompenaars (1993) talks of five dimensions of how people work in relationship to other people that vary across nation cultures. These include:

1. Rules versus relationships

Which of these is more important in a culture? Fons Trompenaars shares a story that highlights the tension between rules and relationships. The scenario is this: a close friend of yours is driving his car and you are his passenger. Imagine that he hits a pedestrian while driving 15 miles per hour faster than the 20 mph speed limit. There are no other witnesses. His lawyer says that the only way your friend might avoid serious consequences would be if you would testify under oath that he was driving at 20 mph. I remember Fons telling me this story at a training course in Amsterdam, where my colleagues came from all over the world. We then had to choose one of the following options:

- My friend has a right to expect me to testify to the lower figure, as I'm his friend.
- My friend has some right to expect me to testify to the lower figure, as I'm his friend.
- My friend has no right to expect me to testify to the lower figure, even though I'm his friend.

Which of these would you choose? Now decide whether you would testify that your friend was driving at 20 mph to save him from serious consequences. Would you? Or would you tell the truth and leave him at the judge's mercy?

Over 90 per cent of people from Switzerland or North America would tell the truth and not help their friend. On the other hand, more than 65 per cent of people from China or Venezeula would help their friend by testifying he was driving more slowly than he had been. When asked these questions years ago at the training course, I remember thinking that my answer had to be the right one, only to be surprised at how other people had such different opinions from mine! We had a fascinating discussion about it over lunch afterwards.

This is not an easy solution for most people – it is a dilemma – and how we solve dilemmas draws on our national cultures. Here, the dimension is between the rules, order and authority, and the relationships, important as they both are.

2. The group versus the individual

Another cultural dimension covers the conflict between what each person wants as an individual and what is best for the group as a whole. Too much focus on individual freedom and responsibility can tend towards self-centredness, whereas focusing too much on the interests of the group can lead to conformism and slow decision making. Indigenous populations are often group-focused. One such example is the Maori population in New Zealand. If you ask a person of Maori descent who they are, they are very likely to answer in terms of their extended family and tribe, rather than as an individual. On the other hand, the concept of the American dream, where opportunity is available for individuals according to their own ability or achievement, shows the individual focus of that culture.

3. Emotion and reason

National cultures differ whether emotion or reason dominates relationships between people. Where emotion dominates, people show their feelings openly by laughing, smiling or grimacing. Where reason dominates, people are expected to keep their feelings carefully controlled. When asked if they would show others that they were feeling upset at work, most Italians answered that they would, whereas over 80 per cent of Japanese would not (Trompenaars, 1993).

4. How far we get involved

Another cultural difference is how people engage with others and how much personal relationships are emphasized. Let's focus on work relationships. In a low-context culture, the roles that people play at work do not affect their relationships outside of work, whereas in a diffuse culture, people are likely to defer to their bosses even outside of work. For example, how you would react if your boss asked you to come to his house after work and paint the walls and you had other things you wanted to do? A low-context culture would argue that the boss has no authority outside of work. A high-context culture would suggest that you should paint your boss's house, even though you don't want to, as he is still your boss.

5. Where status comes from

Some cultures give people status on the basis of their achievements, whereas others give people status on the basis of who they are: their place in the hierarchy, class, age, gender, education and even their family background.

There is a cultural dimension that relates to the concept of time. Some national cultures see time as sequential or as a series of passing events. People in these monochronic cultures tend to be very focused on planning and doing one thing at a time. Being late to a meeting would be considered rude. I often visit Switzerland, where people fret if trains are one minute late. That is an example of a monochronic culture. On the other hand, people from some cultures see that ideas about the future and memories of the past are very important in shaping the present. These polychronic societies are much more flexible about time, and people are likely to do several things at once, treat meeting times as approximate and accept interruptions. I notice this when I visit the Middle East. It seems that maintaining relationships and socializing is often more important than returning from coffee breaks at the appointed time!

The final cultural dimension deals with how people relate to nature and the natural environment. Some cultures try to control nature and others believe that they are part of nature and should go along with nature.

So how can we use these ideas with virtual colleagues from different cultures?

People in your own virtual teams may be working from very different positions in each of these cultural dimensions and may tackle the dilemmas that you face in a completely different way. This diversity is not just a burden for leaders. It can be a great gift, as it can allow your team to see things from different perspectives and to try multiple ways of doing things.

As with many of the issues in this book, self-awareness is the start. Know your own culture and where you sit on the cultural difference scales above.

Understand how others might perceive you and how they perceive people of your nationality. This will help you to know where you are more likely to clash with others, however unintentionally.

The next step is to be aware of the cultures of others. Explore and seek to understand the cultures of other people in your virtual groups. Be curious and have an open mind. Theory can help, as too can listening to each person's take on things. Remember that each person is an individual and will have variations, no matter what their cultural heritage is. Open questions such as 'What do you think about this?' and 'What have you understood from our discussion?' are much more useful than the closed questions 'Do you agree?' and 'Do you understand?' Outside of work, catch up with films from your team members' national cultures; perhaps ask them to recommend some for you. Reading fiction from their country can be enlightening too.

It can be very helpful to have an adviser or friend in each location that you deal with, someone you trust who can advise you on how best to engage with people in a way that works with their local culture. This will help you to develop your skills to work more productively and effectively with your team.

Some specific issues that come up in virtual working

Working time

How are your remote colleagues likely to want to work? Are they likely to be happy to work late or take work home over the weekend or will they stick to the standard working hours? Will they disappear for coffee breaks whenever they want to or at predictable, fixed times?

A particular issue that I have found is people's cultural attitude to timekeeping. With virtual work, it makes sense to keep meetings short and effective, so starting promptly is key, as it can be very frustrating for people having to wait around for others to arrive late. Unfortunately, just telling people to be on time doesn't make people do it! The most effective, practical strategy that I have found to encourage people to turn up on time is to set aside the first five minutes of the call. During this time, we don't press ahead with the agenda, but instead share social chit-chat and have a chance to catch up with the news and gossip that remote colleagues often miss out on. I have found that people who are not likely to arrive on time will make the effort if they have a chance to connect with others informally. Those who prefer to join at the start of the meeting know that they can arrive five minutes past the official start time without missing any of the planned agenda items.

Social chit-chat

This can be useful to build relationships between members of virtual teams; however, some cultures find it annoying and wish to 'get down to business' straight away. This relates to the dimension of 'how far we get involved'. I have found it helpful to ensure that each team member has an understanding of the cultural differences and realizes that working together as a team involves both doing the work and developing relationships so that the team is high-performing.

Humour

Beware the use of humour, understatement and irony with diverse virtual teams, as cultures vary on what is acceptable. Some cultures do not accept humour in a professional setting. My own British culture tends to use understatement and irony extensively in a way that can be difficult for others to understand. In a virtual team, an 'in-joke' that is only understood by one nationality is destructive, as others feel left out and excluded. If you have people with whom you have a very good relationship, then you could test out humour with them and see how it would land and how it could be tweaked to be more acceptable. On the whole, though, it is best to stick to safe, inoffensive topics, as what you think might be harmless may cause offence!

Focus on face

An issue that comes up again and again is that of 'face'. Many of my clients work with outsourced or offshore colleagues remotely. Daniel is one of them. He is from the United States but is based in Zurich, Switzerland, and he leads a team of software developers offshore. Over lunch one day, I heard from Daniel about his frustrations on his project. 'When I asked my developers if they could get some work done by Wednesday, they all said yes. Now it's Friday and there is no evidence that the work has even started. It drives me mad!' This sounded familiar and I asked Daniel if his colleagues were based in the Middle East, India, China or elsewhere in South-East Asia. He told me that they were from India.

The trouble was that Daniel had unwittingly come across a big cultural difference. In India and many other countries, there is a very strong concept: 'saving face'. It is a deeply rooted cultural characteristic, which people have grown up with all their lives. It is about avoiding humiliation or embarrassment, maintaining dignity and preserving reputation. In strongly group-oriented societies, it is imperative to protect others from losing face too. In societies where status comes from hierarchy, junior employees will work especially hard to prevent their bosses losing face. On top of that Daniel has another difference to cope with: time orientation, so people are less likely to report delays immediately.

Let's analyse what happened when Daniel asked his question and see what he could have done differently to work more effectively and to have 'saved face'. Daniel asked the whole team in a virtual meeting: 'Can you get the work done by Wednesday?' To save face for themselves and for Daniel, there is only one possible answer: 'Yes'. To answer 'No' would imply that they were not good enough and it would also reflect badly on Daniel, even if 'No' was correct. Daniel's flaw was asking a closed question, with 'Yes' or 'No' the only options for reply.

So what could Daniel have done better? Ideally, he would have got to know the team members and understood their cultural perspectives. He should have used open questions, such as: 'What steps do we need to accomplish to deliver this piece of software?' and 'How long will it take to complete these steps?' It would have been better to discuss things one-to-one with the individual tasked with doing the work, making it easier to discus challenges and how to overcome them. Daniel could have explained about what would happen next and worked through with his colleagues why certain deadlines were important to the delivery of their work and the context for the timings. That would help with the cultural differences around time. Daniel could also have asked for regular updates on progress, making sure that they were very specific about what had been completed.

Ultimately, the best person to decide what to say in any cross-cultural conversation is the person in it. So build up your own understanding of your culture and others' cultures and harness your curiosity to help you to develop the ability to bridge cultural differences.

Generation

Why generation matters for virtual leadership

In my surveys on virtual working, generational differences do not really come up as an issue. Only just over 1 in 10 people raised it in my surveys. However, just as cultures are different and people are hugely influenced by culture in which they are formed and exist, so are the experiences of people of different generations. Their lives have been moulded by their shared experiences and this will make a difference to how they work with you and your teams. As a quick example, 'baby boomers' are likely to try to make things right first time. They may well have used typewriters when growing up and maybe at work, where there was no undo, so typing has to be right first time. On the other hand, 'millennials' have always had an undo button, so tend to just type away and then go back and correct things later. Try giving a baby boomer and a millennial a piece of writing with mistakes and see how differently they react!

To quote Graeme Codrington, who spoke at my Virtual Working Summit in 2013, 'I think communication and connection is difficult between the generations today because we have such different value systems and such different expectations of how things should happen – what is normal, what is right, what is good and what is weird, bad and wrong. Some of the frustrations that people have with communicating with younger and older people than themselves, with getting themselves understood or making connections, are actually amplified in the virtual world because in the virtual world we lose some of the signals that you pick up in the real world; you lose body language, you lose some of the visual references that we have. As a result, things that might be hard in a physical world become even harder in the virtual world' (Codrington and Pullan, 2013). So that is why generation matters for virtual leadership.

Different generations in the workplace

Let's look quickly at the different generations in, and those about to join, the workplace, using the categories defined by Codrington and Grant-Marshall (2011):

1 Silent generation: born between the 1920s and the 1940s, there are not many left at work. For them, the global depression of the 1930s and the tumultuous events of the Second World War are key, with the themes of economic instability, social upheaval, loss and austerity. Their attitude to work is that it is their duty to work hard. When they started work, the only technology they used regularly would have been a telephone and, perhaps, a typewriter.

2 Baby boomers: born between the 1940s and the 1960s, they are often in positions of power or starting to retire. Key events when they were growing up included the first man in space and moon landings, the Vietnam War, the invention of the contraceptive pill, The Beatles and hippies. Their themes focus on growth and development, along with

grand visions of the future. Work is self-fulfilling rather than a duty, and makes them feel important. When they started work, there might have been a computer somewhere in the building, but desk telephones were everywhere. Naturally, face-to-face is often their preferred style. Jobs were easy to get when they started work, and rapid economic growth was normal.

3 Generation X: born between the 1960s and the 1980s (or so), Generation X people are often in key leadership positions in companies. This is my generation and I remember hearing about the first micro-computers, AIDS, the end of the Cold War, the Berlin Wall coming down and the events of Tiananmen Square in China. Themes for this generation include uncertainty, instability and change. Lifestyle is important and a key part of work is funding that. When we started work, which we were not guaranteed to find easily, there were more computers in the workplace than before and we used e-mail, as well as telephones.

4 Generation Y or millennials: born between 1980 and 2000 (or so), these so-called millennials are true digital natives, who have known computers all their lives. Growing up, they experienced the world wide web, Google search, 9/11, social media, wars in Iraq and Afghanistan and international terrorism. This generation was very protected as children and their themes include promises of a bright future, which does not always come true. Work is to help to change the world. When they started work, which was often hard to find, computers were everywhere. They might not bother with a landline and tend to use mobile phones instead, at home and work. They really are digital natives, usually very happy to use technology to work virtually. They value flexibility, networks and the ability to learn and grow. They share and collaborate and respect talent rather than hierarchy. Even in India, which is traditionally a very hierarchical society, companies such as Infosys are reorganizing into matrix organizations to attract millennial talent (Mendonca, 2015).

5 Generation Z: born from 2000 onwards, these children have often had far less physical interaction face to face with others than in previous generations. They tend to communicate virtually with their schoolfriends after school rather than going around to meet up face to face. Their ease with technology comes from wide experience of it from an early age and they will no doubt expect to have access to all of this at work too. They do not like e-mail and often prefer to send short messages using their phones.

A glimpse into the future with Charlotte (13), Julia (13) and Amadea (14)

As Generation Z have yet to enter the workforce, but will do in a few years, I thought it would be useful to interview a few of them. Rather than meeting up face to face, they invited me to join them in a conversation online, using Facebook messenger. Here is some of the conversation. Please note that the original spelling has been left uncorrected to highlight yet another difference between Generation X and Generation Z:

Penny

> Hello everyone. I'm writing a book about virtual working (ie working when you're not in the same place). In one part of it, I talk about how different generations approach virtual working. There's not much on teenagers, so thought I'd start by asking a group of you. Thank you in advance for being part of the group and, if you'd like to, I'd be happy to name your first names and ages in the book, along with some of the conversation.

Charlotte

> Mum, have you ever heard of the 'no too long text' rule?

Penny

> No Charlotte I haven't! First question: what do you feel about working virtually with others (like this group?)

Julia

> i feel that it is good if you work virtually if you know who you are working with.

Penny

> Do you mean that you already know them face to face, Julia?

Julia

> yh. so like in this group it is my friends from school which i see everyday (when at school) and also you which i have met you and you are charlotte's mum

Amadea

I have no problem with it.

Penny

Question 2. People my age often feel more comfortable talking on the phone 1–1. How do you feel about the phone?

Julia

i think the phone is good if you are not good at writing and it is technically faster

Amadea

People do use the phone as its useful but mostly people prefer texting

Penny

Question 3. How do you feel about e-mail and how much do you use it?

Julia

i think email is good because you can contact people formally for example emailing teachers. i don't use it too often

So what have I learnt from my virtual conversation with members of Generation Z? A few things: it is important to keep text messages short! I've noticed that I am much fussier about proper grammar, punctuation and spelling than the teenagers are in their messages. While they are happy to interact virtually, it is best if they have met beforehand. While they occasionally use e-mail and their phones, they are much more comfortable with instant messages. They don't usually use Facebook but were kind enough to use a platform that I could communicate with them on.

How to work virtually across generations

I have given you a short introduction to the contexts within which each generation at work now grew up. Use these to understand how different people have different perceptions of the world and different expectations. Of course there will be individual variations, so consider what people want from you as a virtual leader and how you can create a virtual working environment and team that meets their needs. Of course, it is easy just to assume that everyone else wants what you would like, but you know that that isn't true, don't you? Ask people what would make your virtual team work better for them and see if you can find a way together that works with the particular mix of generations, and cultures, that you have.

Of course, it does not just apply to your teams. Your own leadership style will be influenced by your own experiences growing up and the context at the time. Both will have affected you and your attitude to life and leadership. So be aware and think about how your own style will differ from others and what changes you could make.

A day in the life: Mauva

Mauva works as an interim manager for a private-sector utility company in England. The whole industry is engulfed in change as the government works to open up the market to competition. Mauva is playing the role of an Agile business analyst on a project to update existing IT systems and to implement new systems to meet these changing needs.

8.00 am Mauva arrives at work early, unless the motorway is busy, which happens from time to time. From 8.15 am she is straight into meetings and calls with the development team, half of whom are based in India. To make sure that things are progressing well, they have daily calls, which everyone in the team attends. Mauva finds that her IT colleagues in India, unsurprisingly, know little of the industry in the UK and the major changes going on and so she needs to explain the business context for their work as well as passing on business requirements for them to develop into software. She uses a combination of video and audio conferences, e-mail and a shared collaboration tool for documents.

12 noon Mauva breaks for lunch as the Indian office has now closed for the day. She takes an hour, which helps her to switch into a more focused work mode for the afternoon.

1 pm Now is the time to focus on writing documents and face-to-face meetings and workshops with her local colleagues.

4.30 pm It is back on the motorway for Mauva. Hopefully by leaving a little bit early, she will get home before the motorway hits gridlock! However, with all the virtual tools available, she can catch up with work at home in the evening if there is something important to deal with. Mauva also work collaboratively with her partners in the Caribbean, providing Agile business analysis expertise, so the evening is a good time to deal with them, virtually of course!

Mauva's hints and tips:

- Working with Indian colleagues is different. We are lucky to have half the development team onshore with us and the other half in India, which helps as we can clarify things with local contacts if we need to.

- From my experience over many years working with offshore developers in India, I have found that it really helps if the developers write down their questions for me. I answer these over the phone and ask them to reflect back their own understanding of my answer in writing. This way, I find that the misunderstandings are picked up immediately. There really is a language barrier, even though we all speak English!

- Something else that has worked very well for me is that I review key requirements documents with the team of developers, going through them line by line with the document shared with them so that they can see as I go through it. This means that I can deal with questions as they arise.

- In today's market, working virtually is the norm for the types of job that I do. Every contract over the last four years has stipulated virtual working.

Summary

To summarize this chapter, here is Richard Pooley. He asked highly successful, very experienced international managers 'What is the quality most required to be a successful international leader?' The vast majority answered that it was curiosity. He says, 'You really genuinely need to want to know how other people operate and how other people think. To do that, you need to ask a lot of questions and you need to be a very good listener. Listen, observe and keep your mouth under control!' (Pooley and Pullan, 2012).

I think that this applies very well to those who are navigating the complexity of wide time zones, language, cultures and generations.

Questions for reflection

1 Which virtual working complications affect you as a virtual leader and the people you work with?

Time zones

2 How will you work across wide time zones? Do you need to generate some overlap to meet at the same time or can you split into groups? How do you intend to do this?

3 How will you create a very clear, shared calendar so everyone knows what is happening when?

4 How can you make the most of asynchronous working to reduce the need for meeting live?

Language

5 What issues have you already faced in terms of language?

6 How will you make it easier for both native and non-native speakers to take part fully in your virtual meetings? Might offshore English work for you?

7 What can you do to model the behaviour that you would like to see?

Culture

8 Which different cultures are present in your virtual teams? What issues arise as a result?

9 Where do you lie in each of Trompenaars's cultural dimensions? What about other members of your team? What will you do with this knowledge?

10 What actions would you like to take now to help your team to work effectively despite the cultural mix?

Generation

11 Which generations are present in your teams? What issues arise as a result?

12 What stands out for you from the descriptions of other generations? How does this relate to what you notice in your virtual work?

Overall

13 What will help you to stay curious, self-aware and interested in others? How easy will it be for you to listen more than you speak? What might help here?

References and further reading

Carté, P and Fox, C (2008) *Bridging the Culture Gap: A practical guide to international business communication*, 2nd edn, Kogan Page, London

Coats, K and Codrington, G (2015) *Leading in a Changing World: Lessons for future focused leaders*, TomorrowToday Global, Johannesburg

Codrington, G and Grant-Marshall, S (2011) *Mind the Gap: Own your past, know your generation, choose your future*, 2nd edn, Penguin, Johannesburg

Codrington, G and Pullan, P (2013) Managing across the Generations in a Virtual World, interview recorded as part of the Virtual Working Summit 2013 (www.virtualworkingsummit.com), Loughborough

Livermore, D (2015) *Leading with Cultural Intelligence: The real secret to success*, 2nd edition, Amacon

Mendonca, R (2015) [accessed 27 January 2016] Infosys May Opt For Matrix Organization Structure To Woo Millennials [Online] http://economictimes. indiatimes.com/tech/ites/infosys-may-opt-for-matrix-organization-structure-to-woo-millenials/articleshow/49574587.cms

Pooley, R and Pullan, P (2012) How to be a Successful Communicator When Working Virtually Across Borders, interview recorded as part of the Virtual Working Summit 2012 (www.virtualworkingsummit.com), Loughborough

Settle Murphy, N (2013) *Leading Effective Virtual Teams: Overcoming time and distance to achieve exceptional results*, CRC Press, Boca Raton

Trompenaars, F (1993) *Riding the Waves of Culture: Understanding cultural diversity in business*, Nicholas Brealey, London

Trompenaars, F (2003) *Did the Pedestrian Die?* Capstone Publishing, Oxford

Potential pitfalls 08 and how to overcome them

This chapter deals with some of the practical problems that people face when working virtually. As a reader, you will be able to prepare for and avoid these pitfalls. The chapter is full of real business situations faced by virtual leaders, gathered from people from around the world.

It is structured into four broad categories:

- Issues that impact virtual leaders and team members.
- Issues when running virtual meetings.
- Issues outside of virtual meetings.
- Issues when trying to create a culture where virtual work is effective.

There is more detail elsewhere in the book, but this chapter is meant to give quick, practical advice that you can apply immediately. I suggest that you flick through the issues listed below to find those most relevant for you right now.

By reading this chapter, you will:

- Understand a range of practical issues that face virtual leaders.
- Identify ways ahead for each of the issues raised.

Figure 8.1 A mind-map of this chapter

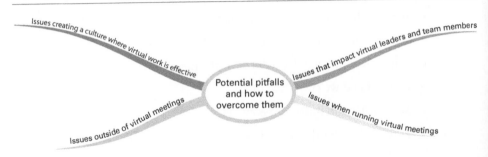

Issues that affect virtual leaders and team members

Working late

Remember Janet from Chapter 1? She was permanently exhausted from running a virtual project from the UK, with her US-based team. As a conscientious project manager, Janet found that it was easiest to spend her evenings on one-to-one and group calls from home, but this was causing her to get more and more exhausted and negatively impacting her work–life balance.

In this case, something needs to give. It seems that Janet is working almost entirely through live meetings with the team. I would advise her to use technology to help her to work asynchronously with her team, keeping only the most important issues and relationship building to live meetings.

'I'm frazzled after my virtual meetings'

What with taking notes, writing down actions, keeping time as well as facilitating the session, some virtual leaders find their meetings exhausting. But why are they choosing to take on all the work? Sharing the load is a very good way of keeping other people engaged – after all you cannot nod off to sleep if you are responsible for timekeeping!

I usually allocate a timekeeper and a scribe, preferably someone who can share the actions on a shared screen or via chat during virtual meetings.

'Virtual meetings take up most of my day'

Many virtual leaders and team members spend over 20 hours in virtual meetings each week. When do they have time to focus on the work itself?

It is all too easy for meetings to multiply. Before arranging a virtual meeting, ask yourself some meeting start-up questions:

- What is the purpose of the meeting?
- Is a meeting the best way to achieve this?
- What outcomes will we achieve at the meeting?
- How should we spend the time?
- What roles will different people play?
- How will we work together effectively?

- What will happen as a result? (You can see a visual reminder of this in Figure 5.2 on page 132.)

When you are asked to attend a virtual meeting, use these questions to see if it makes sense to join. Instead of being there for the whole meeting, perhaps you can just join for a part.

'I'm spending too many days sitting in front of a screen all day'

As a virtual worker, it is all too easy to become sedentary. There is no need to move as you can work, join meetings and contact team members from your desk. To get into a healthy routine, plan movement into your day. Go for short walks at lunchtime and get up from your desk regularly. A standing desk might work for you. Use a pedometer to count your steps and aim for 10,000 per day. One of my readers, Ian, suggests using a monitor to alert you when you have been stationary for too long. He says that it is amazing how easy it is to forget to move!

A pain in the neck?

Andrew spends a lot of time on the telephone, as he leads a project team spread across several countries. He used to develop headaches during the day, with his telephone handset jammed between his head and his shoulder. Now he has a wireless headset and the headaches have disappeared. With his hands free, it is much easier for him to take notes, open files and walk over to the recycling bin.

It is easy for virtual workers to focus on work over their own needs. Make sure you have the equipment that you need to be effective, without causing you physical problems. Many companies will provide ergonomic assessments and equipment; there are legal requirements for this in some countries.

'I'd like to be better at virtual leadership, but don't have lots of spare time'

Well, you are holding a book full of ideas and practical strategies to help you. Read a few pages a day and try out the ideas at work.

You can get better and better, while still continuing with your virtual work. At the end of each virtual meeting, take 5 to 10 minutes with your colleagues to look back and reflect on 'What went well?' and 'What could we do differently next time to make it better?' (Some people use 'What went wrong' but this can lead to moaning and a lot of negativity. My more positive suggestion works better.) Then use these lessons learnt to keep doing what works and to change what doesn't before your next virtual meeting. Small improvements on a daily or weekly basis soon add up!

Of course, you can visit the website for this book at www.virtualleader shipbook.com, download resources and join in the discussion!

Issues related to live meetings

There is detailed advice about virtual meetings in Chapter 5. In this section, you will find some quick tips to help you avoid common pitfalls when you are running live meetings.

'People are always late!'

Why don't people turn up on time to live virtual meetings? For some, it is about organization (or lack of it) and for others it is cultural. Sometimes technology can be slow or previous meetings overrun. How to solve this problem depends on the cause.

As a virtual leader, encourage anyone who doesn't know how to use your meeting technology to have some training and a practice run before the first time they use it for real work. As it can take several minutes for systems to be up and running, make sure that people receive a reminder of your meeting a few minutes before it starts, along with any phone numbers, codes and links that they need in order to join.

Too often, people start meetings on the hour to run for an hour. That leaves no time for a bio-break, a quick cup of tea or even the previous meeting overrunning a minute or two. Try starting your meetings at five minutes past the hour and plan to finish at five minutes to the hour.

In some cultures, being late to meetings is acceptable. (See polychronic societies in Chapter 7.) If this causes you problems, then what will encourage people to join on time? One thing that often works with my clients is to include some gentle office gossip and chit-chat for the first five minutes of a call, as remote workers often miss out on this information.

'My meetings overrun'

Virtual meetings often take longer than expected. The most powerful way I have found to plan and start meetings is to run through my start-up questions (see Figure 5.2 on page 132 for a visual guide). Start by gaining clarity on the purpose of the meeting and the objectives that you would like to achieve. Are your objectives realistic given the length of time you have? Then plan your time carefully, taking into account lessons learned in previous meetings. It is helpful to have a plan B, and perhaps others up your sleeve, so that you are able to be flexible if you need to be.

Run through each of the steps with all the participants to gain their agreement and ensure that everyone is clear. This makes your meeting far less likely to overrun.

Should something unforeseen happen and you cannot finish what was planned, it makes sense to let people know that things have changed. Gain their agreement to do things differently, which might mean postponing some of the content to a later date or for the team to work on asynchronously after the meeting.

'Could you repeat that last question please? I missed it'

Often when Bill asks a direct question to an individual in a virtual meeting, there is a pause. Then they come back to him saying something like: 'Sorry, can you just repeat the question?'

This is a point that I've heard from almost every virtual leader I've worked with. Coming back after a pause by asking for the question to be repeated indicates that they were: 1) not expecting a direct question; 2) not listening.

The first point is the easier to fix. When you set up each meeting, agree how you will work together. Make sure that people realize that you will be asking each participant direct questions throughout the call. I plan in times to poll participants – to go through the list of participants asking them for their input by name, one at a time. If people know this is going to happen, they are much more likely to be ready to answer.

The second point is harder to fix. Why were they not listening? Can you find out? Perhaps they were not engaged and involved in the meeting, which I'll cover next.

'People aren't engaged in my virtual meetings'

The biggest challenge with virtual working is to engage remote participants in remote meetings. There is so much else to draw their attention away from your meeting, especially on conference calls. Are they answering e-mails or catching up on social media? Or playing a game? Or, like Zoe in Chapter 1, are they half-asleep?

Polling participants will help. So will using stories to engage them. Add visuals to your virtual meetings and share screens with live annotations. Help people to relate to the others in the meeting by using video and having a team photo, including the faces of each team member. When designing your meetings, plan participation rather than presentation. (There are many more ideas for engaging people in Chapter 5.)

'Who just offered to take on that action?'

Kate is a senior executive who leads large conference calls with organizational leaders from all around the globe. There is just one problem. She does not always recognize the voices on her calls. So Kate doesn't know who has volunteered to take an action or who has objected to a decision.

That is not an effective way to work! It is impossible to follow up an action that an unknown voice has agreed to take on. Unfortunately, this situation plays out on calls over and over again every day.

There is a simple solution; however, it does takes some practice to get used to it. The best way to introduce it is to model it yourself, then others will follow. At the very start of the call, agree that each person will state their name immediately before everything they say. Here is an example: 'Penny here, I will take that action.' For the first few minutes it can feel a bit strange using this rule with a new group, but that feeling soon disappears. The advantages of knowing *who* has agreed to *what* far outweigh the slight discomfort at the start. This is a good habit to keep for all your virtual sessions, as it makes life so much easier for new members of the group, even if all the other participants recognize everyone's voices and know exactly who is speaking.

Silence

Often when leaders ask for input in their virtual meetings, the line goes dead. There is complete silence. What is going on? Is everyone thinking? Are they preparing to share ideas? Have they gone to sleep? Are they catching up on e-mail? Unless you can see their video stream, you really do not have a clue.

I suggest that, instead of asking for input in a general way, you poll the group. Ask each individual by name for their input, one by one. Of course, if they have nothing to say, they can pass.

The sudden interruption

In a meeting, a loud noise interrupts the audio stream: station announcements, airport announcements or a dog barking or, worse still, a loud flushing noise. Have you been there? The call had been going well and all of a sudden it is impossible to talk because all you can hear is a nasal tone announcing the departure of the 9.10 am train from Paddington, or a colleague's dog barking.

What can you do about this? Once again, it is all down to how you agree to run the meeting. A useful rule to agree is that people in loud, or potentially loud, environments put their phones on mute unless they are speaking. This does mean that there will be a slight gap before they speak while they are unmuting, but it makes the audio quality so much better. This is particularly important if your call is being recorded for others to listen to later.

What gender are they? I haven't got a clue...

Remember Tomás's dilemma from Chapter 1? He said, 'I had been working with someone from India via e-mail for a while, but had no idea if they were male or female. Their name didn't help me. I couldn't tell when I heard their voice, as it could have been either male or female. In the write up afterwards, I had to refer to this person as "they" when everyone else was "he"' or "she". It was very embarrassing!'

With situations like this, it is far better to ask questions upfront when it would be a normal part of a team getting to know one another, rather than leaving the situation to get worse over time. I would probably request a one-to-one meeting with the person and say something along the lines of, 'I'm very sorry, but I'm not very used to Indian names or listening to your accents yet. Please could you let me know a bit more about yourself?' If this didn't work, I would need to ask directly, 'I'm very sorry but I can't work out if you are male or female – please could you help me out by letting me know?' Usually, making out something like this to be a deficiency on my part seems to work much better than just ignoring it, and team members are usually very happy to help put me right.

'Why can't they answer me truthfully?'

We heard about Daniel's frustrations with his team of software developers in India in Chapter 1. Daniel said, 'When I asked them if they could get some work done by Wednesday, they all said that they could. Now it's Friday and there is no evidence that the work has even started. It drives me mad!'

This is a case of 'saving face' and Daniel needs to work out a way to find out what he needs to without causing loss of face to himself or his remote colleagues. I suggested that he could use open questions to find out how long the team would need and what was involved in the work, rather than a closed question, to which the answer could only be 'Yes'. (There is much more in Chapter 7 on cultural clashes.)

'I need a break. Now!'

I joined a virtual project risk management review for an international manufacturing company. This review ran all morning, using a conference call with a shared screen. The screen showed a few cells of a very large spreadsheet, which recorded all the risks. After three hours, I was desperate for a bathroom break, as the conversation had not stopped.

This happens far too often in virtual meetings. Leaders assume that people are able to operate like machines. In a face-to-face meeting, people would stop for bio-breaks, but in a virtual situation, it is very difficult to flag that people need a break.

Once again, it comes down to the design and start of the virtual meeting. As a leader, keep your virtual meetings to no more than an hour, or possibly 90 minutes, before stopping or taking a reasonable break. We are human beings after all and function far better with time to recharge and refresh.

'I wonder who is on the line?'

Who is on your call? Has anyone extra joined, perhaps uninvited? Could they hear confidential information? This is a common issue.

When you design your virtual meetings, plan who will be present and how you will ensure that you do not have other, uninvited participants. Have some security in place – use a code to gain entry. Use technology to make all of the connections visible. At the start of your meeting, check who is present. It is useful to have a discussion around confidentially, especially if people from different organizations are joining in – and we will look at that next.

Consider confidentiality

Laura joined a conference call with a very important client, but it went horribly wrong. She had arranged her call for the time she would be travelling to the airport in a pre-booked company car. However, due to cost cutting, her firm had arranged for three other people to share a local cab with her. The environment had changed and, rather than playing a key part in the call, which was of a highly confidential nature, all she could do was say 'Yes' or 'No' at the right places. She felt gutted.

In this situation, I would suggest being transparent with the client and letting them know that, rather than breach their confidentiality, you would only answer closed questions during the call. Of course you would follow up afterwards via more secure means. An alternative would be to request that your clients postpone the call once it became apparent that there was a confidentiality issue.

Out of sight should not mean out of mind

Michael works remotely from the rest of his team. He is often the only remote participant in meetings, where everyone else is sitting together in a room with poor acoustics. He feels like a second-class citizen or, as he describes it, 'some sort of pariah'. The people in the room forget that he is there and often enter into heated discussions together, which he cannot hear properly, let alone take part in.

My suggestion here is to have a 'level playing field' with equal access to information for all. The meeting should be designed as if everyone were remote and on the call. Rather than using one central speakerphone, which is often poor at picking up everyone's speech, each individual could use their own phone line. Otherwise, pass the speakerphone to each different speaker to make the audio better for Michael.

'Your "all-day" meeting is not all day for me – it is well into the night'

Like Michael, above, Christopher also had to endure meetings where he was the only remote participant. In his case, it was even worse. He had to attend all-day meetings where the others were in New York. He was based in the UK, meaning that he was on the phone from 2 pm to 10 pm. It was hardly an effective use of his valuable time!

It makes no sense to have people on a phone line for eight hours. Instead the meeting planner should work out in which part of the meeting Christopher was needed and plan a one-hour call focusing on this area, during UK working hours.

'Actions just do not get done after virtual meetings'

All too often, virtual meetings are a bit like the film *Groundhog Day*. Actions from previous meetings have not been completed and end up carried forward to the next one. To break this ineffective cycle, be very clear about actions as they arise during your virtual meetings. Challenge actions if you feel they are inappropriate. It is also important to check people's intent to carry out their actions after the meeting. Put in place some sort of follow-up mechanism to check that actions are being done.

Issues with virtual work outside of meetings

'I can't find anything in our virtual team space'

Virtual collaboration tools and shared team spaces are very useful. Instead of being lost inside people's e-mail accounts, documents are available so that everyone in the team can access the latest version whenever they need to. At least, that is the promise. Too often, though, it ends up in a muddle. Everyone uses it in different ways and no one knows where to find anything.

There are a few things that will reduce the chances of this happening. First, agree upfront how you will use the tools – what structure you will use for storing documents and information. What will happen with old versions of documents? What about working papers that you might not need to keep for long? Then make sure that someone is responsible for curating the information, keeping it easy to access and use. Provide training for members of your team so that everyone knows how to use the tools effectively.

'I'm trying to get work done, but people keep interrupting me'

Time in between virtual meetings is for getting work done. However, if people see you that you are active, they are likely to bombard you with questions and requests via instant message or phone calls. While it is great to be able to interact with team members one-to-one, there is a time for everything. When you need to focus, make sure that you are marked as unavailable in whatever systems you are using. Choose some regular slots when you will be available for team members and encourage them to do the same for you.

'Everything seemed to be going so well but, under the surface, storms were brewing'

I am sure every virtual leader has experienced this one! Everything seems to be going well. You are letting people know what work needs to be done. Everything is progressing, as far as you can tell. The only indication that something might be wrong is that people are rather quiet in meetings. When you ask if everything is going well, the universal answer is, 'It's fine', or, perhaps, silence. Finally you find out that major conflict has broken out and that some team members will not work with others.

Conflict is so much easier to spot in co-located teams. A harsh look, crossed arms or people avoiding each another are all visible. In virtual teams, most of this is hidden away, so keep an eye and an ear out for conflict, so that you can pick it up as early as possible.

It is helpful to talk about conflict early in your team's formation and agree how you would deal with it if it arose. It seems that forewarned is forearmed!

Key elements in virtual conflict include cultural differences, language difficulties and intergenerational misunderstandings. Here, awareness of yourself and the others you work with virtually is key. (Chapter 7 will help you further.)

Issues related to virtual working culture

'If I can't see you, how do I know that you are working?'

Virtual working is an alien concept for some, especially those in older generations. They are used to being able to see people in their teams working and fear that the work will not happen if they cannot monitor progress with their own eyes.

Solving this issue is tricky. It is all about trust and leadership. Try using a virtual team on a small project that they are happy to take the risk on, and build from there. Leaders who prefer to see people working may well like to use a command-and-control leadership style and micro-manage team members. This does not work well. I would advise leaders to use a more facilitative, collaborative leadership style, which is far more effective for virtual working and motivates team members by giving them autonomy.

'How on earth can we develop our own virtual leaders?'

The premise of this book is that virtual leadership has to start with the individual. People need to become aware of themselves and their own leadership style and strengths, which we go into in Chapter 2. The next step is to become aware of working virtually with others, developing skills to build trust and knowing how to set up effective virtual teams, part of Chapter 3. Technology provides tools to use, allowing people to work together in live meetings and in between them. These are covered in Chapters 4, 5 and 6 respectively. With the rich diversity of most virtual teams, it is important for people to be able to handle differences of time, language, culture and generation carefully and considerately, which we cover in Chapter 7.

So, I suggest that you work through the leadership model present at the beginning of the book from the centre outwards (see Figure 0.2 on page 7). To find out more about training packages to supplement this book, visit this book's site at www.virtualleadershipbook.com.

Has your particular pitfall not been covered?

In this case, please join in the conversation at www.virtualleadershipbook.com where I will be delighted to hear from you, share my ideas to solve your issue and open up the discussion with other virtual leaders.

Questions for reflection

1 Which issues in this chapter resonated with you?
2 What will you do differently as a result of reading this chapter?

For further reading suggestions on any of these issues, please consult the References section at the end of each previous chapter.

Inspiration for your virtual leadership

09

This final chapter highlights my top tips for leading virtual work and shares six stories of virtual leaders in different situations. They get the best out of virtual work and virtual teams by being efficient and effective. They live their lives in ways that would have been impossible only a few years ago. I hope that you find these stories useful and that they will inspire you to be the best virtual leader that you can be. The chapter finishes with some further reading suggestions.

Figure 9.1 A mind-map of this chapter

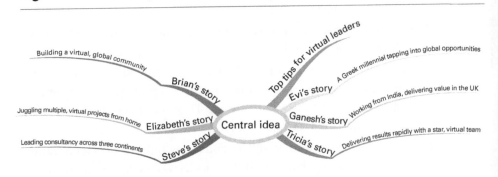

Top 10 tips for virtual leaders

Virtual working can be a fun, rewarding experience, giving you access to the best people in the world. It enables new ways of working that have not been possible before. Enjoy making a difference to your team and to your own life as you work to change the world.

Here are my top 10 tips for your virtual success:

1 Developing your own virtual leadership will make a big difference to the quality of the work delivered by your teams, as virtual work and virtual teams are inherently quite tricky.

2 Choose to be facilitative as a leader. It suits the nature of virtual work, fostering a greater degree of independence and flexibility in your teams and stops you from slipping into command-and-control, which just does not work in most virtual settings.

3 Virtual leaders understand themselves first – their own perspectives and preferences – before moving on to understanding others and how to work with them effectively.

4 Trust is the foundation of effective virtual collaboration and needs to be built.

5 Virtual leaders understand their team members as individuals and their perspectives on language, culture and generation. They are in touch regularly, with communication and feedback flowing both ways.

6 Technology is an enabler for virtual work and leaders must be able to use it effectively and help others to do so, both synchronously and asynchronously.

7 Virtual leaders plan and prepare for their virtual meetings, taking into account participants' needs, and run them well, overcoming the pitfalls that others struggle with.

8 Virtual leaders engage people, in meetings and beyond, using whatever techniques are appropriate and will work for the particular situation.

9 Things will and do go wrong. Virtual leaders should monitor what is happening and be on the lookout for early warning signs of conflict, loss of morale or poor performance issues. They need to be able to stay calm and help the group through troubled waters.

10 Virtual leaders need to be able to find a way through the complications of wide time zones, language difficulties as well as differences of culture and generation in their virtual groups.

Evi's story: a Greek millennial tapping into global opportunities

Evi Prokopi is an example of someone who has grasped the possibilities of virtual working and used them to transform her life. She lives in Greece, where, at the time of writing this book, the economy is suffering and times are hard for many of her generation, with good career opportunities few and far between. Aged 32, Evi is a millennial, who has grown up with the internet and technology. She uses virtual working to grasp opportunities that are not available in her own country. Evi started out as a translator, speaking six languages fluently, and has since developed into a project management consultant. She supervises and assesses Australian students studying for a diploma in project management (from Greece!) and trains project management face to face in Athens. Her main role, though, is to find freelancers around the world to work on projects for a major US company, then to manage these projects to completion.

So what is a typical day for Evi? Although she has three jobs running concurrently, she does not usually start work until 10 am, checking in with her clients in EMEA (Europe, the Middle East and Africa). She uses free software available in the cloud to share documents and meet with her clients, freelancers and students from all around the world. After lunch, she continues until 4 pm, when she stops work to enjoy the afternoon. Evi tends to start work again in the evening and works for around three hours until 10 or 11pm. The evening is particularly useful for working with clients in the United States.

For Evi, her skills at virtual leadership have allowed her to break free from the dearth of opportunities for her generation in Greece and to work with clients from Australia and the United States, managing colleagues from all over the world. With her language skills and complete comfort with virtual working technology, Evi's work is location independent. She can work from anywhere with a decent connection! She loves the free time and flexibility that her work gives her, from free afternoons to a late start in the morning and the ability to work in the evening.

Evi is keen to share her knowledge and skills with others. I met her as we prepared to run a joint workshop on leading virtual project teams at the Project Management Institute Global Congress in Barcelona in 2016.

Ganesh's story: working from India, delivering value in the UK

A consultancy company in India employs Ganesh, who works on projects with colleagues in Chennai and the UK, where his client, a bank, is based. Ganesh often works on upgrades of IT infrastructure and his lead business analysis role means that he needs to interact closely with people. Ganesh spent a year based in the UK with his current colleagues on his projects, so he has met them face to face and has built up good personal relationships with them. He understands their culture and context. All of this supports Ganesh to be really effective. So what does a typical day look like?

Before work Ganesh enjoys the company of his one-year-old baby son, while his wife works. He sometimes meets friends and other family members in the morning.

1:00 pm Ganesh's baby-care shift at home ends and he prepares to go to work.

1:30 pm Ganesh starts work at the office in Chennai. It is 8 am in the UK as Ganesh has shifted his working time to suit his client. He works closely with his colleagues via videoconference, shared screens/whiteboards, and an instant messenger service that lets people know when Ganesh is available to talk, and vice versa. Of course, phone and e-mail are both useful as well. To make sure that everyone is in the picture and up to date on what is going on, each project team meets up for 15 minutes each day virtually. Ganesh told me that the team jokes that the meeting is 'daily prayers'.

5:30 pm Ganesh takes a break at the same time that his colleagues in the UK are going for lunch, so that he is available as much as possible during the day for them.

9:30 to 10 pm Ganesh finishes work for the day and takes the short trip home.

When I spoke to Ganesh, I was impressed by just how far he goes out of his way to be available for his colleagues in the UK. 'If there is a bank holiday in the UK, I often plan my own holidays and trips away to fall on the same days,' he explained. It turns out that shifting his hours for maximum overlap with the UK has some extra benefits for Ganesh too. He can spend time with his young child before work, while his wife works. For many of his colleagues, shifting hours has a very positive benefit as it shortens their commute significantly. By travelling during most people's lunch hour and later in the evening, they can avoid the main rush hour. In India, that can save hours with busy cities and often-crowded motorways, which make London seem relaxed in comparison!

Tricia's story: delivering results rapidly with a star, virtual team

Tricia is a chartered quantity surveyor and project manager in Scotland. Here is her story of planning a new town centre, working virtually with many other professionals, despite the team not being spread around the world:

I used to offer consultancy services as a chartered quantity surveyor. Working from home, I prepared bills of quantities and contractor's quantities for a range of projects, varying in type from school athletics campuses to civil engineering programmes for flood prevention. I never met any of the other consultants face-to-face and I gathered all the information that I needed through the use of technology.

The success of these projects hinged on the availability and quality of information provided by the various design consultants. I was impressed at how quickly they prepared information and responded to queries. I got the impression that no party wished to drop the ball and be the cause of delay! Without meeting face to face, they stepped up to the mark and delivered information I had requested by return. It was as if, by removing design progress meetings, we removed the forum where people could air their explanations on delays. Another advantage was that none of the firms 'buddied up' and defended each other's corner, as often happens usually.

Compare this to the more normal multidisciplinary office. The benefit of working together across the different professions is the ability to have direct contact, to discuss, query and remedy any planning, design, construction, change or legal challenge. However, working in such an environment negatively impacts both output and performance in my view, as time is often stolen and interruptions detract from concentration. Working virtually, when I was able to focus and concentrate on my tasks, I increased my productivity by around 80 per cent. It was hugely rewarding and empowering.

My final project was a new town centre, including retail units, five-storey luxury apartments, underground parking, link to the railway station and new railway platforms. I had two weeks to complete what appeared to be a mammoth task. I knuckled down and completed all the measurement schedules to the delight of the developer and contractor and to the amazement of the design team. While my capability and confidence as a quantity surveyor gave me the knowledge to be able to create a strategy and set up work packages and time targets, technology was a lifeline. Each member of the virtual team cooperated to the success, not only of the entire development, but crucially, to my own ability to interpret all the information and have confidence in my decisions and the format and detail of my works packages.

I remember feeling physically sick when, in the absence of some critical information, I was in limbo for what seemed an eternity, but in reality was less than an hour. I believe that you have to be quick thinking, decisive and confident to perform to the highest standards in the virtual environment. Many quantity surveyors I know say that they couldn't have met this type of challenge, as they are too used to working in a face-to-face group. There they are given set packages of work, under the wing of a group leader who liaises for them. Personally, I enjoyed the experience and felt that I was firing on all cylinders, which was exhilarating.

For this particular piece of work, Tricia chose a 'star' team, where she was the hub and the other professionals liaised with her only, in order to get the work done over very short timescales. In construction projects, time is of the essence and, by working virtually in this way, Tricia was able to focus on this project entirely and avoid distractions, thereby delivering the output much faster than usual.

Steve's story: leading consultancy across three continents

Steve is based in Finland, although originally from the UK, and runs a company that produces tools to help software developers. He recently worked on a consultancy project with a US client from the Midwest. The US-based team consisted of Mark, a US business leader, and Zhao, the technical lead, who was originally from China. Their virtual work together went very well.

Steve suggests that three things contributed to their success:

1 The three people had worked together before, during the pre-sales part of the contract, with quite a lot of personal contact. This really helped the consultancy phase as they understood each other. Steve says, 'By then, we had a good idea of what each other meant. We could tell if things were cast iron or whether we should suggest that we check them out a bit further.'

2 The work that Steve and his company do is really quite complex and deep, so clients often find it hard to grasp the concepts, even when they are sitting right next to Steve and scribbling diagrams on pieces of paper together. As you can imagine, these concepts are even harder to grasp

virtually! Luckily for this project, Zhao, the Chinese technical lead, was very quick to grasp technical concepts, even remotely, and he was able to keep up, which was very helpful.

3 Zhao had to relocate to China part-way through the work. As you can imagine, this wide time zone separation could have caused problems with such little overlap in office hours. In the end, Zhao worked shifts aligned to Mark's office hours.

These three things meant that, what could have been a very tricky piece of work, ended up going well and leading to further work for Steve's company. It is not at all surprising that good interpersonal relationships were the foundations of this project.

Incidentally, there were a couple of technical hitches due to government restrictions. When Zhao moved back to China, he was not able to pick up his Google e-mail, so he had to use a different service. Initially Steve was not aware that his e-mails were not getting through, but once the service was established the work continued as before.

Elizabeth's story: juggling multiple, virtual projects from home

Elizabeth works virtually on multiple projects with multiple teams and multiple clients in two roles, one of which is as the director of a firm providing copywriting to businesses worldwide. She describes below a day in her life. Not much of this would be possible without virtual working!

It's a Friday. I wake up at 5.30 am when my toddlers wake up and check e-mail on my smartphone. I am well aware that I shouldn't do this and that I am bordering on obsessive. This is one of the downsides of virtual working. I am always 'on'.

7-8.30 am Breakfast, getting everyone up and ready for the day. I'm working from home and so I wear whatever is comfortable.

8.30 am Switch on computer and make cup of tea.

About 9 am Start work. By now I am mentally ready for the day. I know what meetings I have and what work is a priority. As a copywriter, I work for a variety of clients. Today I'm using an online content management and scheduling tool to check the upcoming editorial calendar of one of my clients, see what work has been assigned to me and review my editor's notes. We often discuss articles through this virtual work management system although we do have a monthly phone meeting as well. I upload my work when it is done. Using a system like this for virtual work is handy for our team as people are spread across the world. Deadlines change frequently and I get e-mail alerts when my tasks have shifted, without having to join a daily staff meeting.

12 noon Lunch.

1 pm Back out to the office with more tea. Check e-mails. Prepare for a conference call.

1.30 pm It is time for a web conference with a client in India. I join three people on the call and it is great to be able to see them during the meeting. We discuss an upcoming webinar that we are working on jointly, reviewing slides, registrations and the finer details for the event.

2.15 pm Virtual meetings take less time than meeting in person as there is less chat and more focus, in my opinion. Now I'm ready for work again, which means more writing projects and time catching up on e-mails and social media. My job involves being active on a wide variety of channels so I use a number of tools to make staying on top of everything easier.

3.30 pm Phone calls. Although I work virtually, I do speak to a lot of people during the day either on instant message or the phone or Skype. Virtual work doesn't make me feel lonely! I work virtually with clients but also my own team. I delegate work by e-mail to my two colleagues and log it to follow up later.

4.45 pm I get ready for the children's evening routine. One of the benefits for me of virtual working is that I can work flexibly and spend time with my family. We play, do dinner, bath and bed.

7.30 pm I do low brain-power work in the evenings, like reading articles and scheduling them to share with my readers, responding to forum posts, easy e-mails and preparing graphics to go with articles. I also work out what tomorrow's priorities should be and write a note to remind me of the times of meetings and key deadlines, which I leave on the kitchen counter.

8.30 pm I try not to work past 8.30 pm but I will always check my e-mails, social channels and Google Analytics before I turn the light off and go to sleep.

Brian's story: building a virtual, global community

I spoke to Brian who works for a financial services company in the UK and jointly manages a community of specialists. Brian told me about the changes that have happened over the last few years. 'A decade ago, we all worked in small, local teams. Most people probably only interacted with others on the same floor of their building or, at most, 10 miles away. With mergers and restructuring came change and soon we were working with colleagues up to 200 miles away. As a manager, I needed to travel all over the UK for up to three days a week just to see everyone! Initially there was a somewhat negative perception of virtual working. People wanted their expert team members to be onsite with them and not based miles away. It took time to convince managers that my people were really good at working independently and at a distance, using technology.'

Fast forward to the present day. What is different now for Brian? Instead of travelling every week, he finds it hard to remember more than three business trips over the course of the last year. His current team includes partners from two sites in India as well as employees and contractors based all over the UK. Virtual working has become the norm and, now that they have a really good idea of their working culture, practices and processes as well as the technology, it seems to be going well. What has worked particularly well is that they bring most of their Indian partners to the UK for up to a year, to get to know the company, the people and the culture. This supports them to be really effective when they return home.

How does Brian keep his team of experts engaged? Years ago, when face-to-face working was the norm, the experts had little sense of team and little contact with one another. Now, things are different. Brian makes sure that they have a shared sense of identity and do not feel isolated, wherever they are based. All 75 experts meet for a monthly call, with open questions and answers. On the call, they share news, recognition, housekeeping items and changes in the standards and processes that they work to. A newsletter helps to keep people updated with who is doing what. Alongside the virtual connections like this, Brian encourage sites to get together locally on a social basis so that they build relationships. Even the experts thousands of miles away in India feel part of the team. I think that Brian has got it right, don't you?

Questions for reflection

1 Which of the top tips stood out for you? How will you apply these in your own virtual leadership?

2 What inspired you in the stories I shared?

3 What will you do differently as a result of reading this chapter, and this book?

Further reading

To finish, here are some personal recommendations of mine for books to help you further develop your virtual leadership. Please note that these are in alphabetical order, not in order of recommendation:

Carté, P and Fox, C (2008) *Bridging the Culture Gap: A practical guide to international business communication*, 2nd edn, Kogan Page, London. This is an overview of the many topics that comprise the culture gap, and how to overcome it. It includes a whole chapter on making yourself understood in English and a list of 'false friends', those words that are often misunderstood.

Caulat, G (2012) *Virtual Leadership: Learning to lead differently*, Libri Press, Faringdon, Oxfordshire. This book, based on a PhD study, explores the differences needed for virtual working and makes a very strong case for facilitative leadership for remote teams.

Codrington, G and Grant-Marshall, S (2011) *Mind the Gap: Own your past, know your generation, choose your future*, 2nd edn, Penguin, Johannesburg. This book is an easy-to-read introduction to the different generations, with ideas for work, home, leadership and beyond.

Hall, K (2007) *Speed Lead: Faster, simpler ways to manage people, projects and teams in complex companies*, Nicholas Brealey Publishing, London. This book focuses on how to speed up leadership in complex organizations where managers are often bogged down in communication and too much teamwork.

Harrin, E (2016) *Online Collaboration Tools for Project Managers*, PMI, Newton Square. This is a second edition of Elizabeth Harrin's helpful book on how project managers can use collaboration tools to work together asynchronously. It is useful for project managers and others on how to get things done through people with the support of collaboration tools.

Lipnack, J and Stamps, J (2010) *Leading Virtual Teams: Empower members, understand the technology, build team identity*, Harvard Business Press, Boston. A very short, but useful pocket book for virtual teams.

Marshall, G (2015) *How to Be Really Productive: Achieving clarity and getting results in a world where work never ends*, Pearson, Harlow. This book really does what it says on the cover – how to be productive in the sort of world that most virtual leaders inhabit. It is easy to read and covers all of life, not just work.

Settle-Murphy, N (2013) *Leading Effective Virtual Teams: Overcoming time and distance to achieve exceptional results*, CRC Press, Boca Raton. This is a very useful book by my friend and collaborator Nancy Settle-Murphy, which combines many articles into a useful guide for leading effective teams. It contains many bulleted lists, so, while much of the content complements this book, the layout is very different and so is the reading experience.

Trompenaars, F (1993) *Riding the Waves of Culture: Understanding cultural diversity in business*, Nicholas Brealey, London. This is Trompenaars's original book on culture, which I have used since I met Fons in the 1990s. It has stood me in good stead since.

INDEX